AMERICAN FICTION

1920–1940

THE MACMILLAN COMPANY
NEW YORK · BOSTON · CHICAGO
DALLAS · ATLANTA · SAN FRANCISCO

MACMILLAN AND CO., LIMITED
LONDON · BOMBAY · CALCUTTA
MADRAS · MELBOURNE

THE MACMILLAN COMPANY
OF CANADA, LIMITED
TORONTO

AMERICAN FICTION

1920—1940

By Joseph Warren Beach

JOHN DOS PASSOS · ERNEST HEMINGWAY
WILLIAM FAULKNER · THOMAS WOLFE
ERSKINE CALDWELL · JAMES T. FARRELL
JOHN P. MARQUAND · JOHN STEINBECK

NEW YORK · 1941

The Macmillan Company

In Essay Index

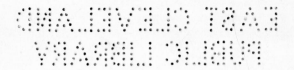
PRINTED IN THE UNITED STATES OF AMERICA
AMERICAN BOOK—STRATFORD PRESS, INC., NEW YORK

ACKNOWLEDGMENTS

Acknowledgment is hereby made to the following authors and publishers for courteous permission to quote illustrative passages, page-references being to this volume:

To John Dos Passos and Harcourt, Brace and Co., for permission to quote a passage from *The 42d Parallel,* p. 65.

To Charles Scribner's Sons, for passages from Ernest Hemingway's *For Whom the Bell Tolls,* p. 117 and Thomas Wolfe's *Of Time and the River,* pp. 183, 190.

To Random House, passages from William Faulkner's *The Hamlet,* p. 156, *The Wild Palms,* p. 158, and *Absalom, Absalom!,* p. 159.

To Harper and Brothers, passages from Thomas Wolfe's *The Web and the Rock,* pp. 182-183, 212.

To Little, Brown and Co., a passage from John P. Marquand's *Wickford Point,* pp. 258-259.

To the Vanguard Press, passage from James T. Farrell's *Guillotine Party and Other Stories,* pp. 274-275.

To the Viking Press, passages from John Steinbeck's *Tortilla Flat,* pp. 321-322 and *The Grapes of Wrath,* pp. 335, 336-337.

PROGRAM

vii

I. THE LAY OF THE LAND

"The proof of the pudding is in the eating."

I. THE LAY OF THE LAND

This book is written at the request of a friend who is a wide reader in many fields, but would like to know more about American fiction in our time and especially about those novelists whom I consider of first importance. His suggestion is that I choose half a dozen of them and discuss them in some detail, so as to make clear to the general reader what there is about each one that gives him a particular claim on our interest and attention. The assumption is that a critical analysis of their themes, their social attitudes, and their literary methods would help the reader to sort out his own ideas and form a reasoned opinion on their performance. It is even hoped that from a study of a few of our outstanding storytellers some conclusions might be drawn as to the general temper of our times—at least in fiction—the prevailing attitudes toward human nature and society, the dominant philosophy of life.

As to my choice of authors for display, the principle is plain. I have picked eight men who, after due consideration, seem to me most worth our thoughtful consideration. I have naturally picked them from writers who interest me. In the last analysis we must be guided in matters of taste by —taste. Nothing will appeal to our taste which does not first lay hold of our attention, and nothing will continue to appeal which cannot maintain its hold on our attention. This is not, of course, as simple as it sounds, for we are anything but simple in our psychological make-up. We can distinguish, among the sides of our nature, mind, heart and imagination, and it might be thought sufficient for a work of art to make its appeal to any one of these. But the fact is that, while we can roughly distinguish these elements in our nature, they are not strictly separate faculties of the spirit; none of them exists in isolation. Each one constantly affects the others, and the thing we call interest is the result of their combined appeal. This is particularly the case with literature, since its medium is words, which have their intellectual as well as their sentimental and imaginative reference. And in fiction, which deals with human nature, it is peculiarly true that deep and lasting interest cannot be roused in intelligent readers unless the appeal to the heart and the imagination is supported by a simultaneous appeal to the mind. The creation of characters might seem to be made primarily by way of the imagination; but it is seldom that, with characters that live, no element of sentiment, of sympathy, enters in to reinforce the imaginative effect. In fiction that deals seriously with human nature, the mind is perpetually on the alert distinguishing motives and passing more or less conscious judgments on behavior. But who can say just where the judgment of the mind begins and the judgment of the heart leaves off? The effort of realism is to present human nature objectively, to label it scientifically. But what scientific labels can be attached to human behavior that have no reference to norms of conduct derived from some notion of social good and bad, some moral standards or preferences? And when we speak of moral preferences, we are using a term which implies the joint action of mind and heart in the estimate of conduct.

The vast mass of popular fiction makes, and has ever made, its appeal to uncritical sentiment. It serves the reader's need for wishful thinking. The plots are so contrived as to gratify the cravings of the heart. The characters are so conceived as to rouse disgust, where they are villains, and, where they are sympathetic, to feed the reader's appetite for nobility, for wit, refinement, altruism, intelligence, and resourcefulness. All romantic stories are success stories; and the reader who identifies himself with the hero or heroine has the gratification of vicariously realizing his ideals and attaining the object of his ambitions. Such fiction serves, no doubt, its useful function in the human economy. It is one of the most innocuous forms of entertainment and diversion; and the provision of such forms of entertainment is one of the most crying needs of urban life. They lend their glamour to drab and commonplace lives, and give heart to readers depressed by what they have seen of the world. I would not think of discouraging the production or consumption of this trashy fiction any more than I would the production and consumption of moving pictures.

I go to the movies a good deal myself and have no apologies to make for that way of passing an evening. It is a form of relaxation as salutary for the tired scholar as for the tired businessman. Besides, the movies offer certain artistic features not present in the trashy novel. They appeal to the love of picture and spectacle and to the love of acting; under present conditions they are the most accessible form of drama. But in their handling of human nature and character they are on no higher level than standard sentimental fiction. In fact, they are on a lower level of seriousness, since the conditions of production are such that they must make an appeal to greater masses, including the mass of the juvenile and the illiterate. Their view of human nature is even more standardized, sentimental, uncritical and childish than that of the average popular novel. Intellectually they are for the most part entirely without interest. And even esthetically—apart from the acting and photography—they are generally most unnourishing food. So that the instinct to seek a balanced diet calls for something as different as possible in the form of reading.

It is even conceivable that the sentimental trashiness of our popular drama works unconsciously to determine the direction of serious fiction—by which I mean the work of our clever men who are aiming at something more than sales. It may be partly by reaction from the taste of the vulgar as shown in our most popular art form that our best novelists lean over backwards in their avoidance of sentimentalism and the pseudo-refinements of bourgeois taste. Now, let me say at once that the authors whom I am featuring as representative of present-day fiction are not necessarily such as I would have summoned out of the void had I been the Proteus of American fiction. Nourished as I was on Dickens and Trollope and Hawthorne, on James and Hardy and Tolstoy— fond as I am, among present-day writers, of Marcel Proust and Thomas Mann and André Malraux—it is unlikely that I should have had the hardihood, not to say the imagination, to have conceived of Ernest Hemingway and William Faulkner, of Thomas Wolfe and John Steinbeck, as standard-bearers of our cultural effort. I might easily have been too conventional, too Victorian, in my taste to have uttered the word which called into being such "questionable shapes" as these. But the threads of fate were not in the hands of any college professor. These figures came by other than academic compulsions to utter other than academic gospels, and satisfy urges powerful and obscure that move like ocean currents through the depths of our national culture.

Now they are very much with us; they are the voices of our day, and we cannot deny them. As for myself I have no wish to deny them. I wish to make them heard, to understand them and appreciate them. My aim is not primarily critical; the time for measured judgments is not yet come. And even for measured judgments, what we first require is sympathetic understanding. We must first live through the esthetic experience and give it descriptive formulation before we can begin to appraise it accurately, assign to each man his rank in the esthetic hierarchy, or even determine whether, in the long view, he is sound or decadent.

It must be obvious, to be sure, that I would not give such earnest study to these eight men if I did not consider them as in many ways superior artists. They have been chosen from scores of meritorious writers, many of whom have claims to inclusion in any list of distinguished novelists. Or rather, they have chosen themselves by something in them that will not brook rejection. Each one of them has something to say about human nature and society that must be heard. And, what is more, each one of them is a master of subtle, powerful and conscious artistry. It is hard to distinguish between the power of thought and the power of esthetic statement. For the mere energy of the spirit, where it is strong enough, has a way of plowing its own esthetic channels, giving to the expression of ideas an accent both original and distinguished.

It would be well worth while, if time allowed, and if it were not invidious, to consider at some length the work of authors who fall just below the standard of distinction which we set for ourselves. For the accomplishment of the first-rate artist appears in higher relief when we set it over against work less distinguished. And the marks of distinction are more easily recognized by contrast with the negative marks of mediocrity. I have puzzled a good deal over the work of writers, like Ruth Suckow, who seem to have all the materials for significant fiction—character, background, feeling and understanding, seriousness and industry—and yet somehow just fail to ring the bell. What she has done for small-town Iowa people in stories like *The Folks* is certainly something which should be done, and it is not marred by provincialism or narrowness of spirit. It cannot fail to interest those acquainted with these localities and these conditions of living, which are in many respects most typical American conditions. The stuff is all there, and there is also in the author the sympathy and insight we should wish for the interpretation of this human data. Yet somehow it fails to take strong hold on the imagination—that at any rate is my own experience—and the farther one reads the more troubled one grows that matter so interesting, presented so faithfully, should prove so wanting in fascination. One admires the sanity of Mrs. Suckow's approach, and one is eager to see the triumph of sanity in art. But one cannot disguise the fact that the interest flags; one wants to skip, not in order to learn the answer to some question, but hoping to find in the next chapter something more arresting than in the present one; and when one puts the book down to go to dinner, one is in no hurry to take it up again.

It is very hard to say just what is wrong. Perhaps one thing that is wanting is rigorous selection of matter. And yet there are plenty of books that are equally crowded with intimate detail which never make this impression of tediousness. It is not so much selection itself that is wanting as a principle of selection. And the principle of selection, which would affect both the style itself and the subject matter presented, would be, I think, some coloring of the mind (beyond mere honesty and goodwill) which would give a more special turn to all that is said. It is not that the effect is mild. For mildness may itself be a coloring of mind sufficient to give distinction, as in Goldsmith and Jane Austen and E. K. Forster, for example, or for that matter in Hawthorne and Howells. But mildness itself must have a kind of intensity or positiveness in order to impress itself on the esthetic sense and not be mistaken for tameness. Subtlety is mild, but it must have a sharpness, too, in order to qualify as subtle. It must have a fine edge, a nicely discriminated accent.

Each one of the men I have chosen to discuss has a marked and individual accent, giving esthetic definition to all his offering, and that precious air of being selective. Let it be the corrosive irony of Dos Passos, the weighted understatement of

Hemingway, the conscious naïveté of Caldwell; let it be the nervous intensity, the rush and incandescence of Faulkner or the lyrical Gargantuan extravagance of Wolfe—even where these qualities are present in excess, even where they lead the author at times along the perilous edge of absurdity— in every case there is something to give the individual stamp of art to the neutral stuff of common observation. It is the mind that is working, but never the mind in its purely scientific and colorless apprehension of truth. It is the mind humanized by emotion and implemented with the rhetoric of feeling. Irony and naïveté are forms of wit; they give point and savor to what might be unimpressive in direct statement.

Even the stark objectivity of Farrell—his bleak, unvarnished recording of things said and done, of brutality, stupidity, obscenity and silliness—even this seemingly photographic method involves the art of self-restraint, self-suppression, so hard for any conscious creator to observe— and from it all, from a narrative in which the author never once appears, there emanates a strong savor of his personal attitude, a sense of the cold fury of loathing with which he contemplates the cultural purgatory from which he made himself so narrow an escape. The very force of the mind, where we are specially conscious of that, as in Jonathan Swift or Michelangelo—to leave for a moment the field of fiction— this is not properly force of mind but force within the mind, power manifesting itself in the operations of the mind. The drive itself comes from the personality, from above or below the mind; the drive is furnished by the sense of values and importance in concepts of the mind, but it is not from the mind that we have our sense of values.

In all these writers we are impressed by their freedom and boldness in dealing with life and character. This boldness is again an esthetic, an emotional quality. There is a kind of ruthlessness or cruelty in their treatment of human nature. Many readers will think this is overdone. They will think it unkind or immoral to tell the truth so nakedly; or they will think that these men give a partial and one-sided view of the truth. And very likely they are right in this last judgment, though they may not be right in condemning this school of writers for being one-sided and partial. It may simply mean that with true artistic instinct they have selected from the social scene, or from certain parts of it, what seems to them most characteristic or what lends itself most naturally to esthetic representation. The rest they leave out of the picture in order not to confuse the effect. And that may be one reason why these men interest us more steadily than certain others who, in the interest of fairness and comprehensiveness, have crowded their canvas with figures that will not come to life and only serve to give a messy effect to the whole.

And that is not all. These writers, like powerful artists in all times, are concerned to render what we may call the very essence of human experience. And for this purpose they have need of characters and incidents that are perhaps more sensational than the average. The peculiarities of human nature are best exhibited in extreme cases. It is about vice and crime that moral problems cluster most thickly. Pedestrian virtue was always notoriously hard to make interesting in literature. Great fiction, great drama, was always too strong meat for squeamish readers. They were as much distressed with the grossness of Ben Jonson, Fielding and Sterne, as they are with that of Hemingway or Steinbeck. American literature has definitely passed out of its Victorian phase, and we need not be surprised to find our writers making liberal use of their new freedom. It would have been so, no doubt, if there had never been a World War, a feminist movement, a Freud, a Marx or a Darwin. But all these things have been. It is not the world of Scott and Thackeray into which these men are born, above all not the same world of the mind. And before considering them individually, it will pay us to take account of certain attitudes common to them all which are directly referable to the times in which they write. These are our own times, and these men are the product of the world we have made.

The most important common feature of American fiction today is that it has all been produced in the interval between two world wars, each one of them greater in scope than the wars following the French Revolution of 1789, and far more disastrous in their effects than those Napoleonic wars. One of these men took part in the fighting as officer of field artillery in France (Marquand), one as member of the Canadian Flying Corps and the British Air Force in France (Faulkner), one as a member of the Italian Arditi (Hemingway), one as a private in the Medical Corps (Dos Passos); two of them also saw service in the ambulance and Red Cross service (Dos Passos and Hemingway). Of the younger men, one viewed the war from the point of view of a college student (Wolfe), and the others from those of schoolboys, farm hands, mill hands, football players (Steinbeck, Caldwell, Farrell). I think we may say that all of them have viewed the first World War with the same horror and dismay; that they all have shared the same doubts as to the ideology that inspired it and that led to our participation in it, the same disgust with that world-wide commercial spirit which was so largely responsible for it, and the same loathing for those traits of human nature which have allowed the dominance of this commercial spirit throughout the civilized world. The disillusionment with human nature, which was already so common among intellectuals before the War, became, we might almost say, universal with them as a result of it.

Few of these men have written extensively about the War; but the first World War was the greatest single cause (among many) of an attitude toward human nature in general which is the most obvious feature of serious contemporary American fiction. Various as are the talents and methods of these men, and various as are the fields in which human nature is shown by them in action, they are at one in their disposition to show it in a distinctly unflattering light. In their general view of it they are uncompromising realists in the historical sense of that term. They are determined not to be taken in by the claims of the heart and the imagination, by man's pretensions to be heroic.

It is somewhat difficult to determine whether this hard-boiled realism in their attitude applies to human nature as it is in itself or as it is molded by social conditions and ideals unfavorable to the development of attractive qualities. At first blush the reader is likely to set down this whole group of writers as arrant cynics. The first impression for many a reader is that they have given up human kind altogether as a race incapable of acting on any but mean and selfish motives, incapable of being guided by the ideals which the reader supposes himself to be guided by. But the reader, if he continues to examine these chronicles with close attention, may come in the end to realize that these authors are not judging human nature according to the same standards as he himself has been accustomed to apply. He is applying the conventional standards of "bourgeois" morality, and is accordingly shocked by conduct which is not so shocking to the authors in question, who apparently make little of these customary standards. They take for granted, it would seem, behavior which the bourgeois reader has been trained to reprobate or, more commonly, to cover with the veil of discreet silence. Or, what is still more distressing, these writers fail to throw over such behavior the light of sentiment by which it may be given a semblance of decency and nice feeling if not made strictly conformable to morality.

What is most irritating about these young fellows is their disinclination to the polite evasions and idealizations of bourgeois romanticism. Man, they seem to say, is less concerned with behaving well than with feeling good about the way he behaves. He is well provided with psychical mechanisms for idealizing what he does—for "rationalizing" his own morality. The novelists we are discussing are in general so bent on exposing the rationalizations of the bourgeois in his business and political life that they will not even leave him a decent covering for his fornications and adulteries. Or, to put it in another way, they seem to regard sexual morality as on all fours with business and social morality in general. All have their basis in natural needs and inclinations; all have their economic bearings. A final judgment upon conduct in any department can be passed only after a careful analysis of the economic aspects of the case. Where economic conditions, for example, put marriage out of the question, one cannot fairly demand that love should be sanctioned by marriage. The bourgeois reader may not share this point of view; and he may accordingly be shocked at the indulgence shown by his author for the sexual freedoms of the proletariat. Nor does he understand why the irregularities of the well-to-do are recorded with a note of irony not exhibited in the case of the dispossessed. Above all, he does not like to encounter in books the descriptive language used by the man in the street. Such language, he considers, should be reserved for the racy stories told in the club by virtuous vestrymen over their cocktails. And he would be very much surprised to hear what the psychologist might have to say about the virtuous vestryman's cocktail story.

It would be a mistake to bracket these eight writers as plain cynics. One or two of them, when you look close, would seem to be too fond of men in their natural state for that—would seem indeed to be convinced of the essential goodness of human beings—or if goodness is too special a word, then of their essential likeableness, or, as we might say, their innocence of evil. Such is the case with Steinbeck, and sometimes with Hemingway. On the whole, however, these writers show men behaving rather disappointingly—rather meanly—and the impression conveyed is that they must inevitably behave rather meanly in the conditions under which their lives are led. The social and economic conditions, the spiritual atmosphere they breathe, the set of values prevailing in their milieu are such that no very admirable or satisfactory behavior is conceivable save in exceptional cases, and the actual exceptions are extremely rare so far as these men report. In general we may say that their conscious or unconscious assumptions are materialistic in the Marxian sense. That is, it is tacitly assumed that men's states of mind are in the last analysis determined largely by the material conditions under which they live, and that these material conditions are largely determined by economic factors, industrial factors.

Of course the thing works both ways. Economic procedures are themselves determined in part by prevailing states of mind, notions of fitness and convenience, as well as operating to reproduce the states of mind which partly determine them. These men are not doctrinaire sociologists, ridden by a rigid theory of economics, and bent at all costs on demonstrating that man is a creature of his own machines. They are sensitive observers of the social scene, well aware of the complexity of causes in the moral world, who have been led by the course of events in their time (including, let us not forget, the great depression of 1929 to 1939) to an acute awareness of the way in which the individual life is embedded in that of society as a whole, and of the extreme disorder and bewilderment and decay of social life in their time, especially among the very large classes of those without anchorage or security.

These men are not dogmatic theorists—their books are not logical demonstrations of the effect of material conditions on character. The case would be simpler if this were so, and the ordinary reader might be made less uneasy by their record. They are, it happens, well aware of native propensities in human nature which tend to shabby or distressing behavior. Several of them, for example (notably Faulkner, Caldwell, Farrell and Steinbeck) are impressed with congenital low mentality as a factor to be reckoned with in any view of the social scene. And while in Caldwell this low mentality would seem to derive from slavish and indigent conditions extending over several generations, the reader sometimes wonders whether the causal sequence may not work the other way—whether low mentality may not in many cases be the cause rather than the effect of slavish indigence. In that view of the case—and leaving eugenics out of account —one may arrive at the very discouraging view that slavish indigence is a condition resulting inevitably from the low mentality which is a recurring feature of human nature, and that the mean and revolting way of life that goes with low mentality is consequently an ineradicable feature of human society.

The same reflections suggest themselves in regard to the inclination to sexual promiscuity so generously exhibited by these writers. There may be some suggestion that promiscuity is a natural accompaniment to economic disorganization, to extreme poverty, slum conditions whether in town or country; and that is doubtless the case. But the very candid record of these men would seem to suggest, in addition, that there is a natural propensity to promiscuousness, likely to be present in all conditions, social and industrial, which is merely aggravated or made more disgusting by poverty and disorganization. And one may further reflect that slum conditions are frequently the effect as much as they are the furthering cause of promiscuity. And so we may be brought to very gloomy conclusions with regard to human nature and the prospects of organizing it in more attractive social patterns.

Another cause of uneasiness and dubiety in the reader of

these American realists is that, with one exception (Wolfe), they are highly disinclined to discuss things with the reader, to come into the open, like Thackeray or George Eliot, and interpret the story for the reader's benefit—to point the moral for him, and explain the underlying philosophy, either in the reader's terms or in their own. In this respect these writers are conforming to the prevailing literary style. Since the middle of the nineteenth century there has been a growing tendency to leave the author out of his narrative, and many considerations have united to confirm writers of fiction in the feeling that it is bad form for them to intrude personally in their story.

For one thing, it is a reaction against the didacticism, the paternalism, of the Victorian writer, inherited by him from the eighteenth-century masters, but given a sentimental and moralizing tone that is particularly offensive to the intellectuals of today. If the author has nothing to say about the behavior of his characters, he feels that he may escape the imputation of being a preacher or a sentimentalist. It is considered to be more in conformity with the principles of esthetics that the work of art should be left to speak for itself; more of an artistic achievement if it is so constructed that it does speak for itself with its own eloquence and is not dependent on the comments of the museum guide. It is thought to be a compliment to the reader to let him draw his own conclusions, recognize for himself the implications of the work of art.

Moreover, it is considered that the *story* is better when it is self-contained. The aim is to "dramatize" the story— free it so far as possible from theoretical generalizations, from painstaking explanations—leave it to work itself out in terms of concrete action, like a stage play. Thus we shall live through the story directly and intimately, and not at one remove as is the case where an author stands there with his pointer and directs us what to see and think.

All these notions are based in real and valid considerations esthetic and psychological, and important values are secured for the reader by the observance of this strict method. It is, however, a method which needs to be applied with infinite discretion; and in any case, we need not be surprised if its benefits are had at the cost of corresponding disadvantages. No work of art can be regarded as so constructed that it speaks with its own eloquence if it leaves the beholder largely bewildered and without clues as to its significance or the principles of its composition. And where the work of art has for its subject matter human nature, it cannot be regarded as entirely successful when it leaves the reader badly confused as to what attitudes toward human nature he is expected to take.

Generally speaking a work of fiction requires no gloss, for the simple reason that the implicit assumptions of the writer and of the reader are virtually identical. They represent the same culture complex, the same scale of values, the same judgments of behavior. But this is not the case with many of these American writers and the average "bourgeois" reader. There is implied in many of these novels a scale of values appreciably different from that held by the average reader into whose hands they will come. And very seldom is there more than a covert hint as to what precisely is the scale of values implied in the story. But more than this— it is not so much the author's scale of values that disturbs the reader as his wish to insinuate doubts as to any scale of values presumably held by the reader. The author wishes to suggest that every instance of human behavior is in need of analysis in terms of causes and effects not always clearly apparent—in terms, particularly, of remote causes and effects in the economic world. He wishes to bring in question the whole set of *mores* perhaps unconsciously held by his reader; and since he is prevented by his self-denying ordinance from stating his doubts directly in abstract terms, all that he can do is to present case after case of behavior, whether conforming to the conventional standard, or conditioned by a social set-up molded by it, or violating the conventional standard as a result of forces not adequately provided for within the prevailing code. He cannot label his cases and show what light is thrown on the prevailing code by the separate instance or the whole exhibit. All he can do is to make his cases as significant as possible and arrange them in such a pattern as to throw what light they can on one another, and then leave it to the reader to draw his own conclusions. And often enough the unwary reader may draw conclusions somewhat different from those intended, and particularly, as I have said, the conclusion that his author has a much too cynical view of human nature.

All of which seems to point the need for an understanding guide and interpreter.

But I have probably laid too much stress on causes for misunderstanding and the "resistance" opposed by the reader to these contemporary authors. And I have dwelt too long, perhaps, on their attitude toward human nature in the abstract. It is only by inference that in reading these novels one arrives at the notion of abstract human nature. What they present is the social scene itself, and this is entirely made up of men and women shown in the concrete. These writers are chosen as much for the lifelikeness as for the truthfulness of their portraiture. And beyond mere lifelikeness, which is within the command of many a second-rate portrait painter, are subtler skills and endowments more difficult to name. There are verve and gusto, imagination and the individual touch; there is skill in composition, in the disposition and balance of parts; there is sense for rhythm and design; there are in the brush-stroke fineness and delicacy, breadth and boldness.

One test of excellence in fiction is the creation of characters that live in the imagination and stay with the reader as permanent acquaintances. In this matter these writers are somewhat at a disadvantage in comparison with those more romantic or more simply theatrical in their characterization. For the heart is a powerful builder of character, and the imagination will often content itself with mere figments of the stage. These contemporary realists will seldom give the heart free reign; and they generally are less concerned with stage effect than with the sober lineaments of truth. But truth itself has carrying power when deeply and intensely conceived. Characters come to life by mere force of being convincing. Besides, these writers are not without their ways of setting the stage and highlighting the actors. And if there are few in their cast of characters who are positively lovable, few who put upon us the spell of a Becky Sharp, a Parson Adams, a Wilkins Micawber or a Tess Durbeyfield, there is still a considerable number who fascinate us, convince and hold us, and who in retrospect are felt to be memorable and significant, and so far as mortal creations can be so, unforgettable.

Thus we have, in Dos Passos, Eleanor Stoddard, interior decorator, and J. Ward Moorehouse, public relations counsellor *(U.S.A.)*; in Hemingway, Lady Brett Ashley, the glamorous "bitch," the Greek-American "count" *(The Sun Also Rises)*, and the Spanish virago and patriot Pilar *(For Whom the Bell Tolls)*. In Faulkner, who is more theatrical, we have a much larger number: in *The Sound and the Fury*, the idiot Benjy Compson, his mean brother Jason and his niece Quentin; in *As I Lay Dying*, Addie Bundren, the dead mother, to name only the most arresting of many characters; in *Sanctuary*, Popeye and Temple, the frantic coed; in *Light in August*, Joe Christmas, the white negro, and the Rev. Gail Hightower; in *Absalom, Absalom!* the portentous legendary figure of Colonel Thomas Sutpen, and the New Orleans half-caste gentleman, Charles Bon. This is the shortest list one could make for Faulkner. In Caldwell, we have the immortal Lester Jeeter, and Ellie May of the hare-lip, and the preacher woman Bessie *(Tobacco Road);* Semon Dye, the preacher man *(Journeyman);* Sheriff Jeff McCurtain *(Trouble in August);* Ty Ty and Darling Jill and Will Thompson the weaver *(God's Little Acre);* not to name any characters from the short stories. In Thomas Wolfe, there are Oliver and Eliza Gant *(Look Homeward, Angel);* Uncle Bascom and Francis Starwick *(Of Time and the River);* "Major" Lafayette Joyner and Esther Jack *(The Web and the Rock).* In Farrell, there are Studs Lonigan (in the trilogy named for him); Ambrose J. McGinty *(Gas-House McGinty);* Jim O'Neill the expressman, the grandmother Mary O'Fla- herty, and Aunt Margaret *(A World I Never Made, No Star Is Lost* and *Father & Son).* In Marquand, we have George Apley, the Boston brahmin *(The Late George Apley);* Aunt Clothilde and Allen Southby, the Harvard housemaster *(Wickford Point),* as well as Mr. Moto, if we go outside of serious fiction into the region of the artistic-commercial. And finally, we have in Steinbeck, Danny and the Pirate (in *Tortilla Flat),* poor Lennie *(Of Mice and Men),* and in *The Grapes of Wrath,* at least Grampa and Ma and the preacher Casy.

The devotees of any of these men will quarrel with me over my omissions, but never, I feel confident, over my inclusions, and not seriously over the proportion of memo- rable characters assigned to each author. I have played my little game without fear or favor. I have got as far as I could from the books and ruled out severely all ulterior motives of criticism and judgment. I have simply sent out a general invitation and held open house for these fictive people as they exist in my imagination; and I have favored those who came first and stayed longest—who cried out most insistently for recognition. I had no idea in advance that Faulkner and Caldwell would head the list for memorable characters, or that Dos Passos and Hemingway would stand at the foot. I am drawing no hasty conclusions. Hemingway and Dos Passos I respect no less than any in the list. Hemingway was best known (till yesterday) for his short stories, which do not give the same scope for building up characters and making us intimate with them. Besides, I do not think that Hemingway was aiming primarily at the creation of character. Dos Passos is greatly concerned with character, but more in its representative and social aspect than for individual picturesqueness and idiosyncrasy. But even these two have more than usual talent for the creation of characters. I could name many others in their stories whom I can never forget—Ellen Thatcher and Bud Korpenning and Anna Cohen in *Manhattan Transfer;* Nick Adams' father, the doctor, in the short stories of *In Our Time,* Joe the jockey's son in "My Old Man," and in *For Whom the Bell Tolls* at least Maria and Pablo and Fernando.

Wolfe has a special gift for Gargantuan grotesques, Caldwell for the naïvely comic, Faulkner for the strange and fearful in character. The characters of Farrell are probably nearest to common painful experience, most simply human and pathetic, though many readers would name Steinbeck in this connection. Farrell is harder, Steinbeck more stagey. Marquand is smarter, more the man of the world.

But I have no inclination to play favorites. What I wish, at the end of this too-protracted introduction, is. to assure the reader unacquainted with these interbellum writers that their pages are swarming with people of the greatest fascination and colorfulness. In no case has the author's seriousness about human nature kept him from meeting his prime obligation as a storyteller, to introduce his reader to interesting and memorable specimens of the genus homo.

II. JOHN DOS PASSOS

The Artist in Uniform

"La peinture opposite the Madeleine
Cézanne Picasso Modigliani . . ."
                                    —DOS PASSOS

II. JOHN DOS PASSOS

The Artist in Uniform

Each one of our contemporary novelists has his favorite subject. It is the Georgia cracker, the Boston brahmin, the Chicago poolroom loafer, the decayed gentry of "Jefferson," Mississippi, or the Okie in search of a job. These subjects are limited and particular, and if the human show is unsatisfactory, it need not be taken as characteristic of the species in general. Elsewhere the picture may be brighter. But with John Dos Passos, the earliest of our group, the case is different. He has taken so wide a sweep in his survey of American living, his destructive criticism is applied so systematically over the whole field, that he leaves his reader scarcely a loophole for cheerful views of human behavior. And this in spite of the fact that Dos Passos appears to hold to a constructive social philosophy which generally leaves its possessor some measure of hopefulness. This social philosophy on its constructive side is so little in evidence in his stories, the world he pictures is so completely dominated by a philosophy at variance with what he holds, that the ordinary reader is left with a dreary sense of human nature as a mean and shallow lot.

This effect is made all the more striking by the rigor with which Dos Passos adheres to his realistic standards. He will employ none of the tricks of romantic storytelling, not even the appeal to terror, to mystery and suspense, which is the stock-in-trade of Faulkner. There is little humor in him; he will seldom give any character the picturesque pointing-up of a Caldwell, let alone a Dickens. His characters are not made heroic by the size of their appetites or by the cloudy splendor of their dreams, like those of Wolfe. He has not Steinbeck's heart-felt love of the earth, the mountains, and of men that toil or that fight together for a common cause. While he has some gift for descriptive words, one does not feel that he has a style of his own [1]; at any rate he has not the sheer literary sparkle and gusto of a Hemingway. His realism is sober, bleak and unrelieved. And the soft reader who begins his reading of interbellum fiction with Dos Passos, as he logically should, must be prepared for a plunge into waters chillier and more bitter than any others that wash our shores. It will mean total immersion in the spirit of the time. And if he survives this baptism by Dos Passos, he need fear no other encounter with contemporary prophets.

The paradox of the case is that, of the whole set, Dos Passos is probably the man of tenderest sensibilities and the most inveterate lover of beauty in the conventional sense of the word. He is, one feels, a spirit that shrinks from the touch of the ugly and the gross; and the whole structure of his fiction is built of materials naturally repellent to him. There are several characters in his fiction that it is reasonable to identfy more or less closely with Dos Passos—the anonymous boy and man who records the impressions of the Camera Eye in *U.S.A.*, Martin Howe of the ambulance service in *One Man's Initiation—1917*, the private John Andrews in *Three Soldiers*. And one even suspects that in *Streets of Night* complementary aspects of the author's temperament as a college man are reflected in Fanshaw Macdougan and David Wendell.

Streets of Night was published in 1923; but it is such a vague and ineffectual composition that one guesses it must have been written earlier and dragged out of the author's

[1] I am not speaking of books like his *Journeys Between Wars* (1938), in which the author speaks in his own person.

barrel after the success of *Three Soldiers* in 1921. It is an impressionistic presentation of moments in the lives of three young people in Boston—Nancibel, violin student, with a maiden aunt in the Back Bay; Fanshaw Macdougan, from Omaha, Harvard instructor in the history of art, living with his invalid mother; and David Wendell (Wenny), son of a clergyman, occupying a post in some scientific museum at Harvard. Wenny is untidy in dress, with a shambling walk like an Italian laborer's. He is ill content with the futility of his life, troubled by the flesh; wants to get a job on the section gang of a railway; likes to take his friends to a dirty Italian restaurant where they drink Orvieto and eat garlic-flavored food. He upsets Nancibel with his direct proposals; throws up his job, tries to lead the life of a bum; tries to satisfy himself with a street woman; pleases his father by taking a job; gets into a hysterical state of mind over the thought that he is just like his father over again; and finally shoots himself.

Fanshaw is the opposite of Wenny. He too thinks their life is futile, but only because they have fallen on evil times. He lives imaginatively in the Renaissance and the eighteenth century. He loves to think of Pico della Mirandola riding into Florence in the time of the lilies and of themselves as people floating down stream in a barge out of a Canaletto carnival; he shrinks from the cheapness of the Italian restaurant and from the vulgarity of Rubens ("more acreage than intensity in Rubens, and all of it smeared with raspberry jam"); he likes the circumspectness and grace with which they went about life in the eighteenth century, never head-long, half-cocked like Wenny. Above all he feels disgust with the usual ways of sex in an ugly world. One must try to be beautiful about life. After Wenny's suicide he makes love to Nancibel in his own delicate way; but she cannot go through with it. (Since Wenny's death she has taken to the Ouija board.) Fanshaw goes abroad on relief work, and after two years returns to the college yard. In Palermo he accompanies a French captain to a high-class bawdy house, with all due sanitary precautions. But he does not share the enthusiasm of the French captain or the American major for a war which brought them so many diversions.

There are several points which suggest that both Wenny and Fanshaw are attempts to dramatize aspects of Dos Passos' own temper as a young man. Wenny finds himself "at 23 penniless, ignorant, and full of the genteel paralysis of culture." (The man of the Camera Eye several times refers to his want of funds, and he clearly found himself ignorant and culture-paralyzed after "four years under the ether cone" at Harvard.) The genteel paralysis is chiefly embodied in Fanshaw; Wenny is the vain effort to throw it off. (In the Camera Eye there are several references to the admiration or the cultivated dislike for the "mucker"—child of labor—felt by the sensitive scion of Virginia bourgeoisie.) Wenny had "lain awake at night thinking of muckers when he was a kid, making himself stories of fights, things with girls, adventures he'd do if he were a mucker, if he were to run away from Aunt Susan and be a mucker." Dos Passos' evident fondness for muckers, the extensive record of the life of muckers in his mature work (Mac, Joe Williams, Charley Anderson), seems to represent psychologically his effort to escape from, to compensate for, the genteel paralysis of bourgeois culture.

It is even conceivable that the sexual adventures of the mucker represent for our author an alternative to the cultural paralysis. Fanshaw's reaction against the grossness of sex is so strong that he almost lands in celibacy; he cannot secure the love of the nice girl; the Palermo bawdy house (reconcilable with Pico della Mirandola) is the final logic of his fastidiousness, though he cannot agree with Major Baldwin that it was a great war while it lasted. Wenny makes a more desperate effort to escape the genteel paralysis so far as his sex life is concerned; but when he goes home with the prostitute Ellen, he cannot stand the sordid conditions of bought "love"—he gives her all the money he has and rushes out into the street. In *One Man's Initiation—1917* Martin Howe has the same, though less violent, reaction; he cannot go with the girls in Paris who offer themselves. "Oh," he says, "if you were only a person, instead of being a member of a profession—" And John Andrews in *Three Soldiers* is nearly as fastidious. It is not for want of understanding of the reactions of "nice" men that Dos Passos has so much to tell of the sexual adventures of the "mucker."

The first published story of Dos Passos was *One Man's Initiation—1917*. It is a record of the impressions of Martin Howe in the ambulance service in France. One suspects that the name Martin Howe is almost the only fictitious feature of the book. The thing most remarkable about Martin Howe, next to his thoughtful, feeling nature, is his esthetic sensibility. He notices things like "the red hand of the waiter pouring the Chartreuse, green like a stormy sunset." In the Gothic abbey where they are lodged for a time, he dreams of the quiet lives the monks must have passed so far away in the Forest of the Argonne; if there were monasteries now, he thinks he'd go into one. While the shells shriek overhead, he and his friends muse in the garden of a ruined French villa, with its dry concrete fountain, its white and pink and violet phlox, chatting or sleeping in the languid sunlight, "pointing out to each other tiny things, the pattern of snail-shells, the glitter of insects' wings, colors, fragrances, all that the shells that shrieked overhead, to explode on the road behind them, threatened to wipe out." The virtual identity of this Martin Howe with the author is suggested by the recurrence of this same concrete (or cement) fountain, even to the phlox and the snails, in the thirtieth Camera Eye in *1919*, as well as of the abbey in the thirty-eighth.

Much the same man appears in *Three Soldiers* as the

private, John Andrews. Here he realizes the childhood wish of Wenny to get out of his class and associate with muckers (the other privates, Bonelli and Chrisfield). He is represented as a good comrade, though given to musing and likely to be seen talking to old women beside a hedge of orange marigolds. He is no mucker himself, but grew up with his mother in a dilapidated mansion in Virginia among old oaks and chestnuts, inventing little tunes to go with the stories she told him. His penchant for the "esthetic" is shown by the recurrence in his impressions of bright orange clay, jade-green rivers, purple-gray church spires, mauve-tinted clouds, picturesque villages with clean red tiles, and by the winey fragrance of apples, and the "smell of damp woods and rotting fruits and of all the ferment of the over-ripe fields." The author of *A Pushcart at the Curb* is suggested by his stopping now and then to look at "the greens and oranges and crimsons of vegetables in a pushcart. . . ." John Andrews is a composer, obvious transposition of Dos Passos' activity as a poet, who is turning the soldiers' drill into *Arbeit und Rhythmus,* planning an orchestral piece, "Under the Yoke," and another on "The Soul and Body of John Brown." His one hope through months and years of hateful military discipline is to "express these thwarted lives, the miserable dulness of industrialized slaughter." That would make it "almost worth while—for him; for the others, it would never be worth while."

The Red Cross man in *1919* has the same esthetic tastes—takes long walks with a friend "along the purple wintry-rutted roads under the purple embroidery of the pleached trees," drinking "good wine full of Merovingian names millwheels glassgreen streams where the water gurgles out of old stone gargoyles Madeleine's red apples the smell of beech leaves . . ." His items are more run together in the manner of a modern landscape; for he has been looking at "la peinture opposite the Madeleine Cézanne Picasso Modigliani."

He still has his passion for what he calls (in *The Big Money*) "landscapes corroded with literature." The drive from Fontainebleau to Marseille is studded with graceful souvenirs—Dumas, Rabelais, Rousseau, Van Gogh. But this thrush has turned catbird. The landscapes of Provence brought them to the eleven thousand registered harlots of Marseille, "posted with their legs apart around the scummy edges of the oldest port." The Italian Riviera was "blue selzerbottles standing in the cinzanocolored sunlight beside a glass of VERMOUTH TORINO," and the eyes of boys and girls in marble Genoa were lighted by the flare of a burning Yankee tanker.

The subjects he would have chosen naturally—this Harvard poet, twenty-one in 1917, mooning in Spain—are those displayed in his *A Pushcart at the Curb* (1922). Picturesque and graceful figures from old Castile—lovers in an alley, the goatboy plying his peaceful trade among grim Moorish towers, and then the fiestas and ceremonial parades, Noche Buena, processions of the Virgin, harlequinades à la Debussy; in Italy, the Queen of Cyprus and Jerusalem entering the gates of Asolo as Cyprian Venus; in Paris, vignettes of Sainte Geneviève, and Watteau Embarquement pour Cythère. Amy Lowell—

> The streets are full of lilacs
> lilacs in boys' buttonholes
> lilacs at women's waists . . .

John Gould Fletcher—

> As a gardener in a pond
> splendid with lotus and Italian nenuphar . . . .

> See how the frail white pagodas of blossom
> stand up on the great green hills
> of the chestnuts . . . .

Alfred Kreymborg—A Pushcart at the Curb. De Falla—fire dance, gypsies, church bells. Respighi—fountains of Rome,

Pines of Rome. Ballet Russe de Monte Carlo—Petrouchka, Three-cornered Hat.

Shy and sensitive soul, delicate spirit, quick imagination, open heart. A good comrade in the ranks or round the café table. Apt at languages, understanding of local ways. He loves the simple life of the Gascon peasant. The Breton laborer gives him a lift in his cart and they exchange sentiments—the Breton boy would go to America, for life is bad in Europe; but life in America is ugly and drab, and men come to the War to seek relief from boredom. "Something sweet and wistful that (Andrews) could not analyze lingered in his mind from Marcel's talk." The gentle ways of peace are symbolized by the rabbit man, with his droll mechanical toy:

> The rabbit was rather formless, very fluffy and had a glance of madness in its pink eye with a black center. . . .
> "Do you make them yourself?" asked Andrews, smiling.
> "Oh, oui, Monsieur, d'après la nature."
> He made the rabbit turn a somersault by suddenly pressing the bulb hard. Andrews laughed and the rabbit man laughed.
> "Think of a big strong man making his living that way," said Walters, disgusted.
> "'I do it all . . . de matière première au profit de l'accapareur,'" said the rabbit man.

Is it humor? Is it the pride of an honest workman, who is his own employer, his own middleman and salesman, and has slipped through the meshes of capitalism and the World War? The rabbit man makes but one more appearance, when he and Andrews exchange the detached impressions of connoisseurs on the beauty of Parisian women and shake hands with sudden vigor. It is the recognition of man for man, across the barriers of language, of class and culture—the acknowledgment of man's essential and individual dignity.

It has the quality of Sterne in the *Sentimental Journey*. And that is not by accident. For this Dos Passos has quite as much of Sterne, or of Henry James, as he has of Amy Lowell or De Falla. By nature he would have written of graceful and humane living—of individuals working out the pattern of their lives without interference—of generous impulse and playful whim—and of landscapes molded by the toil of farmer and forester. But what he found was twisted heaps of brick and iron and officers creeping into shelters. This lover of phlox and honeysuckle met everywhere the smell of carbolic and latrines, of gas and shrapnel, of foul bodies in uniform, and headless bodies rotting in the woods. This lover of freedom and idiosyncrasy found men made slaves, bullied and humiliated, denied all dignity, and kept to their endless drill, their loading and unloading of scrap iron, their window-washing and emptying of slops, long after the War was over. His three soldiers are all good men; but all three were driven by the cruelties of the system to the desperate expedient of deserting. They would have willingly given their lives for their country; but the endless waiting and futility, the bungling and brutality of the War, stifled all remnants of patriotic feeling.

If Dos Passos had had faith in the justice of our cause, he might have had more patience with what are no doubt the necessary conditions of large-scale military operations. But he evidently went in with no illusions. It was the same with the characters who represent him, and they drifted naturally into the company of like-minded people everywhere. The French soldiers did not share the hatred of the Huns so assiduously cultivated by the YMCA men in the name of Jesus. They took for granted that the War was made by financial pirates and feudal lords; that it was but a symptom of the ruthless greed which was the central evil of the world. They believed that all the plain people in all the armies shared this view and that sooner or later they would strike for freedom, for the dignity of man. But their hopes were ill founded, and Martin Howe was destined to witness the death of all those who at the French farm inveighed against the "lies" for which the War was fought.

Dos Passos went into the War as a man of letters, and in the end his contribution was bound to be in the form of literature. The satisfactions of John Andrews took the line of artistic expression; he was bent on giving voice in music to "these thwarted lives, the miserable dulness of industrialized slaughter." Martin Howe was no more resigned than the relief worker who complained of the people being forced to fight and die like cattle driven to the slaughter-house. "I am going to do something some day, but first I must see. I want to be initiated in all the circles of hell." He was soon initiated; and what he did was *Three Soldiers*. The compelling realities of the present took the place of the figures of ballet and harlequinade. His subject was given him. It may not have been to his liking, but he had no choice. It was still a work of art and skill which he labored to fashion. But he had to use the stuff at hand; and the taste which might have been informed by delight and love was guided and compelled by the reactions of disgust and repulsion.

Three Soldiers was the first important American novel, and one of the first in any language, to treat the War in the tone of realism and disillusion. It made a deep impression, and may be counted the beginning of strictly contemporary fiction in the United States. Stephen Crane had come before him with *The Red Badge of Courage*. But Crane's war was imagined, not experienced, and there is about his work an air of the archaic and synthetic. Norris and Dreiser and Lewis are honorable names in American realism, but in many points of tone and technique they belong to the past rather than to the present.

So it was the War that determined the bent of Dos Passos' genius. But the War was just the beginning. The "lies" that made the War were the creation of our society as it operates in time of "peace." And his great work was destined to be the representation of American life on a grand scale, in which the War is shown as a mere incident.

He began with a relatively limited subject. *Manhattan Transfer* (1925) is a survey of life in New York City during the period from about 1890 to about 1925.[1] It consists of a kaleidoscopic succession of moments from the lives of a large number of persons chosen to represent the various classes who may be taken to make up society in the metropolis. If there is one character more central than another it is the newspaperman Jimmy Herf, who may be assumed to represent the general attitude and point of view of Dos Passos. The other characters are largely such as would make the front page of a newspaper, the tacit assumption being, rightly enough perhaps, that the newspaper is the best single index of the American mind. Ellen Thatcher, daughter of a registered accountant who plays the market, a second-rate but successful actress in musical shows, married successively to the actor Jo-Jo, to the newspaperman Herf, and to the lawyer Baldwin; George Baldwin, rising lawyer with a somewhat shady practice, who finally throws over his labor-union friends to run for district attorney on the reform ticket; Jeff Merivale, Jimmy's uncle, who has made his way to the top in banking, and his son James, who goes into business with the same firm; labor organizers and politicians; bootleggers made wealthy by prohibition; theatrical producers—these hold the center of the stage, and represent the classes that prosper most under the set-up. Along with these is a scattering of vocations essential to modern life—realtors, architects,

1 Early in the story, but not at the very beginning, there is a reference to the signing of the Greater New York Bill by Governor Morton, 1895–96; and toward the end a reference to the reform movement against Mayor Hylan. In the course of the narrative, the time is indicated by references to such notable events as the taking of Port Arthur, the Stanford White murder, Sarajevo, the Liberty Loan drive, and the post-War deportation of communists by the Department of Justice.

sanitary engineers, theatrical people living from hand to mouth, together with other types of businessmen whose prosperity is great but precarious—promoters of wildcat schemes, who have to take to their heels, large importers and exporters, who go down for millions in a market crash.

These represent the upper and middle layers of metropolitan society—those who know how to take advantage of conditions, and make up the glittering figures in the social tapestry. And then, weaving in and out among these foreground figures, are the obscure shadows of those who cannot take care of themselves—the misfits, the exploited masses, those thrown off on the slagheap from the great industrial machine. There is Bud Korpenning, from upstate, who slew his father in a moment of frenzied revolt against ill treatment, who seeks to lose himself in the great city, but he is haunted by men in derbies and finally throws himself off Brooklyn Bridge. There is Joe Harland, drunken bum, who could not maintain his favored position in the business world. There is Dutch Robertson, private back from the wars, who cannot make an honest living and keep his girl; he goes in for crime and the law soon catches up with him. There are Jewish garment workers zealous for the union which will win them a decent living. There is Anna Cohen, milliner's employee, who has no place to take her man, and who loses her life in the fire at Mme. Soubrine's.

These are obscure and dreary figures, wisps and straws on the churning surface of our industrial maelstrom; but each one has his moment of spotlight on the front page, which daily serves up for our general entertainment a selection of the disasters and tragedies that grace the progress of civilization. Throughout the book the steady rising lines of those who prosper are crossed in a regular pattern by the falling lines of those who are drifting slowly downward, or plunging suddenly into the darkness like falling stars.

No one's story is told consecutively or with completeness;

but the characters reappear from time to time at significant moments so that we can trace the general outline of their lives. The fragmentary moments are shown with startling vividness in circumstance, and with a certain intimacy in the rendering of sensations and moods. We never question the reality of the character or the situation. But so rapid is the shift from situation to situation, from character to character, so wide are the intervals between appearances, that we cannot quite grasp the thread which binds together the psychic life of the individual. They are individuals, for they have particular bodies and vocations and social status, and they have names and addresses in the telephone book. But they are not quite *persons;* for we are not made to feel that they are self-directing spirits. We are not shown the ideal nucleus round which their emotional life is organized. And so in spite of their vivid reality, they do not have the sentimental *importance* of characters in fiction.

This is no doubt intentional and deliberate on the part of the author. The standard novel of an earlier period was either biographical or dramatic in structure. That is, it followed through the life-history of one person, bringing in as many other characters as were important in relation to him; or it took up a group of characters at the moment in which their story came to a climax and carried it through to its dénouement. In either case, there was a high degree of continuity in storytelling. Our interest was centered continuously on the character and affairs of the leading person; or it was focussed sharply on the problem of a group of persons with more or less conflicting interests and objectives. In either case, there were certain issues to be determined, problems to be faced, either in the successive moments of a single career, or in the urgent pressures of a special dramatic situation. The leading persons were faced with difficulties to be met, decisions to be made, and the way the problem was resolved depended largely on the character of the persons involved, their aims and ideals, their moral prepossessions, their ruling passions. Sometimes they could not have what they wanted because of circumstances that might not be overcome, because of weakness in their own make-up; but character is fate, as Novalis says, and the direction of their effort, at any rate, was determined by the objectives held by the persons of the drama.

This may, in the last analysis, be the case with the characters in *Manhattan Transfer;* but such is not the impression made upon the reader. The manner of narrative is not of a sort to emphasize ideal objectives at all as a determinant of action, but rather to suggest that the whole thing is a matter of stimulus and response. It is true that individuals are differentiated according to gift and vocation, and this is not wholly the result of circumstances. Somewhere along the line there comes in presumably the individual "set" in a certain direction, determined at least in part by the native temper of the individual. But the differentiation is more outward than inward. Human beings have different ways of securing their gratifications; but the gratifications are limited in number and kind. The impulse to make one's way in the world (here measured primarily in terms of money), the craving for "love," for entertainment, and for the avoidance of discomfort—human behavior is pretty well determined by these four considerations; and the word "craving" is perhaps too positive in its implications to suit the case. The working of the human organism would appear to be automatic—certain conditions set going certain types of behavior. The presence of a given organism within the field of vision provokes the response of "love"; discomfort drives one to a more comfortable attitude; a feeling of emptiness provokes boredom and sets one on the track of entertainment and novelty; a business opportunity releases effort and ambition.

Now, this is not a romantic view of human behavior and does not appeal to the ordinary reader of novels. He does not readily identify himself with characters whose behavior is determined in this accidental and piecemeal way. He thinks of himself as *after* something in life, as moved to action by certain ideal aims, which operate continuously, and in reference to which all his effort is organized. There is, accordingly, more coherence to his behavior, and more drama. Many are the difficulties in the way of success in the pursuit of ideal ends: our own weakness, conflict among our ideals, adverse circumstance, misunderstanding, opposing wills. There are odds to be overcome, intricate issues to be resolved. It is in the meeting of such difficulties that the personality makes itself known. And that is one reason why we are fond of drama, even in literature that makes a point of being "realistic."

There are probably several distinct reasons for Dos Passos' denying himself the method of storytelling which is most in favor and which has the great advantage of impressing the reader with the importance, and so—in the last analysis—with the essential truth of his characters. His project is obviously not to present human nature as it might be, as it may have been under favoring conditions, as it may actually be in exceptional cases, but rather as it impresses him in the main as being today under the conditions actually prevailing. He is himself a sensitive idealist grossly offended and disillusioned by what he finds to be the prevailing tone of human feeling in the world that made the War.

There are some faint indications in his characters of ideal objectives which have been missed and which survive obscurely in the depths of souls not strong enough to make headway against the main currents of the time. None of the characters are happy; few are altogether content with the way of life which they feel compelled to follow. Gus McNiel is a milk-wagon driver; he is destined to become a prosperous politician. He has his dream of taking up free land in North Dakota and raising wheat—"pretty curlyheaded Nellie feeding chickens at the kitchen door." This is his feeble tribute

to the ideal. For several of the men, it is "love" that symbol-
izes the ideal values which they have missed in the pursuit of
success. Harry Goldweiser, the theatrical producer, takes
Ellen for an evening's entertainment. He remembers the rap-
tures of boyhood taking a girl to Coney Island. "What I want
to do is get that old feelin back, understand?" When Baldwin
has divorced his wife and is going to marry Ellen, he assures
the latter that "life's going to mean something for me now.
God if you knew how empty life had been for so many years.
I've been like a tin mechanical toy, all hollow inside." Stan,
the reckless Harvard boy, who literally set himself on fire in
a drunken fit, had meant something of this sort to Ellen. It
was doubtless from Stan that she had learned the Shelleyan
formula—"Darkly, fearfully afar from this nonsensical life,
from this fuzzy idiocy and strife. . . ." In the midst of her suc-
cesses and triumphs professional and personal, she has to
remind herself to relax and not "to go round always keyed
up so that everything is like chalk shrieking on a blackboard."
She has been caught in a whirl of meaningless activities
and empty gratifications. She knows: "There are lives to be
lived if only you didnt care. Care for what, for what: the
opinion of mankind, money, success, hotel lobbies, health,
umbrellas, Uneeda biscuits . . . ? It's like a busted mechanical
toy the way my mind goes brrr all the time."

There is one person in the book who has never let the
machine quite run over him; has not delivered himself to
Mammon. At the age of sixteen, through some perverse streak
in him, Jimmy Herf refused to go in business with his Uncle
Jeff; he would not be fed like tape in and out of revolving
doors. He has been a newspaper reporter; he has gone to
Europe as a Red Cross worker; he has been married to the
enchanting Ellen, but has neither converted her from futile
worldliness nor been subdued to it himself; he has tasted of
dead sea apples but will not make them his daily fare. At
length he throws over even his newspaper job; he will no

longer stay "pockmarked with print." He turns his back on the city of destruction like the one good man of Sodom. He gets a lift on a furniture truck headed South. He doesn't know how far he's going, but it's "pretty far." Such is the protest of the self-determining individual against a world that would make of him a sensual automaton.

But there is another consideration leading Dos Passos to his employment of a method which ignores the personal drama dear to fiction. *Manhattan Transfer* is one of the earliest of that type of novel which has come to be known as "collectivistic." The idea is to present a cross-section of the social structure, the social organism; an "over-view" of the subject in which the details of individual lives merge in the general picture of "society." For this purpose, he requires a larger number of characters than can conveniently be featured in the usual storytelling manner; a number and variety of characters such as to suggest general conclusions. The interest is not in the individual dramas of these people, in their personal joys and sorrows, their hole-in-the-corner moral problems; these are of interest only in so far as they are the cellular stuff, the protoplasmic basis, of all social structures. But it is the structure itself which interests the collectivist, the pattern made from innumerable individual cases; the interplay, the working together—the "organic filaments" (as Carlyle calls them) that bind together man to man, and class to class, in the orderly complex of "society." It is the social nexus which the collectivist is seeking.

But the paradox of Dos Passos' world is that the social nexus is just what is lacking. These people live in the same world, the same city. They are subject to the same natural laws, the same economic stresses, and to the same legal statutes. There is a constituted city government—traffic regulations, fire department, milk delivery, sewage disposal—a material organization of the prettiest and most efficient. But for the social nexus binding man to man—affection, gratitude, obligation, cooperation—this is nowhere to be seen. It is every man for himself and the devil take the hindmost. There is hardly a suggestion of any motivation but the four sluggish impulses above referred to, none of which has any but the vaguest reference to interests shared, sentiments reciprocated, ideals held in common. It is an atomistic world, a moral chaos, set in a frame of cosmic order. Society is of necessity collective where so many material needs are served for so many people by so many common agencies, where the stopping of the railroads or the water-supply would result in instant catastrophe and starvation. But in men's relations to man the collectivistic logic is ignored and denied; society is organized on individualistic lines, which means that in effect it is not organized at all.

Everyone denies the connections with his fellows though inevitably bound up with them in the same pattern. Ellen cannot have her hats without the labor of Anna Cohen, but it is only the tragic fire and the death of Anna that bring her briefly to Ellen's mind. Captain James Merivale returns with private Dutch Robertson from the same AEF; but the one prospers in finance while the other drifts into crime; and the only connection between them is the possibility that Merivale may read in the paper of Robertson's getting twenty years. Merivale's banking depends on the commerce of Blackhead and Densch; but Blackhead and Densch fail for ten million dollars, while the bankers still have money to handle. "That's the thing about banking. Even in a deficit there's money to be handled. These commercial propositions always entail a margin of risk. We get 'em coming or else we get 'em going. . . ." George Baldwin is carrying on with Gus McNeil's wife while he is wangling twelve thousand dollars damages for Gus. His going in for political reform means throwing over his friends. The code of the political clansman is simpler. "You know how (Gus) likes to stand by his friends and have his friends stand by him." In marriage people change partners as easily as they change trains at Manhattan Transfer in Jersey; and children are no complication in the world of the abortionist.

Manhattan Transfer is a picture of chaos moral and social; and the narrative technique corresponds to the theme. Each chapter is a loose bundle of incidents from the lives of many different persons or groups, anywhere from four to sixteen in number, completely unrelated save in time and their common involvement in the chaos of Manhattan. There is no effort to mark transitions; each slide replaces the preceding one without preparation or apology, but with something like the flicker of the early silent movies. We pass from the midst of one situation to the midst of another. The characters reappear at wide intervals, without connection or reintroduction. We find ourselves plunged into a situation years later in time and pick up as we can the dropped threads. If Ellen has changed her name to Elaine or Elena, we find this out for ourselves; we piece things together and make our inferences without slowing down, as we read traffic signs on a dark night in unfamiliar country. Within scenes the narrative is often elliptical, with sudden changes from objective action to subjective comment, from what happens to what the character says about it to himself, from third person to first, as the character dramatizes his own experience. The characters' thoughts are not presented formally and consecutively, but by flashes and allusions, as in actual thinking, and with free association of ideas, which do not follow a steady and logical course.

This technique, often suggestive of James Joyce or Virginia Woolf, is dictated by many considerations purely esthetic. There is the instinct to get rid of the author, with his fussy explanations and intrusive comments; to let the situation come to the reader directly with its impact of immediacy and intimacy. But this technique is symbolic too, and corresponds to the philosophical theme. It underlines the dis-

continuity in the psychic life of the characters. We have the
sense of persons not persons—of individuals made up of separate and unrelated moments—at best, a succession of stimuli
followed by their responses. What occurs in the intervals does
not matter, for the personality is not bound together by a
consistency of aim or objective; it is simply uniform in its
responses to stimuli of a certain order. Thus the technique
contributes to the effect of life as sensation, of thinking as
non-purposive, of human beings as puppets on a string. And
since the human mind has difficulty in thinking of itself in
such purely mechanical terms, we have the effect of bewilderment and futility which is so characteristic of contemporary
literature represented physically in the very structure of the
narrative.

Again, this technique serves the social theme. So many
separate lives are shown being led simultaneously, as it
were. There is no need to carry each incident through to
its completion, to follow each individual into all the ramifi-
cations of his private life. What is called for is a representative section, enough of the tissue in each case to determine
its structure; and of such representative bits a vast number,
typical and comprehensive. Each one must be reduced in
scale so that all may be brought under a single survey, as
specimens are assembled under the view of a laboratory
worker whose business is to characterize the whole.

But the whole in this case is a social whole; in a social
whole the important thing should be the connections, the
social relations. And this narrative discontinuity serves again
to emphasize the paradox of social beings ignoring the connections, denying the relations, without which they could not
exist. So that what appears at first a mere eccentricity in
technique turns out to be a peculiarly fitting symbol of something primary in the author's philosophy.

III. JOHN DOS PASSOS

Theory of the Leisure Class

"... that inanimate cold world allowed
To the poor loveless ever-anxious crowd ..."
—COLERIDGE

III. JOHN DOS PASSOS

Theory of the Leisure Class

Manhattan Transfer we have found to be a representation of chaos. But in such an undertaking, the danger is that the representation should itself be chaotic, which would be in direct contradiction to the aims of art. In the fiction of Dos Passos there is much to suggest want of form to readers accustomed to the sort of form which prevails in standard novels of the past centuries. In the standard novel the chief element of form is the plot, with its Aristotelian beginning, middle and end. It is the dramatic issue which is continuous throughout the successive occasions shown and whose resolution determines the dénouement with the strictest of logic. In *Manhattan Transfer* there is no plot in the traditional sense, no dramatic issue to give relevance to each successive incident and leave us with a sense of progress and unity. In the standard novel pattern is provided by the close interrelation of the several characters. But the very point of *Manhattan Transfer* is that the multitudinous characters who represent the city of New York are in the deepest sense unrelated; and by the conditions of the case the author has denied himself this element of pattern.

Or so it seems throughout the first half of the story. As things move forward in time, we begin to realize that the people are not so completely unrelated as we thought. In the deepest sense they are unrelated still; for they continue to ignore and deny the moral bonds that unite them. But it is inevitable, even in so big a world, that some of these people should make contact with one another. Jimmy Herf, the newspaperman, is bound sooner or later to make acquaintance with the popular actress Ellen Thatcher; and once within the orbit of this stellar being he is bound to revolve about her for a certain period. Such a prominent lawyer as George Baldwin is bound to meet with Ellen, if only in the establishment of a world-famous bootlegger; and he too will be drawn within her powerful influence. So it is that some of the more prominent characters are brought together toward the end of the book in contacts more or less casual, and a semblance of plot is produced. More significant perhaps are the connections not positively made but implied; for this is an art that lives by implications more than by front-stage business. When Ellen visits the millinery shop of Mme. Soubrine on the very day that Anna Cohen loses her life in the fire and sees them carry in the stretcher for the dead girl, humanity asserts itself through all the layers of selfish indifference. "Ellen can hardly breathe. She stands beside the ambulance behind a broad blue policeman. She tries to puzzle out why she is so moved; it is as if some part of her were going to be wrapped in bandages, carried away on a stretcher."

It is by touches like this, rare indeed and faint enough so far as action is concerned, that the reader has a sense of progress, if not in the story then in understanding of the author's intention. Formally, however, this book is to be thought of not in terms of plot or dramatic issue, but in terms of themes. The author is not at liberty to develop his themes by personal intrusion and comment in the course of the story; but he has another means of making his comment—that is, in the chapter-headings and in the prose poems prefixed to each chapter in place of the ancient quotations from the classics. Certain chapter-headings, like "Ferry-Slip" and "Nine Days' Wonder," have reference to something that happens within the particular chapter. But more often the title—"Metropolis," "Dollars"— might as well stand at the head of any chapter in the book, and taken all together—Ferry-Slip, Metropolis, Dollars, Tracks, Steamroller, Roller Coaster, Revolving Doors, Skyscraper, with the poems attached—they are one continual reminder of the unsettlement and casualness of life in the great city, its hard commercialism, its crazy pace and the sheer mechanical force of compulsion on all its victims—fed in and out of revolving doors, crushed beneath the anonymous weight of its steamroller.

Under "Metropolis" is a brief enumeration of the great cities of antiquity, with the materials of which they were built, long since fallen to dust, concluding with the steel, glass, tile and concrete of the modern skyscrapers. One chapter is headed with a Sandburgian poem on metropolitan themes—trade (selling out; we have made a terrible mistake), entertainment (dancers in a chop-suey joint), and religion (Salvation Army), the last coming as a consolation for the meagerness of the others, but yielding to the dominant commercial theme repeated. One chapter, entitled "Went to the Animals' Fair," has a fantasy on the stop-go signals, red and green lights, and the endless streams of automobiles mechanically controlled. "Rejoicing City that Dwelt Carelessly" develops the war motives: flags of the nations, bullion-gold (interspersed with soldiers' songs), death and apocalypse, the lure of the French woman (Madymoselle from Armenteers), the Liberty Loan and Red Cross drives, the hospital ships, and again the flags of the nations covering all the other themes with their patriotic glamour. There are glimpses of the suburbs, of the city after office hours, of the streams of people homeward or office bound. "Nickelodeon" introduces a wistful review of the people's pleasures, the cheap pleasures that can be bought for a nickel, newspaper extras, cup of coffee in the automat, popular love songs, naughty peep shows . . . "wastebasket of torn-up daydreams."

These prose poems, like the titles, seldom have particular application to the chapters they head. Their reference is general and universal; they have a backward and a forward glance. They build up the physical background of Manhattan. They are summary and symbolic. Once these themes are sounded, they go on reverberating through every incident of the story, like the jazzy jingle of popular songs. They are cumulative, with the titles they accompany. Dollars after Metropolis is incremental; and then Steamroller, Roller Coaster, Revolving Doors. They reach their climax in Skyscraper (suggesting the Tower of Babel) and their nemesis in The Burthen of Nineveh. And if there is no one else to note the crescendo and heed the warning, there is Jimmy Herf, wise man of Sodom, who takes the ferry to Jersey and shakes the dust of the doomed city from his heels.

Oh, yes, there is progress, direction, in the development of these themes; there is composition in the arrangement of incidents from the private lives of Gotham. The thing has form in its modernistic manner; by suggestion, by implication, by contrast and irony. The more one examines it, the more one finds of studied implication. It has throughout its own hard, bright, clean, crisp realism of presentation. It has its vividness and splendor in recording sensations and pictures. Here is perhaps the most pervasive of the ironies that dominate its tone. The world of Manhattan is so painfully bright and glittering, so garishly magnificent—the colors and sounds and smells so perpetually in evidence; and the moral lives of its people so dull and drab, so lacking in imagination, in daring and splendor. The moral world is so thrown in the shade by the world of material things.

Manhattan Transfer is not a story in the traditional sense. It is an abstract composition of story elements made to develop a series of themes. It would be fun to list the possible influences affecting Dos Passos in the conception of this work. There would be Joyce's *Ulysses,* itself an abstract composition of the utmost daring and complexity, and with a thousand technical inventions to which all subsequent writers are free to help themselves. There were perhaps Dorothy Richardson and Virginia Woolf. There would be Eliot's *Waste Land,* with its thematic development, its discontinuity and ironic implications. There would be the poems of Sandburg. There would be perhaps some of the earlier work of Jules Romains, most famous of collectivists. Above all there would be Gertrude Stein and whatever gates she opened to the young artist when he frequented her circle in Paris shortly after the War. That would mean, more than anything else, the French cubists and post-impressionists—men who chose to paint not one landscape literally, but to pick and choose among the visual objects before them, manipulate them, present them in fragments, arrange them in esthetic patterns, use them as freely as composers in music use the themes they put together. There was also the Salle Gaveau and the modern music of the day, with techniques analogous to those of the painters and the poets. There was the Russian Ballet, with its symbolism, its daring, its free manipulation of human living for visual effect and abstract theme. And then there was the moving picture with its lightning shifts of scene, flash backs and bizarre juxtapositions, double and multiple projection, retarded and accelerated motion, its large facilities for thematic treatment and manifold tricks of magic and legerdemain.

Such models would have been most helpful in freeing the young artist from the conventions of the novel. But no number of influences can abate the originality, the conceptual daring, the technical skill, the freshness, the novelty, the realism and the intellectual power of this performance. Readers were not at first impressed, or knew not what to make of this strange offering. The critics in general were not much better off. Some of the writers had an inkling of its importance; and one of them, the most famous of the time, had the discernment and the generosity to welcome it with warm enthusiasm. One of the most honorable incidents in the career of Sinclair Lewis was his public recognition, in the *New York*

Times review, of the signal importance for American letters of *Manhattan Transfer,* published in the same year with his own *Arrowsmith.* But the stature of Sinclair Lewis has all along manifested itself in his readiness to recognize and welcome what is novel and promising among the younger writers.

Brilliant and serious as was Dos Passos' performance in *Manhattan Transfer,* this work was to yield in significance and impressiveness to his later rendering of the same subject in the three volumes of *U.S.A.—The 42nd Parallel* (1930), *1919* (1932) and *The Big Money* (1936). Dos Passos must have felt that he had not done full justice to his theme in confining his view to the city of New York, even though that is the metropolis of our world, the place where all threads cross. He wanted to bring in the big towns of the hinterland, the prairie farms and lumber camps, the seven seas and the Central America which are the arena of our commerce and imperialism, and the wartime France and Italy that were the playground and the graveyard of our crusading youth. He must have felt, again, that in *Manhattan Transfer* he had given an inadequate selection of our national types; that he needed to lay more emphasis, both on the industrialist, the promoter, and the financier, and on the obscure men who do the chores. Perhaps he felt that, effective as it was in its way, and even a trifle theatrical, his dot-and-dash system of striking the high points in many lives left something to be desired in the way of sobriety and thoroughness; and he now chose to feature fewer characters and give a fuller and more consecutive account of their lives. In the first two volumes, he confined himself to five leading persons; in *The Big Money,* to four. What he gives in each case is a detailed biographical chronicle of the character featured, so that we have a complete case history—parentage, childhood environment, education, occupations, favorite diversions, marital status, down to the circumstances of death, if it occurred within the period of the chronicle—everything that might be required by a sociologist for whom no detail is without significance and who wants his file complete.

The subjects chosen for this thorough biographical study are the following:

Mac McCreary, son of a Connecticut factory hand. He works as typesetter and as migrant laborer at various points in the Northwest, and becomes an enthusiastic supporter of the IWW; but this last yields to the demands of family life. When he decides that his wife is simply milking him, he goes to Mexico, still interested in the labor movement. He sets up housekeeping with a Mexican girl, and ends up very comfortably as keeper of a radical bookstore.

J. Ward Moorehouse, son of a station agent in Wilmington, Delaware. In school he distinguishes himself as a debater and orator and wins a scholarship at the U. of P. He starts life in a real estate office; he finds that he has a genius for promotion, and bright blue eyes, and that he can put on an engaging look that people like. His two marriages are with wealthy women. When his first marriage goes on the rocks, he feels that he is entitled to some compensation for the loss of time he has suffered. In Pittsburgh he becomes an advertising expert for steel products, conceiving the idea of winning the favor of the public for his company with a long-range educational campaign. He then sets up an office in New York as public relations counselor. He specializes in propaganda showing the identity of interest of capital and labor, and in keeping down subversive influences among miners. When our country enters the War, he offers his services to the government and is promptly sent to Paris as publicity director for the Red Cross. He is prominent in shaping the Versailles Treaty, and is able to serve the interests of large investors in oil. On his return to New York he promotes various enterprises and lobbies in Washington against pure food laws which are disadvantageous to his clients, makers of patent medicines. He is a man of great refinement and distinction of manner. While in France he has love affairs with several Red Cross workers, but he never lets women interfere with business.

Janey Williams, daughter of a retired towboat captain of Georgetown, who takes up stenography, and becomes the efficient secretary of J. Ward Moorehouse, first in his New York office and then in Paris. She leads a very limited life, concerned for comfort and respectability; gradually turns into a peroxide blonde; and watches over her employer with jealous care.

Eleanor Stoddard, daughter of a workman in the Chicago stockyards. She greatly dislikes her father, and her ruling passion is the avoidance of all that is ugly and gross. She works in a lace shop, studies at the Art Institute, has a job at Marshall Field's, and goes into business with a friend as interior decorator in New York, where she does the Moorehouse home. She sees a lot of Moorehouse, but his wife is mistaken in thinking that their friendship is anything more than platonic. She follows him to Paris, where she has an important position in the Red Cross and meets all the most interesting people. She brings back lovely Italian panels from her mission to Rome. She has a discreet affair with Moorehouse in Paris; but in the end she marries a Russian prince and burns candles before an ikon while her guests drink tea from a silver samovar.

Charley Anderson, son of a boarding-house keeper in Fargo, N.D., starts life as an automobile mechanic. He works in various places, enlists in the army, becomes an aviator, and on his return from France takes up the business of making airplanes, for which he has a natural gift. But he catches the Big Money fever and goes in heavily for speculation. His relaxations are women and drink, and he goes in heavily for these. He makes and loses a lot of money and marries a Detroit society girl. He has an affair with Margo Dowling, glamorous actress, at Miami, and loses his life in an automobile accident while taking a drive with a girl he met at a night club.

Richard Ellsworth Savage, of a poor but cultured family of Oak Park, is put through Harvard by a lawyer with literary tastes; is prominent there as poet and college editor, then goes abroad in the volunteer ambulance service. After a jaunt through Europe he is called back home for talking too freely about the War; but through influence he is given a captain's commission; he is attached to several high-ranking officials in France, and buzzes about importantly far behind the lines. He has an affair with a Texas girl, but doesn't think he ought to spoil his career by marrying. He gets acquainted with the Red Cross set; and after the War he goes into Moorehouse's firm, carries on a campaign for Americanism and Bingham Health Products, and lobbies against pure food laws. He is a literary prostitute. His talents and charm are sold to the highest bidder; his life is one long picnic, though without happiness, and tending toward sprees in Harlem.

Besides these, there are Eveline Hutchins, daughter of a Unitarian minister, who becomes an interior decorator, a Red Cross worker in Paris, knows a lot of interesting men, marries a rather stodgy one, and dies of an overdose of sleeping powders; Joe Williams, Janey's brother, who joins the navy, deserts, serves commerce through the War as seaman and petty officer, is several times torpedoed, once married, and never amounts to much; Daughter, lively Texas girl, who goes abroad on Near East Relief, has a lot of fun, has an affair with Captain Savage in Rome, but instead of bearing his child, ends her life in an airplane crash with a French pilot; Margo Dowling, the glamorous girl who comes of stage people, marries a dope-taking Cuban, has a series of adventures, and lands very much on her feet when Sam Margolies in Hollywood picks her for a star. And then finally there are Benny Compton, the Jewish communist boy, who strives mightily for the cause of labor and is sent to Atlanta for opposing the draft; and Mary French, who works at Hull House, and for labor organizations in Pittsburgh, goes to prison in Boston for protesting the execution of Sacco and Vanzetti, is a friend of various "comrades," and is jilted by Don Stevens on his return from Moscow.

With the exception of Ben Compton and Mary French, we may say that the characters are pretty much all alike in assuming that the world is their oyster. Only they differ in imagination and opportunity. Ward Moorehouse is the chief of the exploiters, those who know how to make the most out of everything—business, advertising, marriage, the War, relief, and the misunderstandings of capital and labor. Eleanor Stoddard and Margo Dowling stand very high in this category: the one so shrewd in her exploitation of art and charity, the other in her exploitation of art and sex. Charley Anderson had everything for him and was going good; but he didn't have the sense to stick to his honest trade of constructing planes. The Big Money got him, and the little pleasures. Mac and Janey and Joe stand for the small people, seeking their own but without imagination and without opportunity. They are of the race that is used and exploited, and get nothing from the game but hard knocks and prison fare and occasional sprees.

No, Mac is not quite so simple. He had leanings toward something more rewarding and less purely selfish. "A man," he said, "has got to work for more than himself and his kids to feel right." "I wanta study an work for things; you know what I mean, not to get to be a goddam slavedriver but for socialism and the revolution an like that, not work an go on a bat an work an go on a bat like those damn yaps on the railroad." Thus he had a glimpse of some ideal objective, of something more than selfish and casual round which to organize his effort. But he found his socialism was not to be reconciled with the demands of his family. And when he had thrown off the yoke and gone to Mexico, he hardly more than drifted with the current. He was a man of good intentions, but he did not have the stuff of heroes and martyrs. As for Ben and Mary, they are the two characters in the story who consistently worked for something more than themselves. But they were so obscure and ineffectual, such wisps and straws in the wind of fate, that they do not greatly affect the tone of the whole exhibit.

So these are the dozen men and women whose private histories are served up in *U.S.A.* as typical of Americans living in the first thirty years of the twentieth century. Together they form a valuable file of case histories. But how are they brought into form and pattern, how organized into an artistic whole? Again, as in *Manhattan Transfer,* it is not through a central plot or dramatic intrigue. The characters, many of them, come to be associated together in business or in "love," as front-page people are likely to be in so small a world. But their connections are loose and casual; no more is made of these than of many other aspects of their lives; they are not played up in the manner of drama with issue, climax, resolution. The narrative flows along in a steady stream of small events, with a minimum of formal scenes or "constituted occasions." The characters are taken up in rotation, with the smallest apparent regard for the bearings of one on another or upon any "story" in which they are all involved.

Here again, the pattern is largely thematic, and depends on the reference from the private and individual case to matters of general and public import. But here it is not by symbolic chapter-headings and introductory prose poems that Dos Passos suggests the wider reference. He has hit upon a new set of technical devices of startling originality to carry this burden—in which the symbolic and the poetic give way to the literal and the factual, so arranged that the critical attitudes may be supported with the utmost weight of documentation. The first of these devices is called the newsreel. This is a selection from newspaper headlines and articles of a date corresponding to that of action in the private lives which follow; it places the private action in the calendar of history, reminding the reader of what things were of concern to the world at large at the moment when such an individual was dealing with such an item in his obscure life. There is no comment, no reference from public to private; but as the thing repeats itself over and over, there is a growing sense that private and public must be related in the order of things: that the capture of Mafeking or the execution of Ferrer must have its bearing, however remote, upon the career of Mac; that Polish pogroms are of concern to Richard Ellsworth Savage; that the appointment of Daugherty has its long-range significance for Margo Dowling, and the landing of American marines in Nicaragua its importance for Charley Anderson.

Still more, there is the growing sense that the private life is of a piece with the culture complex in which it is embedded, that the spirit of the citizen is deeply colored by the world in which he lives. The topics featured in the newsreel are not chosen at random; they are an exact reproduction of what one reads in the most widely circulated newssheets: disaster, scandal, politics, society, finance, labor. These items are placed more or less helter-skelter in the newsreels as they appear in the newspaper. In the newsreels they are often given in fragments, running into one another and "pied," as they are "pied" in the consciousness of the subway reader, thus making a perfect symbol of the average mentality as it is concerned with public affairs. But gradually the discerning reader will become aware that the choice and arrangement of topics and their very confusion are not so planless and haphazard as one might suppose. Disasters and scandal and society are the screen behind which the serious business of the world is carried on; the dope with which the public mind is put to sleep. And seldom is political news unaccompanied by news of industry and finance and of the organization or suppression of labor. The world in which Joe Williams and Moorehouse represent the opposite poles is a world in which war is closely bound up with the price of steel and sugar, and in which the Treaty of Versailles is followed by the violent putting down of the IWW. The connections are not made in the newsreel any more than they are made by the thoughtless reader; but for the discerning reader they become more and more obvious as the story proceeds. And this is one of the principal means by which Dos Passos gives shape and direction to his work.

Along with the newsreels, and interspersed like them among the records of private lives, are the brief biographies of actual public figures of the time. These are the Representative Men of our country and day; they more or less sum up our national achievement, our official contribution to modern culture. There are twenty-five of these figures: seven from the business world, five from politics, four from applied science and invention, three from the leaders of labor, three from the arts (Isadora Duncan, Rudolph Valentino, Frank Lloyd Wright), two from journalism (the radical John Reed and the liberal Paxton Hibben), and one from social science. The proportion from the several categories indicates the author's general estimate of our cultural effort. Literature does not appear except in the form of journalism, nor pure science at all, unless in the case of Steinmetz. These sketches are for the most part masterpieces of incisive and tendencious writing; they give the author his best chance to show his hand, to indicate his attitudes and bias. The businessmen are most uniformly the object of his irony—Carnegie, the Prince of Peace; Hearst, Poor Little Rich Boy; Insull, Power Superpower. Frederick Winslow Taylor (the American Plan) gives him his chance to suggest the social wastefulness of American efficiency and the speed-up. Minor C. Keith, Emperor of the Caribbean, gives him his text on American imperialism. His political figures are all liberals—spurious and stupid (Bryan), playboy (Theodore Roosevelt), doctrinaire and misguided (Wilson), sincere and forceful but relatively ineffectual (La Follette), and simply heroic (Debs). The one serious thinker in the outfit is Thorstein Veblen, whose analysis of bourgeois mentality and bourgeois economics is (at a guess) the greatest single influence on the work of Dos Passos of anything in print, and whose *Theory of the Leisure Class* offers the most promising clues for the interpretation of *U.S.A.*

Taken together, these twenty-five figures pretty well sum up Dos Passos' notion of what we have to offer in the way of intellectual and spiritual distinction. They do not demonstrate Carlyle's theory of history as the creation of Great Men. But they do suggest the kind of greatness available for the inspiration of Joe Williams and Charley Anderson, of Eleanor Stoddard and Margo Dowling.

One further device Dos Passos has for broadening the reference of his fictitious chronicle. He has left himself out of the narrative proper; but he knows in his heart that perfect objectivity is not to be had in a human record; that even in physical science account must be taken of the position of the observer in reckoning the speed, mass and direction of moving bodies. In presence of documents like these, the reader may well ask: who is their author and sponsor? what is he like? of what authority and bias? Is he not himself an American citizen of our time—involved, like the others, in our common culture, subject to human limitations of knowledge and spirit, faced with the same complex and bewildering problems? Dos Passos has the current reluctance of writers of fiction to mix in his story with sentimental commentary and moral. But he cannot altogether evade the challenge of these natural questions. He has chosen to insert in the narrative a series of flashes called "The Camera Eye," which by fleeting hint and impression suggest the character of the artist whose work it is, his own involvement in the social structure, the conditions that molded him, and his aims and motives in his work.

In *The 42nd Parallel,* we see him as a child in Tidewater Virginia, traveling in Europe, at school in England, his "four years under the ether cone" at Harvard, his presence at protest meetings and cafés in New York on the night of our entrance into the War. In *1919* we have glimpses of him in the ambulance service in France and Italy, emptying slop-pails in the medical corps, and finally in Paris, a civilian going to concerts and witnessing riots of working men in protest against the Versailles Treaty. In *The Big Money,* we see him making a precarious living as a newspaperman, protesting the execution of Sacco and Vanzetti, and raging against the unjust sentence imposed on striking miners in the South.

We see him as a typical product of bourgeois gentility, soft, refined and fastidious, shrinking from the contact of "muckers." But there is in him some protestant strain which leads him to question the assumptions of his class. He envies the freedom of the mucker, and he doubts the legend that he is a dirty fellow who puts stones in his snowballs. He resents the middlemen who milk the profits from the truck-farmers and keep them starving. He resents the snobbishness and the sterile culture of the university. He resents the sacrifice of our boys to save the bankers' investments. He witnesses the waste and horrors of war, and its exploitation by a host of *embusqués,* who occupy posts of safety and make a picnic of the tragedy. He returns to America disillusioned, unwilling to cut the melons of exploitation; he is trying to determine his own moral identity, seeking in Greenwich Village salons a social faith, a formula of action; he is "peeling the onion of doubt." He sees Italian anarchists killed for upholding the principles of Plymouth Rock. He sees the miners enslaved and the bosses triumphant.

They have made us foreigners in the land where we were born
they are the conquering army that has filtered into the country
unnoticed they have taken the hilltops by stealth they levy toll
they stand at the minehead   they stand at the polls . . . they have
clubbed us off the streets   they are stronger   they are rich   they
hire and fire the politicians the newspapereditors the old judges
the small men with reputations the collegepresidents the ward-
heelers (listen businessmen collegepresidents judges   America
will not forget her betrayers).

The wool has been pulled over the eyes of his people. His
rôle is to make them see again: "rebuild the ruined words
slimy in the mouths of lawyers districtattorneys collegepresidents judges." "How can I make them feel how our fathers
our uncles haters of oppression came to this coast   how say
Don't let them scare you make them feel who are your op-
pressors America?"

Such is the project, but how is it to be accomplished? In
what terms shall he "rebuild the ruined words worn slimy"?
What formula of action shall he recommend? It is clear that
Dos Passos has been some kind of a socialist, champion of
organized labor and the cooperative commonwealth. But it
is equally clear how little he trusts the Communist Party or
any other party to bring about what must be essentially a
moral revolution. Already in *The Big Money,* his best man
Benny Compton has been expelled from the party, and his
best woman Mary French has been shabbily treated by Don
Stevens, typical party member. The young man of the Camera Eye is carrying in his pocket a letter from a college boy
asking him to explain why radicals, though right in principle,
are such stinkers in their private lives.

In *The Adventures of a Young Man* (1939) Dos Passos
has given a most illuminating account of the predicament
of a friend of labor who cannot reconcile himself to the
communists' unconcern for the workmen they profess to
champion. This book is not to be compared to *U.S.A.* in

craftsmanship and imaginative power; but it makes, for all that, a precious commentary on the author's *magnum opus*. Its hero, Glenn Spotswood, is a young man of the most earnest devotion, whose father had lost his position at Columbia because of his opposition to the War, and who has himself gone far beyond the compromising pacifism of the old man. He helps organize a strike of miners in the Southern mountains; and then he agitates for the release of strikers who have been railroaded to prison on a charge of murder. The case is exploited by the party solely as an occasion for propaganda; and they refuse to make common cause with labor organizations which might have secured the release of the innocent men. Glenn feels that the cause of humanity will never be won if they lose sight of the human beings who make it up, if friendship and good faith must always be sacrificed to the party line. He argues so vigorously against this policy that he is put out of the party. He cannot find employment in the movement at home, and he volunteers for service in Spain. But there his bad name follows him; he is imprisoned as a Trotsky counter-revolutionary, and almost misses his chance to be the mark for a fascist bullet.

It is an affecting picture of a man of feeling and independent mind made victim to the heartless officialism of a party machine. And the author's gift for irony finds ample scope, besides, in the parlor and bedroom radicalism of New York bohemian society, from which Glenn makes his escape into the life of hardship and danger. The predicament of Glenn was doubtless that of Dos Passos, with this addition, that while Glenn was by nature a man of action—speaker and organizer—Dos Passos is by nature the artist and speculative thinker. He is not at home on the soapbox. His place is the study. And even in the study he has no gift for heartening prophecy and exhortation. He has not the spirit of a proletarian propagandist. The good and honest people he admires—Ben Compton and Mary French—but he cannot invest them with the warm colors of sentiment like Fielding Burke or with heroic glamour like André Malraux. The poor things are so plain and awkward, so homeless and unfavored, that one shivers with discomfort at the thought of them. And for the most part his sense for truth precludes his featuring of characters so well inspired as these. His artistic conscience bids him set down what he has seen. And what he has mostly seen are, on the one hand, boobs and drifters like Janey and Joe, and on the other hand slickers and exploiters like Moorehouse and Savage, with a sample of those, like Charley Anderson, who are boobs and drifters playing the rôle of slickers and exploiters without the staying power required to carry it through.

In the record of these lives the author keeps a curious even tone. One incident follows another without distinction of emphasis, as if they were all on a level of importance or unimportance. The point of view is that of the character concerned, but no one is allowed to build up to a climax of emotion. There is singularly little excitement or depth of feeling. It is as if the author were unwilling for us to get too sympathetic with any of the characters, to become emotionally involved; we are to maintain our distance and objectivity. We are scientists observing the reactions of human beings to stimuli; and at this distance we cannot make out that these organisms are directed by any long-range, any ideal objectives.

It is true that the characters think well of themselves, as is the way with human beings, who cannot see far beyond the limits of their own immediate concerns. Above all, they are persuaded, the more favored characters, of their own "niceness" of sentiment, and totally unaware of their shallowness and confusion of ideas. The crowning exhibits of "bourgeois" mentality are Eleanor Stoddard and J. Ward Moorehouse, in whom an almost complete want of heart and an essentially unsocial and amoral attitude toward the world are compatible with the utmost correctness of senti- ment. These two have developed a considerable tenderness for each other. As the time approaches for our entry into the War, from which they are to profit so shrewdly, they have worked themselves up to a high pitch of sentimentality; but they do not distinguish clearly among their feelings nor understand their connection.

The sight of the French flag excited her always or when a band played Tipperary; and one evening when they were going to see the Yellow Jacket for the third time, she had on a new fur coat that she was wondering how she was going to pay for, and she thought of all the bills at her office and the house on Sutton Place she was remodelling on a speculation and wanted to ask J.W. about a thousand he'd said he'd invested for her and wondered if there'd been any turnover yet. They'd been talking about the air raids and poison gas and the effect of the war news downtown and the Bowmen of Mons and the Maid of Orleans and she said she believed in the supernatural, and J.W. was hinting something about reverses on the Street and his face looked drawn and wor- ried; but they were crossing Times Square through the eight o'clock crowds and the skysigns flashing on and off. . . . When they got to the theatre Eleanor hurried down to the ladies room to see if her eyes had got red. But when she looked in the mirror they weren't red at all and there was a flash of heartfelt feeling in her eyes, so she just freshened up her face and went back to the lobby, where J.W. was waiting for her with the tickets in his hand; her grey eyes were flashing and had tears in them.

This passage will give a notion of the schoolgirl naïveté and intellectual immaturity of a woman of great prac- tical shrewdness, who knows how to make the utmost profit out of every situation. It will give a notion of an insin- cerity and a confusion of mind which are no bar to success in a world of free-for-all competition, where much is gained by the cultivation of the right forms of sentimentalism.

It will give a notion, too, of Dos Passos' skill in rendering the very logic and syntax of his characters' thought. This is perhaps his greatest gift; it is at any rate the gift of which he makes the most effective use. His method is essentially that of irony—an intellectual jiu-jitsu by which a character is left to throw himself by his own weight. This ironic tone is dominant throughout *U.S.A.* And we might have cause to complain if Dos Passos were a socially irresponsible writer like, say, Somerset Maugham, by whom the irony would often seem to be employed for the demolition of individuals, and no philosophical theme is served unless it be a kind of moral nihilism. But the characters of Dos Passos are never merely individuals. They are types of the mentality prevailing in our world of individualistic sentiment and social cynicism. And each one makes his important contribution to the destructive analysis of "bourgeois" sentiment which is Dos Passos' undertaking. This is, as I have suggested, the fictional counterpart of Veblen's theoretic study of the leisure class.

The whole thing is highly credible and diverting. It is most stimulating intellectually. It has for the imagination its architectural grandeur, its bleak magnificence. Its appeal to the emotions is negative. But morally it is most educative. Not so much in a positive way, of inspiration and ideal guidance. But in a negative way, tonic and disciplinary for those who can read its meaning. And it does prepare the way for more positive teaching. If Dos Passos is not himself a prophet of the good life, he is most emphatically the voice of one crying in the wilderness.

IV. ERNEST HEMINGWAY

Empirical Ethics

"Look out how you use proud words.
When you let proud words go, it is
not easy to call them back."

—SANDBURG

IV. ERNEST HEMINGWAY

Empirical Ethics

In certain ways, contemporary American fiction opens with Ernest Hemingway. And much of what he stands for is still strongly active in other writers. Whether he continued to be himself an expanding force was open to question up to October 1940; whether he still had things to offer that would add appreciably to the record. There were signs in *To Have and Have Not* (1937) that some maturing process was going on in him which, if it was completed, might add something to what he had to say. His days in Spain in the fight for the Republic would naturally produce more in the form of writing than had yet appeared, provided that he could manage to bring it into esthetic focus. He is a scrupulous artist, who will use no material—experience or conviction—which he does not see how to assimilate to the terms of his art. Now, with the publication of *For Whom the Bell Tolls*, we have the answer to this question. His latest novel is the largest in scope, the most accomplished in technique, and the strongest in effect of anything he has written. And it demonstrates that he did indeed have something to say, something positive and tonic, which he had never said before, certainly not with the explicitness and power of the present statement.

And more than that. This work of his maturity gives assurance to those of us who have liked and admired Hemingway that we were not mistaken in our reading of him. The cynicism which is such a feature of his work on the surface does not go, and has never gone, to the heart of it or of him. He has never been insensitive to fineness or greatness in human nature; but he has been disinclined to assert the presence of these qualities where he is not certain he has found them. And still more, he has been disinclined to apply to human nature the hackneyed terms of sentimental idealism, for fear of missing the truth. In his study of the truth, he has preferred to follow an inductive, an empirical method, beginning with the simplest, the most palpable elements of human experience, those most readily tested, and to proceed with extreme caution to the determination of "higher" compounds, more complicated formulas. In *For Whom the Bell Tolls* he has reached farther and higher on this road than in any earlier work. And the reason is obvious enough. Here for the first time he has found a subject that justifies the more positive statements about human nature. But it was not abstract theory which led him to this subject; it was not the demands of some literary ideal. It was personal experience. What the first World War did not offer him, nor the bullring at Pamplona, nor the bootleggers and yachtsmen of Key West, was at length brought within his actual range of observation in the Spanish struggle against fascism.

It was, to be sure, his own idealism, his own social sentiment, his conscience, that took him into the Spanish war, as well as, no doubt, his flair for a good subject. But that does not make the experience less genuine, the facts less real. It is true that he might, like many another writer, have come sooner within the range of this sort of facts elsewhere than in Spain. It took time for Hemingway to become "socially conscious." But that again is an effect of his cautious inductive approach to the truth. His social consciousness was not an *a priori* assumption, a matter of literary ideology. It was the slow growth of experience and observation, observation both of himself, his own reactions, and of certain types of people and behavior for which he felt a special affinity. If it had come sooner, it would have been a forced growth, and a denial of his peculiar temper—that skeptical temper which is shy of affirmations but which gives so much more force to affirmations when they come.

This will be our main clue in the survey of his work. It will serve to account for the limitations of his art as well as for its strength. It will in part account for his continuing influence on other writers of fiction, as well as for the fact that so little of his work gives the impression of "dating," in spite of the more than a decade since he first made his appearance. And finally it will prepare us for his own partial transcending of his limitations in the ultimate product of his art.

The naïve reader is too likely to suppose that Hemingway is a naïve writer, whose style and subject matter are limited because of the limitation of his spiritual insight or his intellectual culture. That he has his natural limitations is no doubt true; but before jumping to hasty conclusions in this matter, we must take into account the limitations which he has consciously imposed upon himself for esthetic purposes. The friend of Ezra Pound and Gertrude Stein is not to be lightly accused of want of sophistication. To appreciate what he was up to in his stories, we cannot do better than take into account what he has to say about writing in two of his books which are not fiction—*Green Hills of Africa* and *Death in the Afternoon*.

One of these is a faithful account, presumably, of a hunting trip in a country that he loves; the other is a dissertation on the art of bullfighting in Spain. I don't know how good *Green Hills of Africa* may seem to readers who share Hemingway's passion for hunting. For me it is a very moderately interesting book, and that chiefly in the parts in which he exhibits, in all frankness, the psychology of a man who prides himself on being a good shot meeting with indifferent success. *Death in the Afternoon* is, I believe, a very good book, even though my own concern with the art of the bullfight is not great enough to sustain my interest unabated throughout. There are some very interesting speculations on the psychology of the spectator and on other aspects of human nature well worth discussing over a highball. The point I wish to make, however, before quoting what he has to say about his art, is that the whole book is written, with great competence, in a style quite different from that which prevails in his fiction. The sentences are normal in length and syntax, often enough complex in structure where the thought calls for reasons and reservations; the vocabulary is that of a man of sufficient range and subtlety of thought, who is not incapable of intellectual abstraction and generalization.

From time to time the formal exposition gives way to bits of dialogue between the author and an old lady who is interested in the subjects of his discourse. She is obviously a person of quality and experience, with a quaint air of old-fashioned gentility, who is not afraid of facts of any order provided a certain propriety is observed in the manner of their discussion. The author plays up to her; his own language takes on a stateliness and cadence reminiscent of some classical period, at the same time maintaining that dry succinctness which flourishes in classical periods, and occasionally pointed up to something which in a classical period would be recognized as epigram. I will not say that the best of Hemingway's writing is found in these dialogues. But I will recommend them to the academic reader who is in doubt whether Hemingway knows how to write. He will find here a flavor and turn of phrase which may well remind him of *The Compleat Angler* or of some French dialogue of the eighteenth century. And he will be more ready to acknowledge that the simplicity of Hemingway's style in his stories is not inadvertent but intentional.

Now and then in his talk with the old lady, Hemingway allows himself some cruder expression than usual, gratifying her worldliness with the sense that she is dealing with a man who has been around and speaks a bolder language than the vicar's. In one place when he has taken a speculative flight somewhat over her head, he acknowledges that what he has been saying may be no better than—well, he uses the livery-stable word which we may translate, in scientific terms, as equine excrementa. Her reproof is mild. "That," she says, "is an odd term and one I did not encounter in my youth." "Madame," says the Author, "we apply the term now to describe unsoundness in an abstract conversation or, indeed, any over-metaphysical tendency in speech." "I must learn," she says, "to use these terms correctly."

Hemingway's interest in bullfighting, he lets us know, was in origin secondary to his interest in writing. "I was trying to learn to write, commencing with the simplest things, and one of the simplest things and the most fundamental is violent death." Hemingway came to the Spanish bullring as the one place, now that the wars were over, where he could make a deliberate study of this simple and fundamental sub-ject of violent death. One of the chief difficulties in writing was "knowing what you truly felt, rather than what you were supposed to feel." Another was putting down "what really happened in action; what the actual things were which pro-duced the emotion which you experienced." These were matters of observation and honest introspection. Other diffi-culties were matters of style. There was this "over-metaphysical tendency in speech," which he designated by the crude livery-stable word. There was, again, "that unavoidable mysticism of a man who writes a language so badly that he cannot make a clear statement, complicated by whatever pseudo-scientific jargon is in style at the moment" (more equine excrementa). Another is "journalism made literature by the injection of a false epic quality."

In *Green Hills of Africa* Hemingway relates how he met a German hunter, who questioned him on his literary opinions and aims. To him he explained why the American classic writers were not great: they were too imitative of the English, too would-be genteel. And "they did not use the words that people always have used in speech, the words that survive in language." Contemporary writers were too hurried, too ambitious, too much concerned to make money. "They write when there is nothing to say or no water in the well." As for himself: "I am interested in other things. I have a good life but I must write because if I do not write a certain amount I do not enjoy the rest of my life." Asked what it is he wants, he says: "To write as well as I can and learn as I go along. At the same time I have my life which I enjoy and which is a damned good life." The German asks whether Hemingway is sure he knows what he wants. "Absolutely, and I get it all the time."

There is a certain boyish swagger about this. But there is a refreshing candor too. And he shows a genuine modesty in his recognition that his art is something to be learned. The same note is sounded in the concluding words to *Death in the Afternoon.* "The great thing is to last and get your work done and see and hear and learn and understand; and write when there is something that you know; and not before; and not too damned much after. Let those who want to save the world if you can get to see it clear and whole."

One more quotation before I sum up the points of his program. He conceives the art of prose writing as one which is capable of effects not yet achieved. What he wants, he says, is to see "how far prose can be carried if anyone is serious enough and has luck. There is a fourth and fifth dimension that can be gotten. . . . It is much more difficult than poetry. It is a prose that has never been written. But it can be written without tricks and without cheating. With nothing that will go bad afterwards."

So there we have his project. Writing and living are closely related in his thought. One reason for indulging his love for the bullring is that he can best observe there the fundamentals of human nature. One reason for writing is that otherwise he does not enjoy the rest of his living. Writing is an art to be learned. It involves exactness in recording what happens and in determining the emotion produced. It must not be forced; one must write of what one knows and must not write when there is nothing to say. The simplest subjects are the best, at least for the beginner. The best words are those that people have always used in speech. All tricks are to be avoided. Respectability is not enough and imitation will not do; what one wants is the humble truth. But with all its simplicity, good prose will not be commonplace; there will be subtleties of effect—a fourth and fifth dimension, something beyond poetry.

A purely esthetic program, you say—severely esthetic. No social consciousness; no criticism of life; no ethical implications; nothing to be learned; no ground to be gained in man's battle with the inhuman? Well, it is an esthetic program, as strict as one will often find. But there are some hints of a wider, more human reference. Criticism of life? Do not forget his phrase, "Let those who want to save the world if you can get to see it clear and whole." Doesn't that ring some bell, stir some echo of Matthew Arnold, of all persons! Ethical implications? We find on the fourth page of *Death in the Afternoon* a definition of morality. "I know only that what is moral is what you feel good after." His whole analysis of bullfighting is in terms of a tragic art. "The bullfight is very moral to me because I feel very fine while it is going on and have a feeling of life and death and mortality and immortality, and after it is over I feel very sad but very fine." This may not be the moral standard of an Aquinas, and Hemingway says he does not defend his definition, but if you look, you will find it popping up here and there throughout his stories. There are at least some rudiments of an ethical standard in his writing. The fun will be to discover how, in his morals as in his esthetics, he is dominated by his suspicion of what Sandburg calls "proud words."

Your first impression on reading an early novel of Hemingway's is that he is dealing here with people completely hard-boiled, insensitive, indifferent to moral values. And you wonder what there is about people of this caliber capable of enlisting your interest and sometimes a considerable degree of sympathy if not of liking. On closer examination, you become aware that these very people are actually rather concerned in their funny way with good and bad behavior. Only, they don't wish to be caught "talking a lot of rot" and they don't want to be caught judging of behavior in the terms of Mrs. Grundy or the vicar or George Eliot or their fathers and mothers. They are stubbornly determined not to acknowledge their obligations to any system of conduct handed down to them by the professional moralists. They are determined to find out what they think for themselves, and by actual experiment. They will start without assumptions, and learn inductively. They will begin at the beginning, with the simplest experiences, and build up by trial and error to experiences a little less simple, stopping well short of anything resembling a system or an abstraction. Abstractions are the stronghold of vagueness and sentimentality and dogmatic authority; they are the cloak of hypocrisy and complacency, and the disguise for rationalization.

The test is a very simple one; the good things are those that make you feel good. First, feel good at the time; and then, more complicated, feel good afterward. Immorality is "things that made you disgusted afterward." This is the phrase of Jake, leading man of *The Sun Also Rises*, in agreement with Hemingway in *Death in the Afternoon*. It is easier to be sure about the things that make you feel good than about those that make you feel good afterward; and there is more in the stories about the former. It is easier to be sure about physical sensations than about sentiments and such-like abstractions; and there is more about physical sensations. This is the cautious, the inductive method, the guarantee against sentimentalism and rationalization.

The surest things are hunger and thirst and the sexual urge; and these all come in for a good deal of attention. After dinner in Milan the lovers would stop at the little place where they sold sandwiches: "ham and lettuce sandwiches and anchovy sandwiches made of very tiny brown glazed rolls and only about as long as your finger. They were to eat in the night when we were hungry." No one concerned with the art of living can afford not to provide for the appetite that comes on at midnight or in the small hours. Thirst means generally more than water; it is alcoholic drinks that come in for most lavish recognition. For they make one feel good not merely physically but mentally. It is worth a lot of pains to get the right proportions of whisky and soda—put in the ice and soda yourself so as to be sure not to make the whisky too thin.

But the concern with alcoholic thirst really implies a some-what advanced stage in the inductive process of learning what is good. For it implies generally that there is some bad state of mind which needs to be dealt with. "Wine is a grand thing. It makes you forget all the bad." The lover Frederick is obliged to return to the front where anything may happen to him; his girl is being left in a family way, and no one knows how that may come out; they are not even married, and that is awkward. They are staying for the moment in a station hotel among red plush furniture and gilt mirrors, and it makes the woman feel for the moment uncomfortably like a whore. There is a good deal of bad to be forgotten and it takes a good deal of wine to make them forget it.

One thing that did make him feel good in the Italian barn was lying in the sweet-smelling hay. It "took away all the years in between," and made him think of the barn in north-

ern Michigan where he had lain as a boy and shot sparrows
with an air rifle. But the barn was gone now and they had
cut out the hemlock woods, and "you could not go back."
Most secure of all in Hemingway's scale of values are the
pleasures of camping out, of fishing and hunting. What one
remembers best from the stories, *In Our Time,* is the boy's
sensations as he crawls under the slant of the tent-roof, in
the pleasant light and smell of the canvas, and the "something mysterious and homelike" about the enclosure. With
Hemingway, it is most of all in things like this that the
child is father of the man. In *Green Hills of Africa,* he hated
to see the rains come that put an end to his plans for shooting
kudu; but he could not help acknowledging that on the canvas the "rain was making the finest sound that we, who live
much outside of houses, ever hear." In *The Sun Also Rises,*
Paris dance places are good, and the bullfighting at Pamplona. But best of all is the trout-fishing in the mountains,
the fresh air, the cold water, making a good catch and laying
the fish between fresh green leaves in the basket, and then
the cold wine and hard-boiled eggs, and talking nonsense with
a friend while lying in the shade.

A certain amount of hazard and hardship is an enhance-
ment to any camping-out party. They provide the fatigue
and apprehension which yield so pleasantly at the end to
comfort, rest and security. Notable for gratifications of this
kind was the all-night row across the stormy Italian lake, in
A Farewell to Arms, when the young lieutenant was escaping,
with his girl, from the army and the war. They were risking
their lives and blistering their hands; and it was a great
moment when "Catherine stepped up and we were in Switzerland together." In the meantime they had been well provided with sandwiches and brandy by the friendly barman
in Stresa. Catherine had been plucky and cheerful—an ideal
companion on a trip. They made a good breakfast on their
arrival, and altogether the thing had been a great lark. Above

all, the young lieutenant had had the gratification of proving
to himself that he was still a man.

This is the major theme of *To Have and Have Not*. And
a main reason for bringing in the wealthy on their yachts
and the literary in their cups is, by their soft and decadent
ways, to set off in higher relief the essential manliness of
Harry Morgan. Harry Morgan is a motor-boat bootlegger
of Key West who has been driven into criminal life by a
rich fisherman and a mean revenue officer. He is something
of a Robin Hood, something of a Byronic corsair (without
the pomp of rhetoric and sentiment), and something of a
proletarian outside the "movement." And so here we find
ourselves up to the neck in moral problems and implicit
evaluations. We have even a hint of "social consciousness"
—the honest mechanic and man of action set in opposition to the trader, the politician, and the trifler on a trust
fund. Hemingway's evident preference for Harry Morgan
over any of the sophisticates implies a scale of values—a sort
of moral code—that is carried well beyond the level of physical well-being.

But *To Have and Have Not* is generally regarded as not
the best or most characteristic of his novels. Let us go back
and see how, in more famous work, he has extended the
implications of his simple formula. The first story of length
to impress the public mind was *The Sun Also Rises* (1926).
And I think it is safe to say that the public were chiefly
impressed by what must have seemed the impudence and
irresponsibility of that story. It is a group of newspapermen
and ex-soldiers of the World War, who meet in Paris for
a little dancing and drinking, and then move on to Pamplona for the season of bullfighting. The center of the group
is Lady Brett Ashley, a female given to cocktails and forni-
cation. She is, one must believe, essentially a "good sort"—
likable and companionable, capable of seeing the points of
a bullfight, and of striking just the right tone (for this set)—

in addition to the particular lure which makes them all mooncalves of love. But one certainly gets the impression that she is a hopeless and unscrupulous nymphomaniac—a completely worthless character. In the course of the story certain circumstances gradually come to light which may cause some readers somewhat to mitigate this judgment. It appears that her life with her husband had been no picnic—that he was a brutal character well fitted to drive a woman into desperate reprisals. At present she appears to be engaged to Mike, a Scotchman of good social standing, and a likable fellow, a war veteran who has gone through bankruptcy.

Well, her being engaged to him would seem a poor excuse for her going off with Cohn, the American college athlete, or falling in love with Romero, the young Spanish matador, and going to Madrid with him. Just what her sentiments are toward Mike is never made clear, unless we are to suppose that her affairs with other men are an indication that Mike is not the natural choice of her heart. It is not indeed Hemingway's wont to tell you, like some Trollope or George Eliot, precisely what sentiments one character feels toward another. His way is to tell you what they said and did and let you draw your own conclusions. And the only conclusion you can reach in this case is that Brett is in love with Jake, the newspaperman who has been injured in the War in such a way that he is incapable of making love to any woman. Certainly it is between this pair that the greatest tenderness is shown, and Brett's last word to Jake in the book is: "Oh Jake, we could have had such a damned good time together." To which he replies, with "irony and pity", "Yes. Isn't it pretty to think so?" At any rate, that the one man she loved was out of the question is a circumstance that will relieve her somewhat of the imputation of being a nymphomaniac and a completely abandoned character.

But there is one more point in her favor. She does capture the matador, and he does wish to marry her in spite of the discrepancy of their ages. But she gives him up at least partly for unselfish reasons. She realizes that he is too young; she realizes that marriage will not be good for his career. She does not want to be a bitch, and so she insists on giving him up. "I'm not going to be that way," she says to Jake. "I'm not going to be one of those bitches that ruins children." And then, as if to show that she has made the "moral" choice, the author has her say: "I feel rather good, you know. I feel rather set up." She is a trifle tipsy, and she repeats herself. "You know it makes one feel rather good deciding not to be a bitch." And then she adds: "It's sort of what we have instead of God."

So there comes in, for a glimpse, the most tremendous of all concepts in the realm of moral values. If they had that, they would have everything, there would be no problem. They would have religion and the church, with sin and virtue, and a comprehensive set of prescriptions covering every item of behavior. But that is not what they have nor what they want. What they want is to take nothing on authority or tradition; to find out for themselves; to make their own code. It is a practical question of learning to live according to their own feeling of good and bad. "I did not care what it was all about," thought Jake in a midnight reflection while in pain. "All I wanted to know was how to live in it. Maybe if you found out how to live in it you learned what it was all about."

So here we are back again at the beginning. There is a delightful character who appears in the earlier part of the book, a Greek-American merchant, reputed to be a count, who at least dispenses champagne in a lordly way. He is a man of some ripeness and dignity, who, for all the quaintness of his broken English, manages to impose respect upon Jake and Brett. He is very particular about his wine and the way it is served, wishing everything to be done and enjoyed in the spirit of an artist in living. He is a man of experience, who insists politely that like Jake he has "been around a very great deal," that like him, he has "seen a lot, too." Having been around is evidently an important thing in this set. Unless you have experience, how can you judge? Unless you have been tested, how can one be sure of your quality? It comes out in their talk that the Count has been in seven wars and four revolutions and that he has received most interesting arrow wounds while on a business trip in Abyssinia.

In a way, the Count has the advantage over Brett and her kind. He thinks he knows the values, whereas her experience has led her into some doubt as to what the values are. "Doesn't anything ever happen to your values?" she asks him; and he says, "No, not any more." She wants to know if he never falls in love, and he says he's always in love. "What does that do to your values?" She evidently thinks he is a trifler in love, and that no trifler can have a true notion of the meaning of the word. She is confirmed in this opinion by his reply. Love, too, he says, "has got a place in my values." She says, "You haven't any values. You're dead, that's all." He will not admit it. "No, my dear. You're not right. I'm not dead at all."

This is done in Hemingway's characteristic shorthand. These people are not going to dot their i's and cross their t's either for us or for one another. That is a part of their code. It is for the discerning reader to work out the implications. And here he has, I think, two alternatives. Brett means that love is not love unless it is exclusive and serious—serious enough to upset the cool calculations of an artist in living. And the Count either disagrees—he will keep love in its due place in the system of a hedonist—or else, quite possibly, he agrees with Brett at bottom. He agrees with her, and is actually on the look-out for the kind of love she means. If I am not mistaken, he is another of the men in love with Brett, or prepared to fall in love with her. But he is

a man of a certain delicacy of feeling—her appreciation of
that is another reason for judging him "one of us." What
he is doing on this festive night of champagne-drinking is
feeling his way to an understanding of the relation between
Brett and Jake. If that is serious, he will make no moves in
her direction. For this Greek-American merchant who has
been in so many wars and received arrow wounds in Abyssinia is at bottom a gentleman; that is why Brett recognizes
him as "one of us." No such word is dropped by any of
them. Hemingway would blush to be caught with such a
word on his lips. But that is what it practically comes to.
That is "what he has instead of God."

It is now time to remark that these reckless and profane
young men and women are the product of a special set of
conditions. They are the war generation—the "lost generation," as Gertrude Stein called them. They have lived through
times of violence and disorder. They have been disillusioned.
They have formed habits suitable to war times and been made
unfit for the peaceful routines of civil life. They have been
shaken loose from their moorings, saddened in their outlook,
made restive and skeptical; above all made unwilling to submit themselves to any authority but of their own creation, to
grant any assumptions which they haven't personally tested.
This is not Hemingway speaking; these points are nowhere
explicitly made in the book. But unless these things are said,
the earnest "bourgeois" reader will be unable to do justice
to the strain of earnestness shown by these ne'er-do-wells.
There is, of course, a measure of mere swagger and bragga-
docio in the way they go on—there is something of the show-
off in Hemingway's rebels against convention. And it is that
which has most impressed a large portion of his readers and
imitators. But that is not the whole story with them, any
more than it is with any generation of the young who take
the bit in their mouth. There is something here of serious

independence, and something too, under the flippant disguise, of intellectual criticism. These people are determined not to be the dupes of any stuffed shirt or lawn sleeves.

The amazing thing is, with their start from scratch, that these people go so far on the track of morality—that they recover so much of what is traditional in the civilized code. The case is even more striking in *A Farewell to Arms* (1929). For here there is a positive reaction against something conceived as bad (the War) in favor of something conceived as good, the life together of a man and a woman who love each other.

The Italian action in the World War was notoriously calculating and cold-blooded, not motivated by anything more lofty than materialistic patriotism. The Young American may have entered the ambulance service in Italy as the most available means of serving the cause of "democracy"; but he was early impressed with the seamy side of the whole undertaking as seen from the Italian front. The details given, while meager, are all of a nature to emphasize the mean and unheroic aspects of war; and such discussions of the moral implications of the thing as he hears from others all confirm the impression that this war is no exception to the inherent evil of the institution. The ambulance drivers under his command turn out to be socialists, who see no point in fighting the Austrians but consider that the war was provoked by a class in each country that is stupid and does not realize anything, and that, moreover, makes money out of it. The same view is held by the sensitive and high-minded priest: war is made by the unfeeling and unimaginative, and it would be stopped if the people were organized or if their leaders did not sell them out. Even Rinaldi the surgeon is depressed by the war, though he has been having a fine time in the clinic it provides for him, every day learning to do things smoother and better. Frederick Henry never did feel that it was his war. And when, during the retreat of the army, he is roughly handled by a committee of patriots and has to save his life by swimming down a river, he considers that his obligation ceases. He has done his best to deliver his drivers and his cars to the proper base; and now that they are all lost, he has no further responsibility in this war.

In one minor but significant way, the badness of war is symbolized by the kind of love that flourishes under these conditions. There are houses for officers and men provided with young girls for the comfort of the warriors. And this is the chief form of relaxation and entertainment available. Any more humane sort of love is precluded by the conditions of the case. This situation is more distressing to the American than to his Italian chum Rinaldi, the army surgeon; and the latter gets a lot of fun out of the fine good Anglo-Saxon boy "trying to brush away the Villa Rossa from his teeth in the morning, swearing and eating aspirin and cursing harlots."

Frederick is fond of Rinaldi; but in a way he is even more attached to the priest. He stands between the two; he does not share the priest's chastity nor his devotion to God, but he has no inclination to make fun of these, and he feels that the priest "had always known what I did not know and what, when I learned it, I was always able to forget." This is not precisely his chastity or his love of God. But it is, it would appear, his understanding of the essence of love in general. He does not consider that the experiences with women of which Frederick tells him are love. That is only passion and lust. "When you love you wish to do things for. You wish to sacrifice for. You wish to serve." Such a love he will some day find and he will be happy. When Frederick protests that he has always been happy, the priest says, "It is another thing. You cannot know about it unless you have it."

And the priest, as it turns out, is right. When, in his convalescence in the Milan hospital, Frederick finds himself engaged in an affair with his English nurse, this is not a repetition of earlier casual episodes; he is too much concerned with the object of his affection. The carnal element is no less present; but there is added the circumstance that he is devoted to the woman, wishing to do things for her, seeking her well-being. In the hotel at Stresa he has some talk with the aged and wise Count Greffi; and they come, by way of religion, to the subject of values. "What do you value most?" asks the old man. "Someone I love," is the young man's answer. "With me it is the same," says the Count. And while neither of them acknowledges the hold of supernatural faith, the Count insists that love itself is a religious feeling.

Frederick and Catherine are not married. Frederick would like them to be married for her protection. In Italy in time of war there are too many difficulties. Besides, Catherine has no religious faith and regards the matter as indifferent. She protests that she is an honest woman, and that "you can't be ashamed of something if you're only happy and proud of it." The sanctity of marriage—they seem to feel—is not in the religious or legal ceremony but in the essential nature of the relationship.

It may be worth while once again to remind ourselves of the special conditions under which this relationship was formed. I mean the state of things resulting from the War and the presence of these characters in Europe at a great distance from home. They are singularly detached from all that makes for fixity in the social order. The state of war is an abnormal social state. The point is made that both of these persons have cut the ties of family. These people are not of the lost generation in the sense that they have been damaged by the War and rendered unfit for civil life. But they are living in a social no-man's land, where no one is concerned in what they do but themselves.

I have no doubt that many emancipated readers have taken pleasure in the thought of this love affair on the general principle that it is more fun to "live in sin" than to submit to convention. Somewhere Frederick acknowledges to himself that he has the usual masculine reluctance to submit to the yoke. And sentiments like these are natural enough, though they may be shared by shallow people and expressed in cheap and showy ways. There are enough humiliations and hypocrisies and sentimentalisms associated with the state of matrimony fully to justify the pleasure we take in the thought of a moral holiday, not to speak of our quite natural preference for a free and easy life. And the situation presented by Hemingway is plausible enough and significant enough to absolve him from the imputation of any mere desire to exploit the theme of irresponsible love.

In Switzerland, as the time for Catherine's delivery draws near, it is quite agreed that they will be married after the child is born. For with persons fully persuaded that their attachment is for good and all there would be no point in wishing it otherwise. But this love was destined to be sealed with something more grave even than legal marriage—it was to be sealed with the seal of suffering and death. I used to think that this final episode was artificially attached to the story by Hemingway in order to give it an emotional weight which it did not naturally carry—that it had, in short, a strain of the sentimental or the melodramatic. Later reading has convinced me that the story, from the beginning, is more serious than might be inferred from the tone of irony and understatement that colors the narrative and from the tone of flippancy and emotional reserve that prevails in the dialogue. Once you get the notion that everything has more than its face value, that this is a "religious" passion with which we are concerned, as these things are conceived by the priest and Count Greffi; once you get the notion that Hemingway's generation take some things just as hard as writers with a more eloquent rhetoric, the tragedy of the final chapters follows on with perfect rightness. It may not be necessary to the logic of the story that Catherine should die in childbirth. But it is the most effective means that could be devised for demonstrating the seriousness of her lover's feeling. On present reading I find no sentimentalism in the conclusion that is not present in the whole. I am not much inclined to call it sentimental. Let us say rather that Hemingway, in his severely "modern" and unromantic idiom, has given us a view of love as essentially romantic as any of his predecessors in the long line of English novelists.

The tragedy remains, and a certain saturnine attitude toward the whole show. One thing the author lays himself out to exhibit is the pluck of the heroine—the pluck of a healthy organism not intimidated by the complexities and menaces of life. She realizes, however, that life is a battle, that the hostile powers are many, and that it is accordingly important for her and her man not to be divided in their forces. "Because there's only us two and in the world there's all the rest of them. If anything comes between us we're gone and then they have us." "They won't get us," Frederick assures her. "Because you're too brave. Nothing ever happens to the brave."

In one sense this remains true; for so long as they have the strength of their courage and their love, there can be no complete loss whatever happens. But with the death of Catherine he had not reckoned. Jake in the earlier story was trying to learn how to live in life. "Maybe if you found out how to live in it you learned what it was all about." But now Frederick realizes that one can never learn how to live in it. The rules are too difficult to learn and the masters of the game too ruthless in their application of the rules. Catherine has been trapped by a biological force. She is going to die as a result of her love. "You died," he says to her in thought. "You did not know what it was all about. You never had time to learn. They threw you in and told you the rules and the first time they caught you off base they killed you." That is his judgment in the face of her imminent death. And hers is, "It's just a dirty trick."

It would not be a "modern" novel if this protest were not uttered against the rules of the game. But even so, the reader can hardly feel that he is left with nothing more constructive than the notion of an order given to playing dirty tricks on mortals. Along with that, he is left with certain "values" of which the whole story is a dramatic embodiment—the transcendental values of courage and "love." And these are something, according to this author's formula, to "make you feel good after."

In his novel of the Spanish war, the transcendental values of courage and of love are presented more at length and more explicitly; and to these are added, in positive and explicit form, the social virtues of faithfulness and of devotion to the humane ideal which goes under the name of the Republic. There is the same cult of courage which has been a common feature of Hemingway's writing—mere elemental courage as a sign of manliness. Robert Jordan cannot bear to think of his father, who had denied his manliness by committing suicide. In the conclusion of the story, wounded and in danger of capture and torture at the hands of the fascists, Robert fights to the end his temptation to shoot himself. As long as there is something he can do to prolong the fight he is obliged to cling to the life that remains. Everywhere throughout the story, while Hemingway shows his characteristic interest in the psychology of fear and courage, there is a shift in emphasis. Courage is important in itself, but it is above all important as a condition for meeting one's obligation to one's comrades in the struggle. It takes on a social character which it does not have when you consider only the obligation which one has to one's virility, as with the prize fighters and matadors of his earlier work.

But the thing goes beyond faithfulness to one's immediate comrades. For these are not merely men and women who happen to be in the same boat together and obligated to help one another as human beings banded against death. They are banded together against something worse than death, which is impersonal and amoral. They are fighting, as Robert Jordan says to himself, "for all the poor in the world, against all tyranny, for all the things that you believed and for the new world you had been educated into." So that faithfulness to individuals (an exalted and necessary virtue) passes over into devotion to humanity, which is derivatory and generalized, but which in its greater range and implications appeals to what is broadly called the religious emotions. Robert Jordan is a typical Hemingway character in that he finds it embarrassing to speak of these emotions, almost even to think of them. But the feeling was "as authentic as the feeling you had when you heard Bach, or stood in Chartres Cathedral. . . . It gave you a part in something that you could believe in wholly and completely and in which you felt an absolute brotherhood with the others who were engaged in it. It was something that you had never known before but that you had experienced now and you gave such importance to it and the reasons for it that your own death seemed of complete unimportance; only a thing to be avoided because it would interfere with the performance of your duty."

Thus we find Hemingway, through the thin disguise of his hero, somewhat reluctantly and somewhat tardily, paying tribute to a moral ideal as exalted and as comprehensive as it is possible to conceive. Somewhat reluctantly, because Robert Jordan shares Hemingway's fear of romantic falsification. "Don't lie to yourself," he thought, on one occasion. "Nor make up literature about it. You have been tainted with it for a long time now." Somewhat tardily he pays his tribute to this ideal because, as it happens, "it was something that he had never known before." And even now that he knew it, it would take time before his knowledge could ripen into art. Jordan, like Hemingway, had it in mind to write a book about the Spanish war. "But only about the things he knew, truly, and about what he knew. But I will have to be a much better writer than I am now to handle them, he thought." Such reluctance and such tardiness we have to admire; for they are the guarantee that what is written will be as true as the author knows how to make it.

Another thing that Robert Jordan had never known before was that the love of a woman could be a matter of absolute importance to him. His love for Maria in the camp of the guerillas was to endure for no more than three days and three nights till death put an end to it. But, as he reflected, "what you have with Maria, whether it lasts just through today and a part of tomorrow, or whether it lasts for a long life is the most important thing that can happen to a human being." This affair of Maria is highly romantic. It is a startlingly effective instance of the poetic formula of shining love projected against the shadow of death. It raises more delicate critical questions than there is time to deal with adequately. I will confine myself to the philosophical implications of the episode. However true or untrue, however plausible or improbable it may be from the historical point of view, this episode is highly symbolic in relation to the political theme and to what we may call the writer's metaphysic of emotion.

This beautiful crop-headed Spanish girl serves to concentrate in a single figure the rule of brute force and sadistical cruelty which we have come to associate with fascist ideology and the fascist temper. Robert Jordan finds her in the mountain camp of guerilla fighters, who have rescued her from a trainload of fascists. She had been the object of fiendish cruelty on the part of those who had shot her mother and father (republican mayor of his village), had shaved off the girl's hair to stamp her as vile, and subjected her to repeated outrage. For weeks she has been in the process of recovering from the psychic shock, and it is the tender and passionate love of Robert Jordan that finally restores her sanity by restoring her self-respect. She is, it will be seen, a kind of sacrificial lamb or virgin martyr of the cause of humanity. Her nature is virginal not in the cloistered sense but as we apply that word to the pure-hearted lover of one man. I fancy it is with intention that Hemingway gives her the traditionally sacred name of Maria. By means of this episode Hemingway heightens not merely the romantic glamour of his story but the sense that his theme is that of the agelong struggle of humanity against inhumanity.

But this episode is thematically important with regard to the essential metaphysic as well as to the political alignment of Hemingway. It serves to emphasize the fact that he is not in any fundamental sense a materialist. His hero is fighting under direction of communist leaders, since these have proved themselves most capable of organizing the forces of the Republic. He has made himself acquainted with the Marxian dialectics, but he knows that they are not for him. "You have to know them in order not to be a sucker." His reflections on his political position are brought out by his reflections on his love for Maria. The question is whether he is under an illusion in supposing that his love for her is something more than a purely sexual phenomenon. He asks himself whether it is right for him, a soldier of the Republic, to love Maria, "even if there isn't supposed to be any such thing as love in a purely materialistic conception of society?" And at once he answers himself: "Since when did you ever have any such conception? Never. And you never could have. You're not a real Marxist and you know it. You believe in Liberty, Equality and Fraternity. You believe in Life, Liberty and the Pursuit of Happiness. Don't ever kid yourself with too much dialectics." Another time he is led to similar reflections by Maria's reference to the "glory" of their love—*la gloria*. How different that is, he thinks, from the French conception of *la gloire*. "It is the thing that is in the Cante Hondo and in the Saetas. It is in Greco and in San Juan de la Cruz, of course, and in others. I am no mystic, but to deny it is as ignorant as though you denied the telephone or that the earth revolves around the sun or that there are other planets than this."

Thus we see how far, in matters of both erotic and social sentiment, he has extended the scale of acknowledged values. The test is still the same, of how a given experience "makes you feel," but in type of feeling we have traveled far from the simple physical sensations from which we started. Hemingway has managed to cover a good deal of ground with his very simple definition of the moral.

V. ERNEST HEMINGWAY

The Esthetics of Simplicity

"You'll lose it if you talk about it."
—HEMINGWAY

V. ERNEST HEMINGWAY

The Esthetics of Simplicity

The Hemingway "fan" would surely say that I have laid too much stress on the "moral" element in his writing. And that would certainly be true if the case were left where it is. The morality is something latent in the esthetics. Hemingway is laboring not to point a moral but to produce an effect. But the guiding principle in his general esthetics is the same as in his morality—a reduction of things to their simplest terms. In description, in narrative, in characterization, above all in dialogue, the effort is to say things in words that are most expressive at a minimum cost of philosophy or abstraction.

His favored situations in his short stories are those involving death and danger, and that because the emotions involved are so unequivocal, and there is so little occasion to waste words upon them. In "The Undefeated" the invalided matador trying to make a comeback in the bullring—working against the indifference of managers and spectators, the ugliness of the bulls, and his want of faith in his own powers, doggedly returning again and again to the hopeless fight; in "The Killers" the men in the lunchroom frozen into silence and unquestioning submission before the swaggering brute force of the gangsters, and Ole Andreson, the prize fighter lying on the rooming-house bed with all his clothes on, not daring to go out, making no move to call the police or to get away, so certain he is that there "ain't anything to do now"— just lying there in a kind of torpid jelly of fear, under the spell of his inescapable fate. There is really no need to describe the

97

feelings; they are almost completely rendered in terms of the physical set-up and of what is said on one side and the other. Or if the author feels called on to register feelings, it is generally in terms of unconscious physical manifestations. "My old man sat there and sort of smiled at me, but his face was white and he looked sick as hell and I was scared and felt sick inside because I knew something had happened and I didn't see how anybody could call my old man a son of a bitch, and get away with it." "The doctor chewed the beard on his lower lip and looked at Dick Boulton. Then he turned away and walked up the hill to the cottage. They could see from his back how angry he was."

It will be observed that Hemingway almost altogether avoids the more common practical situations in life, in which people are working for long-distance ends—business, farming, the professions, politics, family life—where a thousand small moves contribute to the piling up of the ultimate score, where the immediate satisfactions are subordinate to the long-range strategy of the game, and where one is seldom confronted with life-and-death predicaments and the naked primary emotions. His people are confined mainly to occupations like sports, war, drinking, and love, where every day brings its showdown, its immediate excitement and challenge. I suppose that he is guided by some sense that business and family life are secondary and instrumental activities, having their value solely in terms of the more primary excitements and gratifications, and that in general the concern with these secondary activities diverts the attention from the primary and ultimate values. In this Hemingway is merely carrying a little farther a tendency which is present in all imaginative writing.

It might seem that his program is to see how far he can go in eliminating from his fiction elements which have been exploited and sometimes abused by earlier writers. He has doubtless the same attitude toward psychology as the founders of the French realistic school in the 1850's. Psychology is to be distrusted because it is so hard to bring it to the test of hard facts—it gives such scope for self-deception and sentimentality, for tricks of rhetoric and fine writing. His double aim is truth and simplicity—the esthetic strain in the realist appears in the familiar phrase, the unvarnished truth. The realist dislikes varnish not merely because it disguises the truth, but also because he dislikes the shiny effect. It is too showy, and a symptom of the "bourgeois" penchant for "conspicuous waste." Hemingway's plainness is an outcome of the movement, as old as Ruskin, in favor of handmade articles. He doesn't care for "nice" people because they are overlaid with so much varnish; it is too much trouble scraping this off to get down to the true vein of the wood. He might satirize these types—but on the whole he doesn't aim at satire; that in itself is too showy a line, whether it be the facetious athletic-club manner of Sinclair Lewis or the smart bookish manner of Aldous Huxley (a foppish Plato), or the earnest sociological manner of Galsworthy. He doesn't want his picture cluttered up with so much paint.

The comedy of manners is not his line—he does not seem to feel that human nature is well represented by its oddities and absurdities. He has no view of society either as an organism (Zola) or as a museum (Thackeray) or as a training school for souls (Tolstoy). His canvases are not panoramic; there is none of the symphonic interplay of groups of characters, as in Tolstoy or Wassermann. Of "nature" he is unaware—whether as pastoral landscape with figures (Hardy) or as the vast indifferent background of sea and sky and jungle which gives its splendor and pathos to the epics of Conrad. His work is mostly lacking in the richer colors of the romantic imagination. His fiction will not be thought of in terms of painting. It is black and white line drawing. And its special merits are such as are to be had in this medium.

In all this elimination of what other writers seek, while he is doubtless following his natural bias and temperament, it is also clear that he is following a theory deliberately held— that he is making a virtue of his limitations. His work is *stylized,* as they used to say in Paris. There is a conscious effort to simplify the outlines, to cut out all that is fancy and leave the basic design to make its effect without interference from incidental graces and coquetries. It is like the furniture that came into style at that period on the continent—great masses of wood uncarved and unmodified by fluted pilasters and brasses and curlicues—with straight metal pipes in place of curved and claw-footed legs, and the fewest possible pieces in any one room. It is like the chic street dress of Parisian women, all in one color and stuff, without flounces or ruffles, and with lines as simple as a ship under sail. Today we should call it streamlined, except that this implies more sweeping, more continuous lines—a broader and smoother effect—and more seductive curves.

Hemingway's style is more a matter of separate statements, with no legato, no holding over of the effect with the blurring of the pedal. Most of his sentences are short and simple, a single statement, subject, predicate and object. And most of the rest are strings of simple statements held together with *ands.* The rarest thing with him is the statement modified by subordinate clauses indicating reasons, causes, conditions, concessions—intrusive refinements of thought, which only serve to clutter things up and blur the simple behavioristic sequence. Stimulus and response—gesture, speech, action. Let them speak for themselves; the effect is neater and cleaner. And leave to James and Proust the fussy articulations and qualifications of sentimental logic.

I went out the door and down the hall to the room where Catherine was to be after the baby came. I sat in a chair there and looked at the room. I had the paper in my coat that I had bought when I went out for lunch and I read it. It was beginning to be dark outside and I turned on the light to read. After a while I stopped reading and turned off the light and watched it get dark outside. . . . There was a crowd of kids watching the car, and the square was hot, and the trees were green, and the flags hung on their staffs, and it was good to get out of the sun and under the shade of the arcade that runs all the way around the square. . . . I drank a small bottle of chianti with the meal, had a coffee afterward with a glass of cognac, finished the paper, put my letter in my pocket, left the paper on the table with the tip and went out.

All the English teachers in the country are trying to get their pupils to discover the varied relationships of ideas, and to range their ideas in the proper order of subordination. Hemingway is just as strenuously working to reduce all ideas to a single order of relationship, the conjunctive coordinate relationship, in which no one item is subordinated to any other. It is the great leveling democracy of the *and*. Both Hemingway and the English teachers have their reasons. The teachers are concerned with the logical structure of thought and hoping to raise their pupils a few degrees in their level of understanding. The writer of fiction is concerned with the esthetic projection of images. The understanding spirals back upon itself and ties itself in subtle knots that will hold the thought firm. But the writer of fiction is telling a story and he wants it to flow and not be lost in eddies of logic.

And there is another reason—another difference of aim. The teacher is trying to lift his pupil to a higher level of intellectual sophistication. The writer of fiction—if it is Hemingway—is generally trying to render the reactions of characters whose intellectual level is that of the eighth-grade pupil. I am not referring to the reader of Hemingway but to the people he reads about. The simple-minded reader may be grateful to Hemingway for putting up so few obstacles to his understanding. But the simple-minded reader does not understand the half of what the man is driving at. The point is that Hemingway has set out to record the behavior of people not precisely simple-minded, but who have not learned, or who

have deliberately unlearned, the language of intellectual
sophistication. Such are the boy Nick Adams, the prize
fighters and rum runners and barmen and jockeys, who may
be shrewd enough in their way, but whose way is not that of
Aristotle and Hume. And such are the newspapermen and
army men, the Italian counts and American college girls, the
sportsmen and Hemingways, who may have been reared on
Balzac and Herbert Spencer, but whose particular dread is to
be taken for highbrows and blue-stockings. Such being the
people he will represent, it is imperative that in their talk
there should be no hint of bookishness.

And not merely in their talk. Hemingway is of the school
of those who identify themselves in tone with their characters. The narrative portions are assimilated as nearly as possible to the tone and idiom of the characters to whom they
refer. And the vocabulary is chosen with the same eye to simplicity as the syntax. Hemingway admires and emulates the
discipline of Flaubert. But he does not follow the principle
of the *mot précis*. The exact word of Flaubert and Maupassant is the discriminating word, the most expressive word—
chosen from the widest range accessible to an author trained
in language and thought. With Hemingway the exact word
is the word most likely to occur to the unsophisticated, or the
consciously unbookish, character. It is the word which puts
the least strain upon the intellect, the most simple and so
undiscriminated word. How do you feel? I feel fine. What
kind of a day was it? "It was a lovely day, not too hot, and
the country was beautiful from the start." What kind of a
torero was Belmonte? Belmonte was very good. What kind of
a Catholic was Jake? He was a rotten Catholic. What were
my reactions to Cohn's nervousness? I enjoyed it. "It was
lousy to enjoy it, but I felt lousy."

The dialogue is equally standardized in its simplicity and
even more idiomatic in the manner of the day. The reader
can easily verify this for himself. It would take too much

room and cost me too much in publishers' fees to give an adequate notion of it in quotation. It is enough to note that it is skillfully constructed so as to render the cultural tone of the characters and secure the effects at which the author aims.

And now, I am only too well aware that the reader is asking himself what Hemingway means by the fourth and fifth dimension which can be got in the writing of prose, and wondering what possible subtleties are to be rendered in writing which labors under so many self-imposed or congenital limitations as this we have described. And while I have, I believe, more than an inkling of what he has in view, and feel myself that he has had no small success in reaching these further dimensions in his art, I realize that these are things which are going to be very hard to catch in this crude net of analysis. And the fish we catch may be very different from what Hemingway intended. But perhaps it doesn't matter provided they are something equally good.

I will begin with the dialogue; for it is here that I discern what we might call a fourth dimension. It is not to be inferred from my account of his style that his dialogue consists of the vulgar remarks of vulgar people under the stress of vulgar emotions, and that consequently the effect is too cheap to be interesting. The mistake would be in applying the word "vulgar" to these people, remarks or emotions. The emotions are too urgent and primary to be vulgar; the people may be crude but they are seldom vulgar; and the same thing applies to the remarks. Vulgar and cheap are words implying more of the showy and factitious than is here the rule; they are "bourgeois" characteristics, and they suggest the self-consciousness of Babbitt, his ineffectualness, his exaggeration and salesmanship. The speech of Hemingway's characters is colloquial and lowbrow; but what is more remarkable is its edge and economy. His dialogues are lean and stripped. The number of things said is reduced to a minimum; and they are rendered in the smallest possible number of phrases chosen for their expressiveness and pertinence, and brought into relief by the device of repetition.

In his repetition of key phrases in dialogue, it is clear that Hemingway is proceeding in the manner of a composer more than in that of someone making a literal transcript of ordinary talk. People do repeat themselves, and they do take up and repeat the phrases used by others in conversation. But this is an occasional and incidental feature in ordinary talk, which is less selective and more formless and featureless than this stylized dialogue of Hemingway's. There is a curious likeness in this respect to the dialogue of Henry James, otherwise so very different from Hemingway's. In both these writers there will be passages of a page or more in which the changes are rung on a single phrase, exactly repeated by one character from another, or repeated with slight change, and then taken up by the original speaker in exactly the same words or with some slight, significant variation. The difference is that in James the effect is more intellectual and dialectic —carrying forward some subtle point of interpretation; while in Hemingway the effect is more often emotional, deepening the sense of fear, of strain, of pathos.

In both cases the effect is incremental, as in ballad refrains. The repetition of the phrase by the second person gives to it the special coloring of recognition from his point of view; the repetition of the phrase in a new context gives it new associations and impressiveness; and the variation of the phrase by some slight change in wording, or the substitution of something virtually synonymous, makes us appreciate its full significance for thought or feeling. In James we are advanced in our understanding of the complicated or puzzling situation. In Hemingway we are brought more and more under the spell of the mood he aims to evoke. We come to recognize the tune under its changing phases; and we feel that it amounts to more than the several notes of which it is composed.

Another matter that concerns Hemingway is that his phrases should have the right sound. I don't know whether Robert Frost would care for Hemingway; but he ought at least to appreciate the scrupulousness with which he listens to the "voices." It is Frost's theory that in ordinary speech what counts as much as the overt logical sense of the words is the latent sense they yield to the ear when spoken aloud by virtue of accent and inflection. The plain prose denotation of the words is less important than the emotional connotation they carry when shaped by the living breath. He is particularly concerned in poetry with the rendering of those intimate tones of the speaking voice which most closely fit the unself-conscious utterance of the heart. He feels that he cannot write a line unless he hears the natural inflections of the voice which the words carry in their context. And he is the chief of that large band of American poets who have sought in this century to keep close in their verse to the natural inflections of unrhetorical speech. In this respect the school of Hemingway owes perhaps as much to the work of our poets as to any prose influence.

This is a very difficult and elusive matter, and it can never be determined with any scientific precision without the use of machines for recording the inflectional curves of the voice, as well as some adequate means of noting on the printed page the variations of pitch and emphasis that go with the reading of a phrase or a sentence. In the absence of these conveniences I shall have to ask the reader to try over certain pages of Hemingway for himself, reading them aloud as naturally as possible, with as close attention as possible to the changing pitch of the voice as it follows the shadings of thought. In the seventh chapter of *The Sun Also Rises* let him read the page (60 in the standard Scribner's edition) where the Greek count discusses Brett's "class"; the page following where he expresses the wish to hear her "really talk"; and that following where he discusses how charming she is when drunk, and how much he has "been around"; and finally, the page where he discusses with her what love does to your "values." If I am not mistaken, and if the reader has an ear for these things, he will find that in each of these cases Hemingway is playing a subtle tune upon these key words; he will note the rising and falling inflections of the words and the variation of inflection and pitch as they recur in the changing context.

The Count points out to Brett that when she is divorced she won't have a title. "No. What a pity," says Brett ironically. "No," says the Count. "You don't need a title. You got class all over you." Note the high pitch of the first "you," carrying his accent of courtly flattery. There is a slight upward swing of inflection on the second syllable of "title," conveying a note of scorn for mere titles when considered in relation to the essential aristocracy of Brett. The second "you" is comparatively short and toneless, leading to the three heavily stressed words, "class all over." Both "class" and "all" carry what I shall call a circumflex accent. That is, in the lingering emphasis upon them, the voice rises and slightly falls upon each word. In "over" there is a distinct passage from the high to the low register, as we come to the end of the plateau of emphasis in the sentence. Brett acknowledges his good opinion in light ironic tone. "Thanks. Awfully decent of you." "I'm not joking you," says the Count in his faintly foreign idiom. And then he repeats his statement in more emphatic terms. "You got the most class of anybody I ever seen. You got it. That's all." Here are four instances of what I call the circumflex, "most," "class," "seen," and clearest of all, "got." In pronouncing these words as they stand here, the voice slides through several degrees of rising or falling or rising and falling pitch so as to prolong the relish taken in the thought of Brett's "class" and the unmistakable fact of her possessing it.

We are not to suppose that Hemingway is primarily concerned with the slangy inelegance of the terms used. Everything goes to show that his dispenser of champagne is a man of experience and discrimination. In such language as is natural to him he is paying this lady the compliment of recognizing her social and personal quality. He is paying deference to something rare and fine. There is no single word which so effectively connotes all that he has in mind as the slang word "class"—no word so short and direct nor one that will carry so well the tones of voice appropriate to his intention. And there is no word signifying possession that has the force and savor of the preterit "got." Try the equivalent "have" to see how pale it is in comparison. "You have it!" It is true that "class" and "got" are colloquial, and "seen" is positively ungrammatical. But I am not sure that the lowbrow colloquialism of these words does not serve better—if only by the irony of their application—to underline the serious unction of this connoisseur in "values." The fineness of his taste shines through the crudeness of his language.

I do not want to labor the point. The reader may be too much impressed with the cheapness of the subject matter to admit of fine intentions in the handling. For myself, I find a charm and piquancy in this talk, even where it is about drinking and getting "around," that needs explaining. I think I hear a certain clearness of timbre in the inflections, a delicate expressiveness in the repeated words like notes in music. I note the variation of pitch and growth in significance of the word "values" as it is bandied about by Brett and the Count in their playful but covertly serious badinage. The significance grows; the feeling evolves; the sentiment deepens. That is why I have spoken of these repetitions as incremental. They are like phrases in music that broaden and deepen and take more hold upon us as they recur again and again in the progress of the harmonic accompaniment. This, I submit, is not an everyday occurrence in fiction; it means that Heming-

way has carried his prose a step farther than the vulgar practice. And he might well regard this as a fourth dimension in
literary art.

As for the fifth dimension, we might find this in his handling of the situations. It turns out, on close inspection, that
these crude people, as we were rash enough to call them, facing these primary situations, are shown in lights more interesting than one might anticipate from their apparent simplicity, serving to rescue them from the commonplace and
hackneyed. There is something at work here in the author's
imagination which we might call irony, if that were not a
word and a faculty so much abused that it suggests an
effect cliché and banal. Let us call it finesse. This author generally manages to give to his situation what James calls a
"turn of the screw"—a turn of the imagination that reveals
some unsuspected aspect of human nature and raises the subject to a higher pitch of interest and poignancy.

There is "Fifty Grand," the tale of a champion prize fighter
on the decline, who refuses to claim a foul when his opponent gives him a vicious punch below the belt. He fights on
in great pain until he can return the foul, and allows the
fight to go to his opponent. The secret is that he has laid a
bet of fifty grand upon the other man, and he would rather
lose the fight than the money. What he did was doubtless dis-
honorable in the sporting code. But it certainly took guts.
And the "turn of the screw" is in the thought that this exhibition of nerve was not in the interest of winning the fight—
that would be normal—but in the interest of securing himself
and his wife against poverty. There you have something odd
in human nature that is worth recording.

"My Old Man" is a story more appealing to the sentiment.
The story is told by the boy whose father is a jockey dishonor-
able in his way as the prize fighter was in his. For the game
of this jockey is making money on his opponent's horse by
causing his own horse to lose the race. He is very good at this,

but in time his trick is discovered and he has to move on to another race track. The chief technical interest in the telling is the way the sense of this man's skulduggery is conveyed to us through the narrative of his adoring kid. It is not till his father's death in a spill that the full force of his father's meanness is borne in on his childish mind. He had always regarded his father as the finest of men; and he must have been a good father to the boy for the latter to be so passionately attached to him. After his father's death he hears men referring to him as a crook who had it coming to him on the stuff he'd pulled. But there is one friend of his father's who remains loyal— who at least has the grace to try to make the boy feel good about his dad. "Don't you listen to what those bums said, Joe. Your old man was one swell guy." That is a fine touch of humanity. And Joe's last thoughts lend a fine touch of pathos. "But I don't know," thought Joe. "Seems like when they get started they don't leave a guy nothing."

This is a tale of great beauty. I cannot imagine a more touching commentary on the clinging affection of father and son. That the father was a crook makes it no less poignant, or that in the end the son should come to know this. The peculiar triumph is that nothing is said of the tenderness of this relation, and that all the "values" are rendered in terms of the boy's naïve and halting apprehension. An effect like this might well be referred to as a fifth dimension in storytelling. The beauty of it is in the indirection of the approach— the achievement of the effect without recourse to the obvious devices of rhetoric.

Altogether there is a good deal of sentiment in Hemingway; there is much delicacy of feeling. Let the reader try the short stories entitled "Cat in the Rain," "The Doctor and the Doctor's Wife," "A Clean, Well-lighted Place, "Wine in Wyoming." But we are so used to having sentiment laid on with a trowel, delicacy written in italics. Hemingway's aim is to see how much can be conveyed with the least expenditure of words—the sort of vague words that are used simply for heightening the emotion; "proud words," as Sandburg calls them, "tall, opaque words," as Hazlitt calls them. It is as if Hemingway had absorbed Hazlitt's scorn for "sounding generalities . . . splendid, imposing, vague, a cento of sounding commonplaces . . . the most gorgeous, tarnished, threadbare, patchwork set of phrases, the leftover finery of poetic extravagance, transmitted down through successive generations of barren pretenders."

Hemingway goes much further than Hazlitt. He distrusts intellectual elaborations almost as much as rhetorical ones. And he has not Hazlitt's abhorrence of slang words and those associated with "coarse and disagreeable or with confined ideas." His "familiar style" is not, like Hazlitt's, that of the cultivated man but that of the man in the street. He is shy of everything that smacks of what seems to him sophistication, because of the element of inflation and pretense which he has been led to connect with it in his mind. He has had an unfortunate experience with cultivated writers and has learned to suspect them wherever found. He is the burned child that fears the fire. And he is one of a large class. He is one of the war generation, who have learned to dislike big words because they were so much abused both during the War and in the age that prepared the War. As the man says in *A Farewell to Arms,* when one of his companions remarks that the great efforts of the Italian army could not have been in vain:

I was always embarrassed by the words sacred, glorious, and sacrifice and the expression in vain. We had heard them . . . and had read them, on proclamations that were slapped up by billposters over other proclamations, now for a long time, and I had seen nothing sacred, and the things that were glorious had no glory and the sacrifices were like the stockyards at Chicago if nothing was done with the meat except to bury it. There were many words that you could not bear to hear and finally only the names of places had dignity.

The War is but one of many circumstances which has led vast numbers of thinking men, in our times, to distrust abstractions and ideologies. And esthetic taste has evolved along parallel lines. A disposition to behaviorism in fiction has carried with it an indisposition to the use of adjectives and metaphysical terminology. Our artists in fiction have tried to see how far they can go with a mere notation of objective facts. And they have rediscovered the important esthetic principle of economy. They have found that, other things being equal, the best effect is that achieved with the greatest economy of means. There is, for one thing, the great gain of avoiding the obvious. The sentiment is not wanting in Hemingway. But he finds that he can give more point to his sentiment if he does not dress it out in fine language. And all the more so because this method requires more skill than that which depends on fine language for making its point. It requires that the facts shall be so rightly ordered that they will speak for themselves. This is a challenge to the serious artist. The undiscriminating reader may miss the intention and confuse this work with pulp. But if the thing is done with skill and subtlety, the discriminating reader will not long miss it; and he will receive a pleasure proportioned to the difficulty of the undertaking. He will recognize that this writer has what we call "style." For style, in the larger sense, depends less on the words that are used to get an effect than on the right ordering of the words.

The matter goes beyond esthetics in the narrow sense. There is a significant remark in *The Sun Also Rises*. Brett is trying to tell Jake about the way she feels on having given up her Spanish lover. It is for her an edifying experience, something which in earlier times would have been called a "spiritual" experience, for it is a state of the spirit with Brett. But

Jake doesn't like to have these things dragged out into the vulgar light of words. He tries to shut her up. He says, "You'll lose it if you talk about it." That is a deep saying and one to which any man must respond who cares more for actual states of the spirit than for their verbal equivalents. States of the spirit are fragile and tenuous affairs; and in general we feel that the less said about them the better, lest they be cheapened and lost. Man is given to spiritual vanity; and words are liars. This saying of Jake's is as good a clue as we can find to Hemingway's distrust of verbalism, and his reticence on the subject of spiritual states.

Hemingway's system is an interesting one. He has got some very good results with it; and he has begotten a large school of writers, some of whom have got good results. It represents but a small segment of the great circle of what can and has been done in the field of prose fiction. I shouldn't want to see it erected into a dogma and occupy the whole field. I shouldn't want to see all our storytellers bound by the self-denying ordinance to which Hemingway has bound himself. But it is, as it happens, a characteristic feature of our fiction today; and with several of our writers, like Caldwell and Steinbeck, it has proved consistent with high distinction. Like many present-day composers, they have achieved new dimensions in esthetics by taking advantage of limitations, part temperamental, part deliberately assumed, which need not be imposed on all the world.

Hemingway would, I think, be the first to agree to this reservation. He has shown, in *For Whom the Bell Tolls*, that he is capable of applying his own system without too rigid a dogmatism. His subject here—an episode from the fight for republican principles—calls for the frequent delineation of states of mind more exalted and more complex than had often been in question in his earlier work. He is obliged to distinguish types among the foreign communist leaders, and still more types among the guerilla bands in the mountains—gypsies, peasants, village workmen, women. Robert Jordan has been assigned a task of great difficulty and danger, and the problem is, with each person he deals with: how far can he be trusted to follow orders, to understand the requirements of the situation, and to risk his life without flinching? A man's comprehension of the issues of the war, his devotion to the Republic, are but two factors in an equation that involves his personal pride and pride of race, his tribal attitudes, his appetites, his notions of right and wrong, and a dozen other imponderables.

There is the conviction of the old man Anselmo that killing is a sin; he is a brave and stanch Republican, and he knows that killing is necessary to win the war, but he can only do it under orders and with tears running down his cheeks. There is Pablo, the leader of this band, who has a natural bent for killing and cruelty and has performed great services for the Republic, but who has been softened by easy life in the mountain camp and thinks more of successful retreat than of holding the enemy. He is kept in line only by his inability to stand the thought of being alone; he will risk death rather than isolation. There is Fernando, stiff and conventional, who shrinks from the gross language of his comrades, but who is brave and firm in the face of danger, and can be relied on to perform whatever duty requires. There is Pablo's woman, a good cook, formidable master of invective, jealous and passionate, but absolutely devoted to a leader she can trust, and the most tough and resolute of all the comrades. I can only hint the psychological complexities with which the young American has to deal in his Spanish aids, beginning with the vanity and anarchical independence of the Spanish character in general, and including other more lovable racial traits.

And then there are the complexities of his own nature, which he must rule in the interest of his major objectives. He is a college professor and enough of an intellectual to have doubts and misgivings in regard to every value to which his soul is wedded. He is able to master his doubts by virtue of some instinct or power of will; but first he must meet them, and this means a series of sharp debates within himself. In his personal reflections and in his talk with others, states of mind are the ultimate subject throughout—ideals, loyalties, cases of conscience, and the ins and outs of human motivation. And all this gives to the Spanish novel an appreciably more intellectual cast than the staple of his writing. It is more obviously concerned throughout with attitudes and reactions which have their relevance in a system, or at any rate a complex, of ethical evaluations.

It is true that Hemingway still takes pains to keep free from abstractions and sentimental elaborations. He tries to dispense with adjectives, and particularly the sort which serve to inflate the subject rather than render its substance. He tries to express his ethical values in terms of concrete objects, actions, and effects. He tries to keep his sentences simple, by reducing a train of thought to its component elements and ranging them in sequence rather than in the complicated patterns of logical subordination. But in all these matters he allows himself more latitude than formerly. He will not be hamstrung even by rules of his own making. Robert Jordan must admonish himself to keep straight in his thinking on the subject of killing men in war. "Because if you are not absolutely straight in your head you have no right to do the things you do for all of them are crimes and no man has a right to take another man's life unless it is to prevent something worse happening to other people." Here the author has allowed himself in a single sentence four separate conjunctions indicating reasons and conditions. Even in nature-description there is some syntactical build-up allowed, as in his account of Jordan's feeling about the hour of dawn. "He loved this hour of the day always and now he watched it; feeling it gray within him, as though he were a part of the slow lightening that comes before the rising of the sun; when solid things darken and space lightens and the lights that have shone in the night go yellow and then fade as the day comes." There is in that a broader, more lingering cadence than is customary in his choppy writing, evidence of a ripeness that has come to him with his larger subject.

Not all the talk of the ragged band is in obscenities or in words of one syllable. There is much that is in a tone of dignified self-respect, and there is the formality and elevation of republican ideology. They are all agreed that they must first win the war; but there is some difference of opinion as to what should be done with the undesirables. Agustín would have them shoot the anarchists and communists "and all this *canalla* except the good Republicans." But Anselmo disagrees. "That we should win this war and shoot nobody. That we should govern justly and that all should participate in the benefits according as they have striven for them. And that those who have fought against us should be educated to see their error."

Hemingway has undertaken in this book a linguistic feat of the first magnitude. Nearly all the dialogue is supposed to be talk in Spanish rendered in English, and his effort is to suggest throughout the flavor of the native idiom. I don't know how it will seem to a reader not trained in languages, but to me the effect is charming, picturesque and dramatic. Hemingway's ordinary English is so American, so modern, and so uncompromisingly vernacular that it would hardly do on the tongue of these Spaniards, whose language is in many ways so much more stately and at the same time has its own vernacular idioms that are often more racy than the American equivalents. The stateliness is largely a matter of the longer and fuller words that betray the Latin origin. Of a foreign name hard to remember: "It is a name I could never dominate." Of reinforcements from another camp: "Advising them in time, it should be possible to unite fifty rifles of a certain dependability." "How dependable?" "Dependable within the gravity of the situation" *(dentro de la gravidad).*

Such expressions are well enough in their way, lending a quaint dignity to the characters and reminding us of their Roman heritage. But they need to be used with discretion, as I think they are. The genius of the foreign language is heard more often in homelier and more intimate turns of idiom chosen for some raciness of flavor. Pithy understatement: "less bad" for "excellent," or "why not?" for "yes indeed." Crispness and succinctness with gravity: "I go down now with Anselmo"; "Go now to thy bridge"; "Thus should men move" (that is, like the owl by night, the wings beating quickly, but with no noise of feathers as the bird hunts). Pride and elevation of feeling suggested by inverted word order: " 'For us will be the bridge and the battle, should there be one,' Robert Jordan said and saying it in the dark, he felt a little theatrical but it sounded well in Spanish." Sober precision of statement: " 'It should be of the highest interest,' Anselmo said and hearing him say it honestly and clearly and with no pose, neither the English pose of understatement nor any Latin bravado, Robert Jordan thought he was very lucky to have this old man. . . ." (But it *is* understatement, is it not? Referring to an enterprise in which they stand the greatest chance of giving their lives for the Republic—"it should be of the highest interest . . ."!)

But let me give, with publisher's permission, a longer passage of consecutive dialogue so that the reader may feel how much strength is lent to the situation by the native idioms lovingly cherished by Hemingway and faithfully transcribed in English. Fernando has been seriously wounded and has been borne by two of his comrades to a steep bank which they have to scale in making their escape. He asks them to leave him where he can still get in a shot or two at the enemy. Fernando is a stiff and pedantic person, but the soul of loyalty and courage.

"Leave me here," Fernando said. "It hurts much and there is much hemorrhage inside. I feel it in the inside when I move."

"Let us get thee up the slope," Primitivo said. "Put thy arms around our shoulders and we will take thy legs."

"It is inutile," Fernando said. "Put me here behind a stone. I am as useful here as above."

"But when we go," Primitivo said.

"Leave me here," Fernando said. "There is no question of my travelling with this. Thus it gives one horse more. I am very well here. Certainly they will come soon."

"We can take thee up the hill," the gypsy said. "Easily."

He was, naturally, in a deadly hurry to be gone, as was Primitivo. But they had brought him this far.

"Nay," Fernando said. "I am very well here. What passes with Eladio?"

The gypsy put his finger on his head to show where the wound had been.

"Here," he said. "After thee. When we made the rush."

"Leave me," Fernando said. Anselmo could see he was suffering much. He held both hands against his groin now and put his head back against the bank, his legs straight out before him. His face was gray and sweating.

"Leave me now please, for a favor," he said. His eyes were shut with pain, the edges of his lips twitching. "I find myself very well here."

All this, of course, is incidental to Hemingway's main purpose, which is to picture the Spanish character as exhibited in certain obscure and humble adherents of the republican cause. The Spanish character, and especially that of the Spanish peasant, has exercised for years a strong fascination on Hemingway's imagination. And he has made the three days of this Homeric episode the framework for a magnificent delineation of his subject in all its variegated picturesqueness and strength of appeal—the pride and dignity and gravity, the grossness and cruelty, the homely earthiness and lofty gallantry, the loyalty and treachery, the passionate intensity of feeling, and the resolute devotion and idealism of the Spanish race. This is the subject for a chapter by itself.

I have only space to say that Hemingway has here shown an unsuspected genius for character-creation. Most impressive of his Spanish characters are Pablo and Pilar by virtue of their heroic stature and colorfulness taken in combination with all-too-human weaknesses and contradictions which make them so appallingly unpredictable in speech and action. But the canvas is crowded with minor figures *muy simpatico* and nicely individualized, from the stanch and tender-hearted Anselmo to the crazy commissar Marty, the heresy-hunter of the Communist party, brief apparition of the night before the attack.

There is no space for developing this theme. Instead, I will make one further remark on the Spanish flavoring of the dialogue in which the mountain band give outward expression to their character. The reader will note the constant use in their speech of the second-person singular "thee" and "thou," which alternate with the plural "you," as the feeling of the speaker fluctuates between affectionate intimacy with the person addressed and a more formal and distant attitude. It is the same fluctuation that is seen in the speech of young Hamlet and Gertrude, felt now as his mother and most intimate friend and now as Queen of Denmark and party to his father's murder. It is true that in Shakespeare's time the singular and plural forms were both current, and there was nothing foreign and poetic in the use of "thee" and "thou." They were the homely forms, and "you" was for stateliness and formality. In a contemporary writer in English "thee" and "thou" are archaic, suggestive of poetry and the Bible. Hemingway is of course aware of this, and has taken deliberate advantage of it to give to his dialogue an elevation of tone which is suited to his present subject. Any reader familiar with the English Bible or with the English prayerbook is certain to be affected in some degree by the solemnity of feeling associated with these now obsolete forms.

But that is not the whole story. Hemingway is surely relying on the literary culture of his readers to respond to the other range of associations established by these forms as they are still used in German and the Latin languages. Along with the Biblical solemnity go the intimacy and familiarity of the second-person singular in these languages, the homeliness and earthiness of forms that suggest not the ceremony of aristocratic life but the friendliness and warmth and familiarity of the plain people. This is a stroke of great subtlety and daring. Hemingway has managed by the use of this idiomatic device to link together in our feeling the secular homeliness of the republican cause with the poetry of religious sentiment. And, moreover, since "thee" and "thou" is the language of lovers, it is another means of establishing a connection between the two idealisms which run parallel through the story of Robert Jordan, the idealism of love and the idealism of political sentiment. "I love thee," Jordan declares to Maria, "as I love all that we have fought for. I love thee as I love liberty and dignity and the rights of all men to work and not be hungry. I love thee as I love Madrid that we have defended and as I love all my comrades that have died."

And so it is that, while still resisting the temptations of rhetoric, Hemingway has by no means neglected the resources of language. By skillful use of the idioms of a foreign tongue and the poetic associations of the Bible, he has added another "dimension" to his English prose.

VI. WILLIAM FAULKNER

The Haunted South

"Quoth the Raven 'Nevermore.' "

VI. WILLIAM FAULKNER

The Haunted South

William Faulkner is a novelist who has won to a place of distinction in American letters in spite of peculiarities which might naturally have alienated every group of readers to whom he looked for a backing. There is the type of reader who regards himself as normal and wholesome, who considers that life is not fairly represented unless in the dramatis personae of a novelist the sane people outnumber the insane, the good people outnumber the bad, and unless from the whole social picture some hopeful and practical lesson may be learned. This type of reader will be outraged by the emphasis laid by Faulkner on characters of mentality perverse or moronic and by the general air of self-complacent pessimism and romantic cynicism which pervades the world of Faulkner. I call the pessimism of Faulkner self-complacent and his cynicism romantic because one is constantly given the impression that no intelligent observer can make any but a pessimistic interpretation of human nature, and that somehow cynicism is the only possible recourse of the feeling soul in the presence of the record. As for deriving any useful lesson from the spectacle, it seems to be implied on every page that human behavior is too inveterately tragic and fateful to be corrected and that, in any case, a utilitarian attitude toward human behavior is sign of a simplicity and stodginess unworthy of a person of imagination or aristocratic breeding.

There is, again, the type of reader who wants his story

told straight off without evasions, postponements, and circumlocutions. And he is repelled almost invariably by Faulkner's disposition to tell his stories in a round-about and riddling manner, with the most brazen neglect of chronological sequence, and the most wanton use of every trick for confusing the reader, leading him astray, putting him off, and generally teasing and bewildering him. So there is the second large group—the largest of all—whom he seems to have set out to insult and alienate.

And then there is a smaller group, but an influential one, who prefer simplicity to affectation, natural idiom to showy rhetoric; and Faulkner has often done his best to set them against him by his penchant for "fine writing"—for the precious and strained and euphuistic in style. He has the clever schoolboy's fear of the obvious; and there is hardly one of his novels in which he has not occasionally made himself ridiculous by his determination to be "different." This desperate fear of the commonplace is shown not merely in his style—in adjective and figure and allusion, in tight-rope sentences and thorn-hedge paragraphs; it is equally found in his predilection for motives of action once or twice or three times removed from the familiar and ordinary, and strained to such a point that sometimes the reader cannot be sure even at the end what the true motivation was—he can only have a reasonable certainty that the motives of action were such as unaided he never would have thought of.

So then we have a writer of stories morbid and repellent in subject matter, often affected in style and strained in motivation, and almost invariably teasing and eccentric in manner of narration—one could hardly imagine a more formidable array of barriers set up by an author between himself and his audience. And yet the fact remains that the man has an unmistakable fascination for thousands of readers, who will often turn to him in preference to writers wholesome, natural and straightforward. If we could resolve this paradox, we should discover some of the secrets of genius. And we should realize that there are things more intriguing —for many readers, and under certain circumstances—than the obvious, the wholesome, and even the natural. Faulkner's strong points will appear in the course of our discussion; and paramount among them all is the power of his imagination. This is the one faculty, I should say, which is most indispensable in a writer of fiction. Whatever virtues a novelist may have, he will be little read if he cannot impress the reader's imagination; and whatever his shortcomings, he is sure to find readers and maintain his place in literature if he knows how to evoke a vivid world of people and events.

With Faulkner, too, his defects are closely bound up with his qualities; and as we give an account of his world, we shall often be in doubt whether to lay our emphasis on the defect or on the quality which it dogs as a man's shadow dogs his substance. There is here a kind of ambiguity or ambivalence, which is best suggested by saying that the man is too clever. Well, it is a comfort to think that any man who is too clever must at any rate be clever, and there are so many of our professional entertainers who are—candidly—not clever enough! Perhaps we shall find that Faulkner's cleverness is a clue to his merits and defects in every direction—in his style, his technique, his choice of subject matter, and his attitude toward human nature.

Let us begin with his subject matter, his world of people and events. His first published novel *Soldiers' Pay* deals with the return of a desperately wounded aviator to his Georgia home, and with his fiancée, a shallow glamorous Southern belle, who proves unequal to the challenge of the situation. The mission of salvaging his damaged spirit is taken over by another woman, a young war widow, who is making up in this way for an earlier failure of her own to satisfy her humane ideal. The stage is full of other characters, including a fat young man who quotes Horace and is seeking without much success the right system for seducing women. The book appeared in 1926, and does not fail to play up the "lost generation," hard drinkers returned from war and at a loss how to adjust themselves to the ways of civil life. If it has a theme, it is that indicated in the title; the cynical implication is that the rewards of patriotism are slim in a world of unheroic selfishness and bitchery.

The strongest character is Margaret Powers, the war widow with a heart; and here the cleverness of Faulkner takes the form of a sort of strained and ambiguous sentimentalism. In immolating herself upon this hopeless altar, Margaret Powers gives the impression—to change the figure—of taking up a cross that was not properly hers. One is not even convinced that the marriage ceremony was the right prescription in Donald Mahon's case. One feels that Margaret might have done better, whether in the way of nature or of right feeling, to marry either of the other soldiers that she was stringing along. But that wouldn't have been so handsome a gesture in the Southern manner. And that would have given the wrong tone—and a happy ending—to this resolutely sophisticated story. It would not have suited the book of young Faulkner—injured aviator, *fin-de-siècle* modernist, poet of nymphs and unicorns, reader (I assume) of James Branch Cabell and Ezra Pound. The spiritual note for Margaret Powers must be one less commonplace—a note of transcendentalism in worldliness. Her soul must be a freaked and pallid orchid taking its nourishment from an atmosphere of disillusion and decay.

With the two following novels I will be very brief. *Mosquitoes* takes us on a yachting trip out of New Orleans with a party assembled by a rich woman who collects artists and doesn't know what to do with them. During the five days of the trip the men spend most of their time below drinking whisky and telling tall tales, while the women play cards above. Nothing happens except that Mrs. Maurier's niece tries to elope with the steward, and they get lost in the swamp among the mosquitoes and have to be rowed back to the yacht. But there is an unconscionable amount of talking, blasé and sophisticated. The older people exchange a considerable amount of middle-aged wisdom. There is one character (the sculptor with a torso) who is meant, we feel, to appear less futile than the rest. His higher wisdom may be gathered from his remark to his friends at an advanced stage in the whisky drinking. "Only an idiot has no grief; only a fool would forget it. What else is there in this world sharp enough to stick to your guts?"

The third novel *Sartoris* has more plot than *Mosquitoes*. But its chief interest lies in the fact that Faulkner introduces so many characters who are to reappear much more significantly in later novels—Horace Benbow and the Snopeses in *Sanctuary* and elsewhere, Colonel Sartoris in *Light in August* and *Absalom, Absalom!*—and the fact that many of these characters and episodes are modeled on persons known to William Faulkner or ancestors of his. Bayard Sartoris, daredevil returned from service in the British air force, is the second character in Faulkner's novels suggestive of his own case. His great-grandfather, John Sartoris, who built the railroad that runs past Jefferson, corresponds to the great-grandfather and grandfather of the author-aviator, Colonel William Falkner *(sic)* and his son John, who built the railroad running past Oxford. And there are many other parallels. The town of Jefferson is to all intents and purposes identical with William Faulkner's native Oxford, except that in certain novels Oxford exists independently as the seat of the state university of Mississippi.

The narrative is crowded as full as it can hold with anecdotes, high-spiced and amusing and grounded in fact, many of them destined to be more seriously developed in later novels and short stories. More than either of the other early books it anticipates the sort of material that Faulkner was going to exploit in his masterpieces. The note of futility hangs over it all as it hangs over *Soldiers' Pay* and *Mosquitoes;* but more significant than that is the note of decadence. The decadence of Southern character and society following the Civil War. That is to be the major theme of all his most important books; and it is this theme which will be found to give them their chief importance considered as social documents. It will also prove to be the main source of that element of mystery and terror, of horrid fascination, that makes of William Faulkner the Edgar Allan Poe of contemporary fiction.

The novels which have the greatest significance in the development of this social theme are all laid in the same general district as *Sartoris,* the imaginary town of Jefferson, Mississippi, and its immediate neighborhood. This is Faulkner's "Wessex," the country that he knows best, to which he can give the greatest air of reality as well as representative importance. The novels in question are *The Sound and the Fury* (1929), *As I Lay Dying* (1930), *Sanctuary* (1931), *Light in August* (1932), *Absalom, Absalom!* (1936), and *The Hamlet* (1940).

The Sound and the Fury is an intimate study of four members of the Compson family—representing four types and degrees of degeneracy. Maury (later called Benjy) is a congenital idiot, dumb and partially deaf, incapable of feeding or otherwise caring for himself—a great hulking man at thirty-three—who apprehends but little of what goes on about him, though he has the faculty of second sight and can smell death at a distance. The section dealing with him is dated April 7, 1928; but Benjy cannot distinguish between past and present events, or rather sensations, for it is in them that he lives; and sights, sounds and smells of the present are forever carrying him back to earlier days. There was the winter evening in early childhood when Damuddy (grandmother) died, when his brother Quentin (nine) and sister Caddy (seven) splashed each other with water and the mean brother Jason (five) told on them; the day of the funeral when the children were kept out of sight in the negro quarters; the day when T.P. (negro boy) drives them out to the cemetery; the evening when Benjy is told he is too old to sleep with his sister; the day when Caddy, now fourteen, tries to assure Benjy that she is not going away; and the later day when Caddy's lover comes between them. There are still later days, when Miss Quentin (Caddy's daughter) and her man with the red necktie come into the picture. And that has brought us back to the seventh of April, 1928, when Benjy and Luster (his negro guardian) are running along by the fence that separates their place from the golf links, watching the players knock the little ball and hearing them cry "caddie!" More than anything else the word "caddie" sets Benjy's dim mind off on its re-enactment of the past; the reminder of his dear lost Caddy sets him moaning and whimpering in his loony way. For it was her tenderness and the good smell of her (she smelled like trees) that brought to the poor fragment of humanity such satisfaction as he could find in life.

In the course of these scenes we catch glimpses of the in-valid mother, her brother (Uncle Maury) who lives on the Compsons, and the father who is drinking himself into his grave. The mother lives mainly in her sense that her family is superior to her husband's, that she has burdens heavier than she can bear, and that all but Jason and Maury are in a conspiracy against her. Uncle Maury is dimly seen carry-ing on the gallantries of a Southern gentleman with a neigh-bor's wife and being beaten up for it. Behind these whites and supporting them by their service and their moral strength are the negroes: the boys who look after Benjy, the man Roskus, and the one upon whom all depend, maternal Dilsey the cook. If in anything I have misrepresented the facts, it is that Benjy is a poor interpreter, and we have to piece out our knowledge of things altogether from the rubbish heap of his mind.

The second section is that of Quentin, June 2, 1910. It was on that day that Benjy's brother drowned himself in the Charles River in Cambridge, Mass. If I am not mistaken this is the day of his sister's marriage to a Southerner named Sydney Herbert Head, whom Quentin abhors as a man who has been put out of his Harvard club for cheating, but who promises to give Jason a post in his bank, and whom Caddy marries to save herself from disgrace. Quentin's mind has been disordered by the knowledge of his sister's wantonness, and as much as anything else (one is made to feel) by the jealousy he bears to the other men who have possessed her. For he has come to depend on her love as on her honor; and in the devious turnings of his mind he cherishes the notion that he was the one who was most guilty—guilty of incest. This is giving a very modern turn to an ancient theme. Critics have likened the tragedy of the house of Compson to that of the classic house of Atreus. And one ingenious student has even suggested that Caddy's real name (Candace) may have been picked—to suit the motif of (imaginary) incest—for its likeness to that of the legendary Canace, ruined by the love of her brother Macareus.[1]

The mental condition of Jason is sounder, but his moral complexion is meaner. The only suggestion of disease is his liability to headaches, his painful susceptibility to the smell of gasoline. His day is that just preceding Benjy's, April 6, 1928. He is working in a store; for Herbert Head turned Caddy into the street, and he never took Jason into the bank, if he ever had one. Instead, Jason has to slave as a clerk in a store, and bear alone the burden of the family. In spite of

[1] The story was treated by Euripides in a tragedy, and may be read in Ovid, Gower or Lydgate. The connection with Faulkner is highly speculative, but it will do no harm to credit him with ranging scholarship. The suggestion was made by W. A. Deahofe in an admirable study of Faulkner, a master's thesis on file in the University of Minnesota library.

being his mother's favorite, he labors under an ugly sense of wrong. And he gets his revenge by making life intolerable to his niece Miss Quentin (Caddy's child, whom they have taken to bring up), embezzling the money which her mother sends her, and finally driving her to run away with a man from a traveling show. The final section of the story relates the events leading to the flight of Miss Quentin. To her grandmother, Quentin's depravity is God's curse on her for her mother's wickedness. To the reader it seems that Quentin is a decent enough girl driven to the devil by the meanest of uncles. It is in the form of moral obliquity that the hereditary taint displays itself in Jason Compson. We have the satisfaction of knowing that Quentin carried with her the three thousand dollars which her uncle had sequestered, and that Jason can never recover this without endangering both his life and his good name.

The next of Faulkner's novels in date of composition was *Sanctuary*. This novel, Faulkner tells us, was written with a view to selling; and for that purpose he invented "the most horrific tale he could imagine," dealing with what, so far as he could tell, "a person in Mississippi would believe to be current trends." The central event is the victimization of a college girl by a bootlegger and gangster, who is at the same time sexually impotent as the result of an inherited syphilitic taint. The principal events take place in a desolate decaying farmhouse in a lonely grove of cedars, haunt of the bootleggers, to which the girl has been taken by a good-for-nothing young man in search of more liquor. This young man, who has attended the University of Virginia and there learned to drink like a gentleman, is one of Faulkner's most sardonic commentaries on Southern gentility gone to seed. The girl is not much better—a second version of the sort of Helen of Troy whom he presented in *Soldiers' Pay*—childish, heartless, vain and vicious—hothouse rose of Southern womanhood, cheap and tragic lure of love. Without conscience and without courage, she brings three men to their deaths —one for defending her against the redoubtable Popeye, one for arousing Popeye's jealousy, and one convicted on her testimony of a murder actually committed by Popeye.

Three relatively admirable figures relieve the gloom of this sordid chronicle—Ruby Lamarr, gangster's moll, possessed of such primary virtues as can flower in this soil; Tommy the shambling yokel, victim of his chivalrous instinct to protect womanhood; and Horace Benbow, lawyer and thinker (albeit a fool by Ruby's scale of values), who makes a vain attempt to save the life of her man. He proves unequal to that task of making justice triumph; but at least he has the reward of good intentions and of their verbal equivalents, this man who believes that God may be foolish at times but at least He's a gentleman. When Ruby wants to know how he will pay himself for what he has done, his answer is: "But can't you see that perhaps a man might do something just because he knew it was right, necessary to the harmony of things that it be done?"

In view of Faulkner's own account of the making of this book, it would be foolish to try to read much into it of social significance; but it does contribute its mite to the natural history of "Jefferson" in its decline and, in the portrait of Popeye, it adds the most "horrific" figure of all to Faulkner's gallery of sub-human monsters.

Before he had found a publisher for *Sanctuary*, Faulkner had written and published the next in his Jefferson cycle, *As I Lay Dying*. Here for a time he has left both bootleggers and good families to deal with poor whites on the cultural level of those treated two years later by Erskine Caldwell in *Tobacco Road*. And in its own somber and sardonic way, *As I Lay Dying* sets the tone of farce that Caldwell was destined to sound in all his novels. If there is degeneracy here, it is not that of the best families, in whom good blood turns bad by virtue of some mystical curse attaching to aris-

tocracy. It is the decadence engendered by poverty and ignorance. And for the most part the Bundrens, whose farm is not
far distant from the bootleggers' hideout of *Sanctuary,* are
not so much decadent as culturally degraded, afflicted by the
sordidness that attaches to want of scope and means. The action of the story is limited to less than two weeks, covering
the death of the mother Addie and the transfer of her body
for burial in the cemetery at Jefferson. It was her wish to be
laid to rest among her own people. But her wish is hardly
more than a pretext on the part of several of her family—the
pretext of her husband Anse for getting himself a new set of
teeth, that of the girl Dewey Dell for seeking at a drugstore
the means of checking her pregnancy. The coffin is fashioned
in the mother's sight and hearing by her son Cash, and when
she is dead it is loaded on the farm wagon together with the
family and driven the thirty miles to Jefferson.

Many ill chances delay the progress of the strange cortege,
and chiefly the flooded river which has carried away two
bridges. Days before they come to Jefferson the body has
begun to smell and they are followed for days by growing
flocks of carrion fowl. Many weird incidents enliven their
monstrous saga, which climbs through an ascending scale of
somber hilarity. The burning down of the barn where they
have lodged for the night gives Jewel the chance to display his
filial devotion by rolling out his mother's coffin after saving
the horses and cows. The fire was started by Darl, the loony
son, and reveals to them all that his gift of second sight is
truly the sign of madness. Before they return to the farm he is
overpowered and sent to the asylum at Jackson. The curtain
falls on the tableau in which the father, spruced up with his
new set of teeth, presents to his widowed family their second
mother, together with her prized possession, a gramophone.
" 'It's Cash and Jewel and Vardaman and Dewey Dell,' pa
says, kind of hangdog and proud too, with his teeth and all,
even if he wouldn't look at us. 'Meet Mrs. Bundren,' he says."

The story is told by the characters, turn by turn, each in his own voice and personal idiom, with the utmost vividness and poignancy of individual characterization. The best of them all is Cash, who is a good and conscientious workman, building his mother's coffin with every refinement of solid carpentry. The most poetic characters are Darl, with the weird philosophy of a disordered mind, and Jewel, son of love and sin, who takes out his mute rage and sorrow in the violent management of his savage horse. The greatest of them all in spirit is Addie the mother, who had found in sin what she could not find in the empty words of her sanctimonious Anse, and who then had given him two more children to make up for what she had robbed him of. Addie was great, in a woman's way, by her power of feeling, by her complete possession of reality, and by her painful awareness of the distinction between words and things.

He had a word, too. Love, he called it. But I had been used to words for a long time. I knew that that word was like the others: just a shape to fill a lack; that when the right time came, you wouldn't need a word for that anymore than for pride or fear. Cash did not need to say it to me nor I to him, and I would say, Let Anse use it, if he wants to.

It is perhaps an error to speak of these people as decadent or even as degraded. They are not bad people; their motivation is normal enough, natural enough for the most part. What makes Anse ridiculous is his selfishness and ineffectualness where his position calls for competence and the suppression of self; and still more, it is his need to put a good face, a pious face, on actions which are crassly egotistic. As for their Odyssey of misadventures, these were the fault of their poverty, their helplessness. They were the victims of mean circumstances. There was no undertaker to put a gloss of decency on the rites of the dead. And the very elements conspired to humiliate them and make them look obscene and monstrous. They were human beings stripped of all the adventitious aids to dignity and elevation—human nature reduced to its meanest elements.

Which is not to say that Faulkner gives a rosy view of human nature!

The next in the series is *Light in August*. And here we can say with some assurance that Faulkner has given us a story loaded with social significance. What I refer to is the sense one has that individual souls in the South today are shadowed by evils inherited from a pre-war social system and ideology. In this story there are four persons who above all others are thus ridden with the ghosts of slavery days. There is the Rev. Gail Hightower, Presbyterian minister, whose heart is less in the mysteries of faith than in the daredevil glories of the Civil War. In his childhood his imagination had been fed on stories of his grandfather, Confederate officer, who had killed so many Yankees and had himself been shot while robbing a hen-roost in the course of a heroic raid on the military stores at Jefferson. To all intents and purposes he has grown up to be his grandfather; he has married his wife and pulled all wires to secure appointment to the church in Jefferson in order to identify himself with that heroic past. His sermons are troubled by crazy allusions to the galloping horses and crashing guns of the ancient war; his wife is driven to distraction and disgrace by his all-absorbing obsession. In his own disgrace he functions obscurely as a confessor of souls, but he figures mainly as a spirit haunted and destroyed by the ghosts of an earlier frantic time. "I know that for fifty years I have not even been clay: I have been a single instant of darkness in which a horse galloped and a gun crashed. And if I am my dead grandfather on the instant of his death, then my wife, his grandson's wife . . . the debaucher and murderer of my grandson's wife, since I could neither let my grandson live or die . . ."

Hightower is one of the most strained and obscure of all

Faulkner's creations. Less dark in significance, and better worked out in action is Joe Christmas, the white negro, central character in the tragic history. He was son of a white woman and a high-yaller man, one of a circus troupe. His grandfather, old "Doc" Hines, is a combination in extremes of religious and race fanaticism, one who advocates the extermination of the negroes in the interest of racial purity. His way of dealing with miscegenation in his own family is to shoot the father of his grandchild, let the mother die of neglect, and then arrange that the child be adopted by as great a hater of sin as himself, the pious and cruel farmer McEachern. But before his adoption, Christmas was confined in an orphanage, where the other children called him nigger because of his curly black hair; and after he is grown and his own master, his life consists of a series of efforts to work out of his blood the sense of his racial inferiority. He has relations with many white women, invariably letting them know at some stage in the affair that he has negro blood. Sometimes he is abused and beaten up; at other times he is all the more passionately received because of the strain of color. The last of these affairs is with a middle-aged woman, Miss Burden, living in a lonely house in the neighborhood of Jefferson, while Christmas occupies a cabin on the run-down estate.

Miss Burden comes of New England Calvinists and nigger-lovers, and has spent her life helping and counseling the negro women of the neighborhood. In her affair with Christmas animal passion merges with a sense of her inherited mission of raising the negro to a level with the white man. Her brother and grandfather were killed in Jefferson by Colonel Sartoris, ex-slaveholder and Confederate soldier, who resented the interference of nigger-lovers in the affairs of the South. In her father's view, they were "murdered not by one white man but by the curse which God put on a whole race before your grandfather or your brother or me or you were

even thought of. A race doomed and cursed to be forever and
ever a part of the white race's doom and curse for its sins."
She told her father that she wanted to escape from these sinister involvements; but he assured her that that was impossible.
"You must struggle, rise. But in order to rise, you must raise
the shadow with you. But you can never lift it to your level.
I see that now, which I did not see until I came down here.
But escape it you cannot. The curse of the black race is God's
curse. But the curse of the white race is the black man who
will be forever God's chosen own because He once cursed
him."

With the years Miss Burden's passion wears itself out and
piety comes flooding back. It is the attempt of a woman, now
grown old, to force on Christmas the role of repentant sinner
that drives him to the desperate fury in which he cuts her
throat. It remains for him to be hunted and tried for murder. Something like peace descends on Christmas now; he has
run through the whole cycle of automatic movements unconsciously directed toward wiping out the negro stain. But the
fatal inclination of whites to mate with blacks calls for more
violent forms of purgation than those provided by law. And
it remains for an officer of the American Legion—compensat-
ing, himself, for his having missed service in the Great War—
to shoot him down with his own automatic and mutilate the
dying mulatto, so that "now he will let white women alone,
even in hell." Fiercest of all in stirring up the spirit of lynching against the white nigger is his grandfather, old Doc Hines,
prodigious incarnation of all that is most unreasonable in
fanaticism, whether religious or racial.

There is much more to the story than I have indicated.
But this will be sufficient to show that, in this novel, Faulkner was deliberately attacking a theme of wide social bearing.
In Hightower we have the new South haunted by the ghosts
of the Confederacy. In Miss Burden and Doc Hines we have

the perverse troubled conscience of the white race (North and South) haunted by the ghost of slavery. In Christmas we have the problem of race made flesh.

The problem of race recurs in still more formidable guise in *Absalom, Absalom!* hand in hand with the more comprehensive, the all-inclusive problem of social caste. Central figure here is Thomas Sutpen, born poor white in the West Virginia mountains. When the family moves down to the settled Virginia lowlands, the ragged barefoot boy comes to realize that there are white families in comparison with which his own people are beggars and slaves. Turned away like a nigger from the door of the great mansion, he conceives the heroic project of himself founding a family which shall be forever exempt from such humiliations. He makes himself wealthy in the sugar plantations of Haiti, and marries the daughter of a planter of French descent. But when he learns that his wife has negro blood, he puts her away, at the same time making ample provision for her support. He comes with his Haitian slaves to Yoknapatawpha County, Mississippi. By dark devices he becomes owner of a hundred square miles of Indian land, which he clears for farming; builds himself a great mansion, which he furnishes suitably, with the help of funds secured again by obscure tricks of dubious legality. He marries the daughter of a poor and unexceptionably respectable trader of Jefferson, and starts to build up his dynasty on the secure foundations of wealth and race. Son and daughter he begets to carry on the aristocratic tradition.

But once again the dark fate strikes. His son Henry attends the state university at Oxford, and there becomes the intimate friend of Charles Bon, a wealthy and plausible young gentleman from New Orleans. He brings him home to Sutpen's Hundred, where it is taken for granted that he will marry Judith Sutpen, Henry's sister. But Thomas Sutpen knows that this Charles Bon is no other than his own son by the earlier mulatto wife, now living in New Orleans. When he tells Henry that Charles is his half-brother (not mentioning the question of blood), Henry, in blind loyalty to his college friend, will not believe him; he breaks with his father and gives up his inheritance. Now the Civil War intervenes; and all three men serve through the war with the Confederate troops, Henry and Charles fighting side by side and saving each other's lives. By this time, Henry is convinced of the truth that Charles is his brother, and is simply postponing till the end of the war the decision as to what he owes to his sister and what to his friend. But when, toward the end of the war, he encounters his father in a Southern camp, and learns that Charles is not merely his own brother but a half caste, the problem of miscegenation is added to that of incest. Charles Bon has a grudge against his father for the way he has handled the matter; he is grimly determined to go through with the wedding. He and Henry ride back to Sutpen's Hundred together; and at the gate the white man shoots down his mulatto brother to prevent his sister's disgrace. Then he disappears and is not again heard from till the year 1909.

In the meantime Thomas Sutpen has returned from the war and is making a last desperate effort to restore his ruined dynasty. During the war his wife has died and her sister Rosa has come to live at Sutpen's Hundred. He proposes to her that she marry him provided that issue results from a preliminary trial. Rosa Coldfield is outraged by the indelicate proposal and goes back to live in Jefferson. Sutpen's only hope now is to bear a son by Milly, granddaughter of Wash Jones, a low-born squatter who resides in a fishing camp at Sutpen's. Sutpen is an old man now, and this is his last throw of the dice. When he learns that Milly's child is a female, he deliberately provokes Jones to the point of killing him. Jones makes a clean sweep by killing Milly and the infant before giving himself up to the law.

Such was the end of Thomas Sutpen, but not the end of his grandiose project of building a citadel above the treacherous wash of money and caste. There still remained several of his blood living in the great mansion. Two of them lost their lives in 1910 when Sutpen's Hundred burned to the ground. And so the whole great idea, with all its passionate and tragic accompaniments, had burned itself down to ashes—all but the somewhere surviving half-breed half-wit, Jim Bond, who remained as sour memorial, and perhaps continuer through casual breeding, of the blood and dream of Thomas Sutpen.

We may be sure that William Faulkner is not the mind to have devised without deliberation this gargoyle irony of Southern racism. The story is conveyed to us for the most part in the form of midnight conversations between Quentin Compson and his Harvard roommate from Canada, Shreve McCannon. The two young men work out together the complicated facts and obscure motivation of this prodigious chronicle with equal excitement and concern, equal appreciation of it as a social document—equal sense of the horror and fascination, the romance and tragedy of the old South and its fateful inheritance. To one, born far north of the Mason and Dixon line, it is the fascination of the foreign and scarcely believable. "We don't live among defeated grandfathers and freed slaves . . . and bullets in the dining room table and such, to be always reminding us to never forget . . . a kind of entailed birthright father and son and father and son of never forgiving General Sherman, so that forevermore as long as your children's children produce children you won't be anything but a descendant of a long line of colonels killed in Pickett's charge . . ." To the other it is the more horrid fascination of matters in which he is personally involved, from which he can never hope to escape. This is the same Quentin Compson who, in *The Sound and the Fury*, left the room which he occupied with Shreve and drowned himself one June day, together with the memory of his sister's disgrace and the general ruin of his family.

Both young men are pledged in their youthful idealism to

put some not too discreditable construction on human motives and behavior; both are pledged by their hard-boiled modern code to disguise their idealism under a mask of cynicism. They are both romantic, and Shreve is also inclined to generalize on the sociological implications of the story. With Quentin it is more a question of reconciling his opposed emotional reactions. Between them we may suppose that they sum up the attitudes of the author, emotional and intellectual. "I think," says Shreve, "that in time the Jim Bonds are going to conquer the western hemisphere. Of course it won't be quite in our time and of course as they spread toward the poles they will bleach out again like the rabbits and the birds do, so they won't show up so sharp against the snow. But it will still be Jim Bond; and so in a few thousand years, I who regard you will also have sprung from the loins of African kings."

So much for sociological inference. Now for emotional attitudes toward the South which are Quentin's heritage. Shreve is well aware of Quentin's shrinking from whatever is repellent in Southern life and history. And so he says to him, "I want you to tell me just one thing more. Why do you hate the South?" " 'I don't hate it,' Quentin said quickly, at once, immediately: 'I don't hate it,' he said. *I don't hate it* he thought, panting in the cold air, the iron New England dark; *I don't. I don't! I don't hate it! I don't hate it!*"

There is something suspicious about the promptness with which Quentin replies to the suggestion that he hates the South, as if this were a question uppermost in his own mind, and an imputation to which he feels obliged in his mind to say no. His repetitious vehemence in denying it to his conscience is again suspicious, as the author doubtless meant it to sound, reflecting his own divided mind. Of course William Faulkner does not hate the land of his own nativity, whose legends and people have been the subject of all his dreaming, the very essence of romance, whose passionate fertility and haunting honeysuckle fragrance disturb the slumbers and madden the brains of so many of his characters. It is not the cold air and iron dark of New England to which his heart owes allegiance. But there is so much in the life of his beloved South that is cruel and ugly, obscene and graveyard-smelling—so much that is lost and hopeless and perverse, for which it is impossible to make excuse before the bar of European and Northern civilization, that he finds his heart filled with distress and loathing. He cannot hate the South any more than a man can hate the mistress that is his ruin—mistress of incomparable charms and savage corruptions—without whom he cannot exist, with whom he cannot live in peace or conscience, and whom he scarcely dare acknowledge to the world.

Faulkner is a second Edgar Allan Poe, Southern artist in mystery and terror. But Poe was Southern in culture and spirit more than in subject and reference. He was romantic poet, where Faulkner is realistic novelist. His locale is synthetic and imaginary—European and Renaissance—Usher and Ulalume—peopled with bodiless essences, attached to no county, fed from no cornfield or country store. Faulkner's world is a real county, in an actual Mississippi—farmers' shacks and ruinous mansions and negro huts among the cotton fields and pig pens, the ditches and bottom lands and pine ridges, rutted and dusty roads, galleried crossroad stores and courthouse squares and bungalows among magnolias and wistaria. His people are farmers and lawyers, merchants and bootleggers, horse-traders and preachers, poor whites and negroes and people of long established social standing—deep in the struggle to maintain themselves against nature and the trickery of men—ridden with greed and lust and pride and fear—burdened with guilt and madness—and spurred on, many of them, by desperate obsessions of ideal good. Over them hang the leaden skies of past glory and present ruin. And pressing on them from all sides are the insoluble problems of caste and race; with hordes of poor whites living like beasts, and the countless race of half-breeds whom the tides of white and black blood pull asunder with opposing impulses.

Faulkner is like Poe, by natural disposition, an artist in mystery and horror; but he is likewise, by disposition and training, an artist in familiar truth and fact. Of all Southern writers Faulkner is the one who has been least restrained by regard for convention or for the sensibilities of his own people. And mainly for that reason, he is the one who has done the most of all Southern writers to bring the South to life imaginatively. For that very reason—and in spite of a sort of reckless irresponsiblity there is in him—he may have done something to prepare the Southern mind to meet the dark and intricate problems of its inheriting.

VII. WILLIAM FAULKNER

Virtuoso

"The object of a novelist is to keep the
reader entirely oblivious of the fact
that the author exists—even of the fact
that he is reading a book."
—FORD MADOX FORD

VII. WILLIAM FAULKNER

Virtuoso

It is hard to do justice to Faulkner's range and at the same time to the quality in him that gives homogeneity to all his work and marks every piece as unmistakably his. There is a kind of cold ferocity about all his writing, a strained intensity, which makes one think of the painful state of nerves, the actual physical pain, which (according to an early sketch of Sherwood Anderson's) he used to carry with him without intermission as heritage of his flying in the first World War. It is as if whatever he does, whatever appearance he makes in the world of men, he must grit his teeth and dominate by force of will pain which might otherwise make him soft, and that the personal suffering to which he will not bow was always filtering through into his general statements about human nature, giving to them a tone of suppressed rage. The voices of men are in Faulkner "sweet bells jangled out of tune and harsh." Human society is "an unweeded garden run to waste." It is a garden of the deep South, with black soil fertile and unexhausted, but with no one left to tend it but old ladies who remember the Civil War and idiots who cannot tell weeds from flowers, the present from the past. It is a strange combination of civilization and savagery, like a colonial mansion in a cypress swamp. There is force without measure, like an unbanked Mississippi. I do not mean without design; for the man is a prodigy of contrivance. I have in mind a certain extravagance in him that makes one think of the Elizabethans—

Jonsonian realism and Shakespearean passion for figure and fustian. The Elizabethans lapsing into Jacobeans, abounding strength and passion haunting the charnel house.

His characters almost invariably represent deviations from the norm, as if he feared that normal people would land him in commonplace. He is by temperament an idealist as opposed to utilitarian common sense. His most sympathetic characters are persons obsessed with morbid ideals, or morbidly obsessed with ideals. His mean people are monsters of selfish calculation.

In his latest novel *The Hamlet,* he traces the rise of the Snopses, often met in his earlier stories. They are a family of human weeds obscure and prolific, amply provided with every device for making the best of their environment. At the period of *Sanctuary* they are shown in their third stage as prosperous tradesmen of Jefferson, with one cigar-chewing member of the state senate, battening on corruption and betrayal. In *The Hamlet* we see them in their second or transitional stage. They have come out of the backwoods and taken root in the country store. And this is a chronicle of the tricks by which they made themselves rich enough to move on to town. Unloading worthless IOUs on country cousins, and worthless Texas horses on their neighbors, unloading worthless real estate by making the buyer think there is buried treasure on the land. They are marvels of the sort of shrewdness more generally assigned to Yankees, and in their later deals they have to do with men nearly as shrewd though several shades less mean and unscrupulous. It is a farcical drama of rascality in the Jacobean manner—diamond cut diamond. The comedy reaches its climax in the hunt for buried treasure on the Old Frenchman Place, when the buyers find that the supposed ancient coins consist of recently minted quarters planted there by Ab Snopes' nephew within the week. The idealism and poetry (such as they are) are furnished by an idiot brother of the Snopeses' in love with a cow. The whole show is grim enough, though marked by many characteristic touches of the bizarre and fantastic.

Among other recent novels *Pylon* (1935) and *The Wild Palms* (1939) exemplify what I mean by morbid idealism. One is never quite sure, indeed, whether the emphasis should rest on the idealism or on the morbidity; for it is never clear to what extent the author's sympathy goes with the exponents of idealism, and to what extent he means to represent them as fools and degenerates. That is, of course, the trouble with idealism when it contravenes the conventions of society; one knows not whether to judge it by its own standards, which are subjective and capricious, or by the standards of society, which are capricious and arbitrary. In *Pylon* we have the story of a New Orleans reporter, soft-hearted and Quixotic, who is sent out to the airport to get a story on the races. His imagination is deeply impressed with the odd and desperate way of life of pilots, mechanics, and their dependents. They are completely absorbed in their racing, looking forward perpetually to the purses they may win, penniless for the most part, homeless and comfortless, and willing to risk their necks on any crazy gamble. The reporter becomes particularly attached to a family group of four people—the woman, the two men with whom she lives indiscriminately, one of them her husband, and the little boy who does not know which one of them is his father. The newsman's sympathy is enlisted by the poor waif, by the hard-boiled, heroic woman (with whom we may suppose him to be in love in his confused way), and even (so large is his heart) by the reckless cynical men in overalls whose fortunes are so queerly bound together by their common craze. When they have no place to stay he lodges them in his own room in the Vieux Carré; he gets drunk with them on absinthe; he moves heaven and earth to get them a "ship" when their own is disqualified by the jury; and when the husband is killed in a crash, he sends the others off together and makes himself responsible for the body. He more than once risks his job on the newspaper in his devotion to these vagabonds.

It would take too long to follow the windings of the fantastic nightmare in and out of the littered carnival streets, or the involutions of this disoriented psyche. It is sufficient to note the somber and lurid colors in which the whole composition is invested, and the sort of tailspins, nosedives, and other dizzy maneuvers indulged in by the idealist soul when once he leaves his earthly moorings and abandons himself to the treacherous weather above.

Somber and lurid throughout is the color scheme of *The Wild Palms*. Here Faulkner tells in alternation two separate stories, which seem to have for him some inner connection of tone or theme. The first is that of a poor medical student of New Orleans who falls in love with an artist-woman and takes her away from her husband, a conventional and high-minded man. Until he met Charlotte Rittenmeyer, Harry Wilbourne had been a chaste and hard-working student, determined to keep out of all involvements and at all costs restore the ruined fortunes of his family. But now he is carried away with the obsession of love as the central value of all living. Nothing else is of importance but that he shall meet the challenge of love, prove equal to its exalted and exclusive claims. This idealization of love he shares with Charlotte and they undergo the greatest hardships in order to maintain it. The one thing they are not prepared for is the support of a child, and when she becomes pregnant, she insists that the young doctor shall perform an abortion. This he is reluctant to do. He has shown himself capable of doing it successfully in another emergency case; but where his own woman is concerned he dreads the ordeal. When finally, in a late stage of pregnancy, he yields to Charlotte's insistence, his worst fears are justified. So great is his emotional disturbance that he botches the job, with fatal results to his mistress. He is tried for his crime and sentenced to fifty years of hard labor in state prison.

At the last moment Rittenmeyer generously brings him a dose of cyanide so that he may put an end to his misery. But Harry reasons that the memory of his love is all that remains to him; without that, there would be nothing. And between nothing and grief he prefers grief.

The parallel story is that of a convict in the state prison at Parchman, a no-account youth who had been sent up for an attempted train robbery, inspired by his love for a no-account girl. During the great river floods, the prisoners are removed, and to this convict is given the commission of taking a rowboat and saving the life of a stranded woman. This he accomplishes, but the boat is caught in the blind fury of the waters, and the two of them are driven about on the great leaden wastes, downstream and upstream too as the Mississippi floods back into its estuaries, for days at a time. They are stranded on mudflats infested with mocassin snakes; they live for a time with an alligator hunter in the midst of a swamp. The convict helps to deliver the woman's baby. But in spite of long and intimate proximity he has no inclination to make free with her person. After many frightful and laborious adventures, he manages to work his way back to Parchman. For to this bumpkin, prison is home, and labor in the fields is associated with peace and security. His early experience was such as to give him no notion of a fairer way of life. As for "love," his experience had been more exalted but not less disillusioning. He has learned to think of women as perilous beings who betray. He welcomes the ten years extra sentence he is given for his supposed attempt to escape. To one of his mates who asks him what he will do for women in all that time, he replies with one contemptuous word, "Women . . . !" which eloquently sums up the meaning to him of that passion through which Harry Wilbourne got life in the same penitentiary.

Thus the obscure convict from the backwoods is a sort of counterpart by opposites of the man for whom "love" was the

one supreme ideal value; and together they make their mutu
commentary on the devastating and triumphant force tha
more than any other shapes the destinies of men. As for the
lurid and somber color-scheme of which I have spoken, it i
suggested by the titles given to the alternating panels of thi
panorama. Each section devoted to the convict is headed b
the title "Old Man," referring to Old Man River, which
takes on in the course of this prodigious Odyssey the propor
tions of a nature-god, a terrifying force beyond understand
ing or control. Never perhaps was so much literary passion
spent on the description of power and desolation, of puny
man at the mercy of the elements. The sections devoted to
Harry Wilbourne and Charlotte are headed "Wild Palms,"
for the dreary plumes tossing perpetually in the sea wind
which surrounded the hut in a gulf resort where they spent
their days of agony and alienation while Charlotte bled away
her life.

Faulkner certainly has the faculty of giving, to familiar
scenes and objects, an air strange, sinister and exotic. He has,
moreover, a penchant for certain bloody circumstances in the
private life of women which I will leave it to the psychologis
to interpret.[1] It will be enough to note his fondness, among
ideal sentiments, for those strangely freaked and spotted like
jungle creatures. They make one think of Robinson Jeffers
"striped blossom insanity," which "spread lewd splendors
and lightning terrors at the end of the forest." Also of Jeffers
saying of the poet:

> He brays humanity in a mortar to bring the savor
> From the bruised root . . .

In discussing Faulkner's style, we should distinguish be
tween his own manner when he lets himself go, as he does in

[1] Dr. Lawrence S. Kubie, in the *Saturday Review of Literature* for October
20, 1934, has made a very interesting study of Faulkner's *Sanctuary*, from the
point of view of psychoanalysis, in which reference is made to this peculiarity

most of his later work, and that of his characters when he
has them tell the story, as in *The Sound and the Fury* and *As
I Lay Dying*. The style of his characters is more faultless than
his own; but his own has the greater range. In spite of
all its absurdities and affectations, Faulkner's personal style
is a thing of prodigious force and splendor, perhaps the most
remarkable of our day if we judge by sheer brilliancy, by
richness and expressiveness in characterization and description. His eye and mind are ever on the alert and driven by a
sleepless passion for rendering the very heart of his subject.
His faults are for the most part defects of his qualities, and
chiefly excessive concern for expressiveness, though a measure
of affectation and vanity enters in at times to transform what
might otherwise be mere excess into something ridiculous. For
with vanity there enters the concern not merely for adequate
expression but for display of gifts and erudition. And pride of
power betrays him into carelessness, often leading to faults
of grammar and rhetoric which suit ill with his erudition
and his literary pretensions. The danger here is that too much
attention to his lapses may cause us to doubt for a moment
the genuineness and high order of his genius.

He has the romantic disposition to make too much of adjectives, and not merely of descriptive adjectives but such as
serve to lend glamour and elevation to the subject. He likes
his adjectives, like his nouns, to go in pairs, reinforcing one
another and begetting rhythm and amplitude. He likes them
better if they are of Latin origin and polysyllabic, lending a
certain pomp and magnificence to the whole passage, and perhaps an added touch of elegance where they are used in a
sense now obsolete in English. He says of a parachute: "It
unfolded swaying against the accomplished and ineradicable
evening." He often uses "accomplished" in this strained sense
of something brought to its completion, as De Quincey used
it. As for "ineradicable" (not capable of being uprooted),
one is left with a certain vagueness as to just what it means

when applied to an evening. It is a word of which he is
fond. He speaks of a couple who "had both become inerad-
icably intimate with cold for the first time in their lives, a cold
which left an ineffaceable and unforgettable mark somewhere
on the spirit and memory like first sex experience or the experience of taking human life." He speaks, somewhat con-
fusingly, of "three faces, the one impeccable, the two of them
invincible and irrevocable, the second cold and unwinking,
the third merely unwinking." We understand how a face may
be called impeccable, but not so well how it can be called
irrevocable, nor still less invincible (not the face). We have
the same difficulty with "the impregnably new glow of the
two rose-shaded lamps."

The adjective or adverb often seems to be applied in his
phrase not to the word to which it properly refers, but to
some other word associated with that in his mind. In the interest of brevity and grammatical compactness, and perhaps
with a vague recall of some Latin grace of the wittily *mis-
applied adjective, he attaches the adjunctive wherever he
finds it convenient. We who cannot follow his idea through
all its windings are likely to find this a bit of a nuisance. And
all the more so where, as not infrequently, he simply con-
fuses one fine word with another, as in the following sentence: "It was probably just peaceful despair and relief at
final and complete abnegation, now that Judith was about to
immolate the frustration's vicarious recompense into the living
fairy tale." I think Faulkner knows the meaning of "immolate" (to offer as a sacrifice), and has it in mind in the following phrase, "for one fierce and immolated instant." Even
there, however, it is no little strained, and where he speaks
of immolating a recompense into a fairy tale, he is either
"telescoping" beyond my power to disentangle, or else he is
writing nonsense.

Faulkner has the complacent scorn for English grammar of
one who has construed Cicero and Horace and feels that he

can trust his instinct when it comes to the vernacular. He writes *currente calamo,* like Lord Byron, with results that even Byron would have blushed to acknowledge. "He would merely appear at breakfast in a decent and heavy black coat *in which he had been married and had worn* fifty-two times each year since." "He was the biggest single landowner and cottonplanter in the county now, *attained by the same tactics* with which he had built his house." "That impenetrable tranquillity which a year or so before had been the young girl's vague and dreamy unvolition but was now already *a mature woman's—a mature woman in love*—repose." "Who according to Mr. Compson would no more have sent him acknowledgment that he had beat her than she waited (*whom* Miss Coldfield said was not bereaved) and met him on his return." "He declined to believe that Varner ever had been or ever would be stuck with anything; that if he acquired it, he got it cheaper than anyone else would have, and if he kept it, it was too valuable to sell." In the last sentence it is perfectly clear that he did not decline to believe, but actually did believe, that Varner, if he acquired anything, got it cheaper than anyone else, etc.

I do not suppose for a moment that ignorance of grammar is responsible for these howlers. It is rather a lordly negligence in regard to anything so conventional and pedestrian as grammar; a sense that grammar should be his servant, and not the other way round, that he can bend it to his will—that so accomplished a rider as he can take it over hurdles and hazards so inconsiderable. The trouble is that he does not take *us* over the hazards. And it is not the spills he invites that we mind. It is rather his complete obliviousness to the danger—the nerve of the man in supposing that he is exempt from the normal conventions of writing.

And the same thing holds with regard to his lordly nonchalant use of figurative language and all the other resources of poetic writing. "They are the bright blatant wild daisies

of flamboyant summer's spendthrift beginning." "The rapid
twilight effaces them from the day's tedious recording."

Now he watches the recurrence of that which he discovered for
the first time three days ago: that dawn, light, is not decanted
onto earth from the sky, but instead is from the earth itself suspired. Roofed by the woven canopy of blind annealing grass-roots
and the roots of trees, dark in the blind dark of time's silt and
rich refuse—the constant and unslumbering anonymous worm-
glut and the inextricable known bones—Troy's Helen and the
nymphs and the snoring mitred bishops, the saviors and the victims and the kings—it wakes, up-seeping, attritive in uncountable
creeping channels; first, root; then frond by frond, from whose
escaping tips like gas it rises and disseminates and stains the sleep-
fast earth with drowsy insect-murmur; then, still upward-seeping,
creeps the knitted bark of trunk and limb where, suddenly louder
leaf by leaf and dispersive in diffusive sudden speed, melodious
with the winged and jeweled throats, it upward bursts and fills
night's globed negation with jonquil thunder.

These passages are taken from the chapter which celebrates
the idiot Snopes' mystical passion for a cow. One hesitates to
take them seriously for fear the man may be pulling our leg.
But that, I think, is not the case. The conception is a bold
one and not without its inherent poetry as well as its speculative realism. It is an attempt to suggest, to adumbrate, the
lyrical ecstasy of a sub-human sensibility confronted with
sensations and emotional shades which may be even more
accessible to the earth-bound mind than to the mind that
moves readily in abstractions and ordered systems of behavior. But the author, who made such a great success of Benjy
and Darl (in *The Sound and the Fury* and *As I Lay Dying*),
keeping so resolutely to the objects, terms and symbols which
fall within the range of the idiot's or moron's rudimentary
intelligence, has here given freest rein to his own highly in-
tellectualized and mythopeic imagination.

And that might have worked out well enough and justified

itself as sympathetic interpretation on a higher level of thought. But unfortunately Faulkner was betrayed by the rhetorician in him, the Southern gentleman of literary culture. He was tempted to put on his silver shoe-buckles and embroidered waistcoat to follow the idiot and the cow through woods and pastures and back to the dunghill and the stall. And his finery is a very different thing from that of the old-fashioned Southern gentleman, whose flourishes were ever kept within measure, following without fail the conventional turns of the Walter Scott tradition. But Faulkner, born long after the Civil War, a modern, subject to a thousand assaults from a later romanticism—Browning, Cabell, Lawrence, who knows what?—often cuts loose from all restraints of taste and sense, makes himself drunk with sugared words—"instead is from the earth itself suspired"—"dispersive in diffusive sudden speed"—"fills night's globed negation with jonquil thunder" (shades of Amy Lowell!)—whose affected euphuism obscures more than it illuminates the subtle thought and penetrative imagination.

In telling his story, this man is tireless and indefatigable in exploring every nook and cranny, every twist and convolution, of situation and psychology. And his passion for squeezing the last drop of meaning from his subject plunges him (in some books) into sentences longer and more complicated than any yet produced in English fiction outside of the dreamwork of *Finnegans Wake*. *Absalom, Absalom!* is almost entirely made up of a continuous succession of sentences averaging a page in length; and in *The Wild Palms* the same thing is nearly true, especially in the sections dealing with the convict's adventures in the flood. These sentences do convey a sense of the crowding fury of experience, its unrelenting continuity, its overwhelming volume and complexity. They serve to combine in a single unit many items of experience or understanding which the mind may be supposed to hold suspended in one act of vision, but which, for the benefit of the reader, are generally listed separately. Here is an example from *The Wild Palms,* where the local doctor makes his mental comment on the two curious beings who have rented his cottage by the shore.

But even apart from the wind he could still tell the approximate time by the staling smell of gumbo now cold in the big earthen pot on the cold stove beyond the flimsy kitchen wall—the big pot of it which his wife had made that morning in order to send some over to their neighbors and renters in the next house: the man and woman who four days ago had rented the cottage and who probably did not even know that the donors of the gumbo were not only neighbors but landlords too—the dark-haired woman with queer hard yellow eyes in a face whose skin was drawn thin over prominent cheek-bones and a heavy jaw (the doctor called it sullen at first and then he called it afraid), young, who sat all day long in a new cheap beach chair facing the water, in a worn sweater and a pair of faded jeans and canvas shoes, not reading, not doing anything, just sitting there in that complete immobility which the doctor (or the doctor in the Doctor) did not need the corroboration of the drawn quality of the skin and the blank inverted fixity of the apparently unseeing eyes to recognize at once—that complete immobile abstraction from which even pain and terror are absent, in which a living creature seems to listen to and even watch some one of its own flagging organs, the heart say, the secret irreparable seeping of blood; and the young man too, in a pair of disreputable khaki slacks . . .

So the thing piles up, explanation upon explanation, parenthesis on parenthesis, appositional phrase on appositional phrase, in an ascending (or descending) order of grammatical dependence, till one despairs of ever finding a blackboard big enough to represent in charted form the relations of syntax and subordination of ideas. This type of sentence is particularly serviceable or tempting to the author in books like *Absalom, Absalom!* where there are peculiar states of mind to be explored, to be made imaginable by figure of speech, or made intelligible by reference to differing or similar states of mind.

I was fourteen then . . . so that instead of accomplishing the processional and measured milestones of the childhood's time I lurked, unapprehended as though, shod with the very damp and velvet silence of the womb, I displaced no air, gave off no betraying sound, from one closed forbidden door to the next and so acquired all I knew of that light and space in which people moved and breathed as I (that same child) might have gained conception of the sun from seeing it through a piece of smoky glass—fourteen, four years younger than Judith, four years later than Judith's moment which only virgins know: when the entire delicate spirit's bent is one anonymous climaxless epicene and unravished nuptial—not that widowed and nightly violation by the inescapable and scornful dead which is the meed of twenty and thirty and forty, but a world filled with living marriage like the light and air which she breathes.

Or again, there are situations bristling with questions, with rival and contradictory hypotheses, with insoluble mysteries which yet lure one on from guess to guess, as in the appearance of the drunken half-caste grandson of Supten before the court at Jefferson.

There had been no cause, no reason for it; none to ever know exactly what happened, what curses and ejaculations which might have indicated what it was that drove him [sic], and there was only your grandfather to fumble, grope, grasp the presence of that furious protest, that indictment of heaven's ordering, that gage flung into the face of what it is with a furious and indomitable desperation which the demon himself might have shown, as if the child and then the youth had acquired it from the walls in which the demon had lived, the air which he had once walked in and breathed until that moment when his own fate which he had dared in his turn struck back at him; only your grandfather to sense that protest, because the justice and others present did not recognize him, did not recognize this slight man with his bandaged head and arm, his sullen impassive (and now bloodless) olive face, who refused to answer any questions, make any statement: so that the justice (Jim Hamblett it was) was already making his speech of indictment when your grandfather entered . . .

What were Faulkner's models for these breathless interminable sentences we can only guess. Henry James was famous for the fussy elaboration of his syntax. There was Marcel Proust, with sentences even longer and more involved. Frances Newman, herself a southern writer, made a great and well-deserved hit with the literati in her novel *The Hard-Boiled Virgin,* entirely composed in sentences of extreme length and involution of syntax. These were authors whom Faulkner could hardly have missed, and hardly have failed to admire. But whoever his teachers, he has certainly bettered their instructions, carried to greater extremes their methods, so caviar to the general. The sentences of James are as neatly fashioned and discriminately weighted as those of the most clear-headed and fastidious of philosophers. Proust's are built up and carried forward with an exquisite sense of balance and proportion. *The Hard-Boiled Virgin* comprises the reactions and reflections of a highbrow remarkable for her wit and orderliness of mind.

In Faulkner we are lost for pages at a time in waste and mountainous seas of psychological speculation or hypothetical reconstruction of history. Half the time we are swimming under water, holding our breath and straining our eyes to read off the meaning of submarine phenomena, unable to tell fact from figure, to fix the reference of pronouns, or distinguish between guess and certainty. From time to time we come to the surface, gasping, to breathe the air of concrete fact and recorded truth, only to go floundering again the next moment through crashing waves of doubt and speculation. We are forever on the point of giving up, throwing ourselves upon some reef and letting the ocean thunder by. But so powerful is the spell of this demon, so strong a hold he takes on our imagination and our curiosity, that we yield again our tired bodies to the flood, and go on swimming, gasping, floundering through the charted chaos of his narrative.

For his chaos is a charted one if we take the long view. He knows very well what he is doing, where he is going, and just where he is at any particular point in his devious and looping trail. For this man Faulkner is a born storyteller if there ever was one. He knows how from the first word to intrigue and enthrall his audience, persuade them of the glamour and fascination of his subject, convince them that he has something up his sleeve, and keep them guessing what it is. This is proved by the success of his short stories in the popular magazines, stories which are in their way as teasing and sophisticated as his longer narratives. And if for his novels he has fewer readers, it is perhaps because a full-length novel gives so much more scope for the arts of mystification of which he is a master, and what charms a reader in a work of twenty pages may put too much of a strain upon him when carried through four hundred.

His technique varies from book to book, and is applied with great freshness and originality. The novelist whom he most resembles on the whole in storytelling method is Joseph Conrad, to whom he is akin by virtue of his fondness for bizarre romantic subject matter and his extreme preoccupation with strange and hidden motivation as well as by his virtuosity in the handling of technical devices. Like Conrad, he is given to playing tricks with chronology. In one part of *The Wild Palms* he starts with what is almost the finish of the story, the sojourn of Harry and Charlotte in the dreary cottage by the gulf shore at the time when she is dying. In the other part he concludes with what was almost its beginning— the convict's experience with the girl for whose sake he staged his train robbery and who gave him the go-by after he went to prison. In each case the displacement of matter in time is an inspiration. In the story of the lovers it sets them in a most strange and intriguing light, as they are seen by the doctor whose cottage they have rented, and captures the reader's imagination as nothing else could have done. Nothing essential in the plot is given away; we do not even guess the malady from which the young woman is suffering. When they return, at the end of their flight, to the cottage among the wild palms, the effect is all the stronger for what we have held over from the atmospheric magic of the beginning. In the case of the convict, we had no real need to know that early history until the end, although we might wonder why he could return so calmly and so resolutely to his cage. That wonder simply serves to add a shade of strangeness to this extraordinary figure. The clue to his character is kept for the last, where it brings the curtain down effectively, and throws at length its oblique light on the author's general theme and intention.

In *Light in August* the story pattern is extremely intricate, involving two levels of time which alternately hold the stage. The first is what we may call the dramatic present (the here and now) of the story, comprising some ten days or so in August in and around the town of Jefferson. It is here that Lena comes seeking her vanished fiancé, and is taken under the wing of Byron Bunch and the Rev. Gail Hightower. It is here Joe Christmas, the mulatto, kills his mistress Miss Burden, in the lonely old family mansion, and sets fire to the house (if it was he who did it) on the day of Lena's arrival. It is here that Christmas is confined after his capture about a week later, and is killed by Percy Grimm at Hightower's house when he tried to escape. This is, we may say, the front-stage action, and occupies about a dozen chapters of the narrative. But along with this, at what we may call strategic or convenient moments, is introduced an equal quantity of action from the past, necessary for understanding the behavior of the leading characters, and having its light to throw on the general theme involving the race problem and related matters. There is one continuous block of eight chapters recounting the history of Christmas as a boy and a young man driven from town to town and from mistress to mistress by the obsession of shameful birth and the need to slake the torture of his self-abhorrence, together with the early history of Miss Burden and her Yankee forbears, whose mission was to raise the negro from his degraded status. One long chapter is devoted to the history of old "Doc Hines," Christmas' grandfather, his father's slayer and virtual slayer of his mother, whose hatred of negroes was so strangely blent with his religious preoccupation with sin. A large part of two chapters more is given over to Hightower's early story, accounting for his obsession with the shames and glories of the Civil War and his sense of guilt in relation to his wife's madness and death.

In most cases the front-stage drama is well established before he takes us back-stage, or behind the scenes as we might call it. Our interest in these enigmatic persons is roused to such a pitch that we are eager to follow them into the underground chambers that hold the secrets of their character. In general, we may say of Faulkner that he is a master of innuendo and curiosity-provoking suggestion. Mysterious hints and teasing glimpses keep us pressing forward in the search for solutions. He has a way of making us wait intolerable lengths of time for the satisfaction of our curiosity; but in the interval he keeps us diverted with matter of such vivid interest that we forgive him for his perverseness. Our interest is not confined to matters of fact, but is even more centered on character and motive. We might apply to Faulkner's novels the same label as to Conrad's and Henry James'; we might call them all psychological mystery stories.

I must confess that, in the case of the Rev. Gail Hightower, the psychological riddle is too obscure for me to rede. I am persuaded that there is some mysterious connection intended between him and the theme of Christmas and Hines and Miss Burden. But I have not been able to figure it out to my satisfaction. And I do not think I have less patience and goodwill than the average reader. It is an instance of Faulkner's way of missing his mark through excessive subtlety. This writer wishes above all things not to fall into the banal and obvious; and Lord knows he is never in danger of that!

Most extraordinary of all his psychological mysteries, and most strongly suggestive of Conrad, is *Absalom, Absalom!* It reminds one of Conrad not merely by its cavalier treatment of chronology, but by its way of developing the story with the help of interpreters, who are engaged throughout in a process of reconstructing the facts in conformity with certain hyoptheses they have set up for explaining the characters. The chief of these interpreters (the Captain Marlow of this tale) is Quentin Compson, with whom the reader of Faulkner is well acquainted from *The Sound and the Fury*. We know from that story that he was a Harvard student and drowned himself in the Charles River in the month of June 1910. In the later book, what we may call the dramatic present is made up of two occasions, in September 1909 and later on in the winter of 1910. On the first of these occasions Quentin is shown discussing with Miss Rosa Coldfield of Jefferson, Mississippi, a project she has for going out with him on a visit to Sutpen's Hundred, an estate in the country, and listening to her account of her relation to Colonel Thomas Sutpen, the owner, who was her brother-in-law and whom she had been engaged to marry after the death of her sister. The second occasion was a cold night in Cambridge, Mass., when through many hours he was engaged with his Canadian roommate Shreve, in working out a plausible account of what really happened at Sutpen's Hundred between the early 1800's when it was founded and January 1910, when the house went up in flames, after the visit there of Quentin Compson and Rosa Coldfield.[2] They

---

[2] I say January 1910 and not December 1909 because in the genealogy appended to the book it is stated that Henry and Clytemnestra Sutpen, who were burned up with the house, died in 1910. However, it is stated in the text that the conflagration occurred three months after the September visit of Rosa Coldfield and Quentin; and it is further stated in Mr. Compson's letter to Quentin dated January 10, 1910, that Miss Rosa Coldfield died two days

have a great deal to go on in the way of documents and oral tradition; but most of the events occurred in a now remote past, and the motives of most of the persons involved are a matter of speculation. The tragic events are well established, but they seem incredible to the descendants of the actors. A few faded and fragmentary letters recovered from old trunks and drawers only serve to deepen the mystery. The characters are all there, yet something is missing.

They are like a chemical formula exhumed along with the letters from that forgotten chest, carefully, the paper old and faded and falling to pieces, the writing faded, almost indecipherable, yet meaningful, familiar in shape and sense, the name and presence of volatile and sentient forces; you bring them together in the proportions called for, but nothing happens; you re-read, tedious and intent, poring, making sure that you have forgotten nothing, made no miscalculation; you bring them together again and again nothing happens; just the words, the symbols, the shapes themselves, shadowy inscrutable and serene, against that turgid background of a horrible and bloody mischancing of human affairs.

By touches like this we are made to feel how difficult it is to recall a vanished age, to put the right construction on events so long faded out of most men's knowledge, and above all to comprehend the sentiments, ideals, and passionate objectives which together made up a spiritual whole perhaps unique and for which the conditions are no longer present. Half of the interest lies, as in Proust's *Recherche du temps*

---

before after lying in a coma "almost two weeks," which would seem to place the tragedy at Sutpen's Hundred in the month of December. It is a matter of no importance whatever except that, in an author so monstrously ingenious in fitting together the pieces of his plot, and at the same time confusing the reader, it is a pleasure to discover even a slight discrepancy. If we place the burning of Sutpen's Hundred on New Year's Day, and Rosa's death on the eighth, then we might attribute the discrepancy to Mr. Compson's disposition to stretch the local news by writing "almost two weeks" instead of "an entire week." If that was Faulkner's intention, it is signal example of subtlety expended on matters too small for visibility.

perdu, in the very process of recovery. And we are made to feel the eager excitement of these young men deeply moved by the tragic story, deeply concerned at bottom for the dignity of human nature and the integrity of their ideals, though at times they indulge in a clowning flippancy of manner, which is "just that protective coloring of levity behind which the youthful shame of being moved hid itself."

In the opening chapters it is from Rosa Coldfield and from Quentin's father that we receive the data and the impressions which later Shreve and Quentin try to bring into some kind of order. New information comes to them in a letter from Mr. Compson in January 1910, after Miss Coldfield's death. And when they reach an impasse in the process of reconstruction, Quentin goes back to information had by his grandfather years before from the lips of Thomas Sutpen, and to facts not known to his grandfather which came to his knowledge on the September day when he rode out to Sutpen's Hundred with Miss Rosa. In the two long final chapters the Cambridge roommates are shown engaged in a kind of contest as to which one of them will first succeed in putting together all the pieces of their puzzle-picture.

What is most fascinating is the way the characters, in the course of the story, go through a continuous process of reinterpretation, like ancestral portraits several times retouched. Thomas Sutpen starts, under the brush of Miss Rosa, as a sort of incomprehensible demon of malignancy and perverseness. Later, as we learn from Mr. Compson of the founding of Sutpen's Hundred, we begin to have an awed respect for him as a man of unusual vision and force of character. We come to pity him as we think of his son's repudiation and his predicament in the face of Charles Bon's threat to marry his daughter. Then, with the story of his ideal project as he related it to Quentin's grandfather, our pity is reinforced by admiration for him as a man of feeling. And finally comes the view of him as an old man returned from the war to a ruined estate and family, desperately trying too late to reedify his temple of dreams.

Much the same process is followed in the case of Charles Bon. And with him, it is not so much character and motive which are in question as elements of horror in the basic situation. In the matter of his engagement to marry Judith, we are led through three distinct stages with regard to the gravity of the case, three levels of rising apprehension, as we learn by slow degrees of the reasons for Sutpen's objection to the marriage. At first we suppose that it was merely Bon's having an octaroon mistress (or wife) in New Orleans, with a child of one-twelfth negro blood. We are left rather vague as to the exact legal character of this connection; but it is serious enough to bring up the question of bigamy. And Shreve and Quentin spend a long time trying to imagine the reactions of Henry Sutpen to this marital involvement as it affects his attitude toward his dearest friend and toward the projected marriage of his friend to his own sister. It is much later that we learn that what Thomas Sutpen told his son during the vacation visit of Charles Bon was that Bon was his own half-brother. And now we have to get used, along with Shreve and Henry, to the idea that the projected marriage involves not merely the question of bigamy but the certainty of incest. But this is only the second level of seriousness. For what Henry learns from his father during their final meeting in camp is that Charles Bon is not merely his brother, and Judith's brother, but that he is part negro. So that to bigamy and incest is added the still more abhorrent feature (for a Sutpen) of miscegenation—intermarriage with an inferior race. And so at last we are prepared to accept as credible fact the shooting of Charles Bon by his brother when, after their four years of campaigning, and their ride back across the country together, Thomas Sutpen's mulatto son passes the gateposts of Sutpen's Hundred on his way to mate with Sutpen's all-white daughter.

The way in which Faulkner in this matter keeps the reader

for hundreds of pages barking up the wrong tree, and then a second wrong tree, while all the time his real game is lodged in the branches of a third, is one of the most extraordinary tricks of narrative skill in the history of fiction. And all the more so because it is not a mere trick in plotting. What I have called the wrong trees were not really so. The situations set forth were all correct, and they were bristling with implications for character and theme which called for long and leisurely development. Only by keeping them separate, only by holding back the later ones till the earlier had been fully exploited, could he bring out the full significance of his drama.

We could spend hours in the noting of other examples of ingenious storytelling in this one book. It is not only by looping backward in time that the author advances the understanding of his saga. He frequently gives forward glances, anticipations of action yet to come. These are so handled that they serve to whet the appetite but never to satisfy it. And all the while the story is slowly moving forward in time. All the while, too, the author keeps up his sleeve the crowning incidents of the final scene—the finding of Henry Sutpen in the boarded mansion and the death of Henry and Clytie in the burning house, leaving only Jim Bond, the half-wit negro great-grandson, to carry on the heritage. Even the affair of Wash Jones and his granddaughter and great-granddaughter (child of Thomas) is kept till very near the end. Particularly skillful is the way in which Shreve is held at bay in his effort to explain Sutpen's quarrel with Jones. If it was a son he so passionately desired, why, when his son was born, did he throw up the sponge so unaccountably? Shreve, in his excitement, has confused "son" with "child"—has jumped to the conclusion that the child born to Milly would serve the dream of Thomas Sutpen. He simply cannot imagine that Sutpen's child might be a female. It is not till Quentin sets him right with the simple words, "It wasn't a son. It was a girl," that he can fit in the last piece in his puzzle-picture.

It was indeed a puzzle-picture of the most amazing ingenuity, and of serious artistic significance too, in that the pieces were not so much facts—though these were furnished in great plenty—as sentiments and motives, ideals and ambitions—complete moral outfit of a vanished culture.

It would take an entire chapter to describe Faulkner's technique in *The Sound and the Fury* and *As I Lay Dying,* where the problem of storytelling is complicated by the author's determination to have the telling done in terms of the mental process of the characters. There is something peculiar about the mentality of most of these characters, and constant use is made of the flash-back and of fleeting allusion to times and events far removed from the present action, with an almost complete want of helpful explanation by the author. This stream-of-consciousness technique, inspired no doubt by the example of writers like James Joyce and Virginia Woolf, but highly original in application, results in great bewilderment for the reader, even greater than the ultra-Conrad of *Light in August* and *Absalom, Absalom!* It might easily be dismissed as an example of extravagant modernism, ingenuity overshooting its mark. But it so happens that these two books are, for special lovers of Faulkner, the two most effective of all his novels, judging by vividness and intimacy in the evocation of character and situation. There will be few contented readers of Faulkner's novels, as there are few for Joyce. But these few will agree that he is justified in many of his most extreme deviations from standard technique. So that it would be well worth our while to make a detailed study and interpretation of his method if it would not mean laying disproportionate emphasis on this one man. It is too early to say that he is a more important writer than others—like Caldwell and Farrell —whose technique is so much more normal.

VIII. THOMAS WOLFE

The Search for a Father

"Still nursing the unconquerable hope,
Still clutching the inviolable shade . . ."
—Arnold

VIII. THOMAS WOLFE

The Search for a Father

The chapters of this book were written, all but one, in the spring and summer of 1940. They included a chapter on Thomas Wolfe, dealing with the first three of his vast novels. But this was of necessity tentative in character, so much in the interpretation of what had been published depended on the final volume, which was completed at the time of Wolfe's death in September 1938 but which remained to be published. This volume has now appeared, in September 1940. My one remaining chapter can now be written, and in the light of his final words I can review and correct what was said of the earlier novels. On the whole, however, it will be more interesting, and not less enlightening, to leave what I have said of the earlier books much as it was, and then go on to draw conclusions from the last one. Our impressions of those which came before cannot well be nullified by anything in this. The questions raised in the earlier ones, however they were answered in the last, are the same questions as before. If there is any surprise or contradiction or disappointment felt, it is that provided by the author himself. The course of thought is that which the reader follows in taking the books in order as they appeared. If corrections must be made, they are such as the reader would make who has followed Wolfe's writing from the beginning.

One of the chief criticisms made against Wolfe is that his work lacks form. And one reason why it has seemed to lack form may well be that his scheme was one of vast dimensions, and that it needed to be completed before it became clear what direction it was taking. There was reason to anticipate that much would be made clear in the coming volume. And the numerous readers who have followed his stories with breathless interest could always look forward with strained suspense to what he had still to say.

He certainly stands in sharp contrast in many ways to the other men in our group of writers. In each one of them the subject and intention of the work stand out in sharp definition. They have made their choice of theme with sure selectiveness, have taken their point of view, their tone, have lighted their stage, with the deliberate artistry of skilled craftsmen. Whether it is the New Orleans mulatto, the Boston brahmin, the Key West bootlegger, or the Oklahoma Okie, the subject stands out distinct from anything else in life, clearly delimited, and entirely free from involvement with the author. The author in each case is viewing his theme objectively as something outside himself and capable of being studied, with sympathy perhaps, but also with complete esthetic detachment.

With Thomas Wolfe the case is quite the contrary. No particular social group is the subject of his books, which undertake to comprise as far as possible the whole of American life, South and North, together with a good deal of Europe, and to include people of diverse social station and cultural status. No such specific problem is set forth as that of the poolroom loafer or that of migratory labor or the bored man of wealth and convention. This author is aiming to include the whole of life, in its infinite variety of feeling and manifestation. And he is not viewing life as a detached spectator, who can size it up coolly, but as one passionately involved himself, struggling desperately in its Laocoön serpent folds, blinded by its illusions, confused by its complexities, bewildered by its paradoxes and Protean changes, tortured by its cruelties, and helplessly bound by its Venusberg enchantments. Add to this that Thomas Wolfe is a writer, compared with these others, who appears to be guided more by his emotions than by his reason—is it any wonder that his work should seem, by comparison, formless and wanting in definition and design?

To begin with, it is all very largely autobiographical. In the late books, reacting from the criticism that he had too slavishly followed his own experience, he made some effort to mold and disguise the crude substance of his own life. In *The Web and the Rock,* he changes the name of his central character, and alters the circumstances of his father's marriage. But it is still Thomas Wolfe and his people that form his subject. He does not cover much of the same ground in the different books; for his material was so abundant that he could recount his childhood twice over and seldom repeat an incident or an impression. But the whole thing makes one record and presents one complex of related problems.

Look Homeward, Angel (1929) begins with the marriage of a man from Pennsylvania to a woman from the Carolina hills. He was a stone-cutter, a monument-maker, and she was one of a family now settled in the growing resort of Altamont (Thomas Wolfe's Asheville), with a flair for real estate investment and a gift for building up a fortune. They are an ill-assorted pair—the man a dreamer and drunkard, a prodigious artistic temperament not fully expressed in carving angels—the woman a miser, a money-grubber, willing to sacrifice her whole family to the sordid and anxious idol of mammon. Their children are the victims of this conflict of ideals, and they grow up to repudiate, in one way or another, the parents who made life such a hell for them all. The central character is Eugene Gant (Thomas Wolfe). He is his father's son, artist and dreamer, a sprawling awkward hulking disorderly fellow, overflowing with energy and ambition, a man of gargantuan appetites and a mad drive for experience of every kind. He is abnormally susceptible to all impressions physical and moral, a passionate lover of nature in all her moods, of all her sights and sounds and smells. His sensitive quivering soul is made witness to the dramas and cruelties and shames and humiliations of life in his town; and above all, the turbulent passions and delights of family life. He delivers papers in the early morning in niggertown. He is subjected to the miscellaneous contacts of his mother's boarding house. He goes to school and learns by heart the great lyric poetry of England; he attends the state university, suffers humiliation at the hands of boys older and less callow than himself; his mind is freed from the narrow prejudices of Southern religion and social snobbishness. He is initiated into vice; he has delusions of grandeur; he has his juvenile love affairs; he suffers the death of his brother Ben, and the mortal sickness of his father, dying of cancer. And he says good-by to his mother as he takes the train for Boston to go to Harvard.

Of Time and the River (1935) begins at the point where the earlier story leaves off. Eugene Gant is now Doctor Faustus, determined to attain all knowledge and to know all experience. He studies play writing in Professor Hatcher's (Baker's) class in Cambridge. He returns home to the death-bed of his father. He falls under the spell of the fascinating Francis Starwick, Hatcher's assistant, who stands for all that is beautiful and inspiring in the life of the artist. He sends off his play to a publisher and waits at home for the magic letter which shall seal his fate. It is a rejection slip, and plunges him into despair. He goes on a drunken drive with reckless boys that lands him in jail. He tells his mother he will expiate his crime, retrieve his failure. He becomes a teacher in New York University; continues his frantic pursuit of all knowledge and all experience. He visits the beautiful countryplace of wealthy friends up the Hudson, but finds that he cannot be contented with the still perfection of an order built on the exploitation of the poor and completely shut off from human suffering and turmoil. He continues his pilgrimage in Europe, and leads a hectic life of dissipation in Paris with Starwick and two Boston women. With one of these he falls in love; but she, he finds, is in love with Starwick; and Starwick, alas! is of that lost unfortunate race of men that can give satisfaction to no woman. The two friends quarrel and separate. Eugene pursues his pilgrimage alone. He gets to work on his writing and begins his great opus. When he takes the boat for home, he has a glimpse of a woman and hears her called Esther. "Esther was fair; she was fair; she had dove's eyes."

The Web and the Rock (1939) takes up the story of Eugene Gant from the time he makes the acquaintance of Esther, Mrs. Jack, on the steamer returning to America. But he is now renamed George Webber; and for the first three books the author goes back to fill in the background of his parents' lives and of his own childhood in Altamont (now Libya Hill). His main object is to trace the two streams of blood and tradition—"two worlds discrete"—which struggle for mastery in the spirit of George Webber. There are many new fine sensations from the life of a child; many new and cruel incidents of life in his town; and more is made of the lost and desperate people of the hills, and especially that extraordinary old scalawag, his grandfather, Major Joyner. A new selection of incidents from his early college days is given; and an account of the New York life of Southern men come to the great city of the North to take the world by storm. Then we skip to his return from Europe and his love affair with the wealthy Jewish woman, Esther Jack, designer of stage-sets for smart society theaters. During this period he is teaching at the School for Utility Cultures Inc. (the same New York University) and writing his novel. Esther Jack is a wonderful character-creation and a magnificent woman all round—obviously quite the best thing that ever happened to

George Webber-Eugene Gant-Thomas Wolfe. But there is
a perverse strain in his nature that makes him resent his
attachment to her. He associates her in his mind with all
that is false and sophisticated in the artistic life of New
York, all that is cruel and corrupt in the social system that
floats on the surface of poverty and degradation. She is a
symbol to him of the conspiracy of the world against him,
the genuine artist. When his book is rejected by his publishers, he makes her the scapegoat for all his shame and misery.
He quarrels with her, and goes abroad to pursue alone his
Faustian pilgrimage, which ends up in a fight in a Munich
beer hall and a hospital bed. The last scene shows him
contemplating in a mirror his simian body, and carrying on
a dialogue with that material casing of his soul. He tells his
body how nice it would be to return to the home of his
childhood memories. "Yes," said his Body, "But—you can't
go home again."

So there we have the title for the final volume, to which
one looked so long for answers to the many desperate questions which had been raised by the earlier record. When that
appeared, we told ourselves, we could see the direction of the
thing, and the many incidents and characters would fall into
place in something like an ordered design. I have given the
barest outline of the action, and have had to ignore the vast
number of characters and the varied incidents included in
this bewildering saga. This is anything but the conventional
well-made novel. There is, you might say, no plot, no
dramatic situation to be worked out, no dramatic issue to be
followed through from step to step. And the critics have
largely been unable to explain the force and fascination of
books so lacking in conventional order and form. They have,
I think, been unnecessarily blind to elements of form which
are actually present. We can get further in our appreciation of Wolfe if we think of him not as a novelist but as a
poet or a composer. These books yield their secret to us best

if we consider them as—shall we say?—tone poems. It is not so much the plot as the musical themes or motives that give us a clue to their form. By reference to these musical themes the various characters and incidents take on significance, losing much of their effect of lumpiness and irrelevance. The main trouble is that there are many themes, more or less related but still distinct, woven together in a pattern of infinite complexity; and it takes study to realize how they are composed into something like a harmonious whole.

The dominating theme is what Wolfe calls man's search for a father. He has singled this out himself as the central idea. In his book entitled *The Story of a Novel* (1936), he writes: "The deepest search in life, it seemed to me, the thing that in one way or another was central to all living was man's search for a father, not merely the father of his flesh, not merely the lost father of his youth, but the image of a strength and wisdom external to his need and superior to his hunger, to which the belief and power of his own life could be united." This theme was probably suggested to Wolfe by James Joyce's *Ulysses*, a book that he regarded as one of the greatest of our day, and in which the central character, representing Joyce himself as Eugene Gant represents Wolfe, is shown engaged in a similar search for a spiritual father. This image is perpetually recurring throughout the three earlier books of Wolfe, and it is clear that the entire series is given unity by the idea of life as a pilgrimage, or search for a spiritual essence or being which for the mature man can take the place which a father takes for the child. A father protects the child; he is the source of wisdom and strength; he answers all the questions which the child puts to life; and as it were guarantees to him that life has a meaning and value. The mature man has to face alone the perils and dubieties of experience; and ever he longs for some assurance that he is not morally alone; that there is something in the nature of things which stands back of him to support him against the adversary; some comfort in failure; some assurance of providence or reason in the way things come about.

This image of the father frequently goes along with the image of a door or gate. Life for the pilgrim is a search for some door that will admit him to reality and happiness; some gate that will open on truth and unbare the secrets of the world. To find this door is to find one's father; it is to be no longer alone and fearful; it is to find oneself and make one's way back to the warmth and security of home. All men are by nature lost and lonely; and this is particularly true of Americans. "We are so lost, so naked and so lonely in America. Immense and cruel skies bend over us, and all of us are driven on forever and we have no home." It is this loneliness, this desperate search for a home, that leads us to make so many journeys up and down our own land and in foreign parts; it leads us to so many futile efforts to solve our problems by some childish magic. Of the students in Hatcher's class, Wolfe says they belonged to "this great colony of the lost Americans . . . who feel that everything is going to be all right with them if they can only take a trip, or learn a rule, or meet a person . . . that all the power they lack themselves will be supplied, and all the anguish, fury, and unrest, the confusion and the dark damnation of man's soul can magically be healed if only they eat bran for breakfast, secure an introduction to a celebrated actress, get a reading for their manuscript from a friend of Sinclair Lewis, or win admission to Professor Hatcher's celebrated class of dramatists." Or it may not be in such obvious and extravert things that they will find the open sesame. Perhaps, "it is a face seen once and lost forever in a crowd, an eye that looked, a face that smiled and vanished on a passing train, it is a prescience of snow upon a certain night, the laughter of a woman in a summer street long years ago, it is the memory of a single moon seen at the pine's dark edge in old October—and all of our lives is written in the twisting of a leaf upon a bough, a door that opened, and a stone."

A related theme to that of lost Americans is the theme of the South seeking its homeland or its realization in the North. This is especially the case with Eugene Gant, George Webber; his father is represented as having come from the golden North to the dark and glamorous South. His blood was mixed there with that of the lost and ineffectual people of the mountains. And in his son there is a perpetual longing to return to his father's land, the golden land of the North. "Then his spirit flamed beyond the hills, beyond lost time and sorrow, to his father and his father's earth; and when he thought of him his heart grew warm, the hot blood thudded in his veins, he leapt all barriers of the here and now, and northward, gleaming brightly there beyond the hills, he saw a vision of the golden future in new lands."

Closely associated with the image of the father and the door is that of the word. Every person in whom the author has an interest is a reminder of the secret door, the magic word; and he can never forget them because they are so vividly connected with the object of his search. There was the mysterious English family with whom he lived in Oxford, having so little to do with them. He could never forget them. "Although he had never passed beyond the armor of their hard bright eyes, or breached the wall of their crisp, friendly, and impersonal speech, or found out anything about them, he always thought of them with warmth, with a deep and tender affection, as if he had always known them —as if, somehow, he could have lived with them or made their lives his own had he only said a word, or turned the handle of a door—a word he never knew, a door he never found." Returning with his uncle from a walk in the mountains, he views the houses of his home town. "The sight of these closed golden houses with their warmth of life awoke in him a bitter, poignant, strangely mixed emotion of exile and return, of loneliness and security, of being forever shut out from the palpable and passionate integument of life and fellowship, and of being so close to it that he could touch it with his hand, enter it by a door, possess it with a word—a word that, somehow, he could never speak, a door that, somehow, he could never open."

The image of the word is of peculiar importance because this is the record of an author's life. His natural weapon and tool is the word. And his goal is inevitably conceived of in terms not merely of happiness, of experience, of possession, but in terms of understanding, of expression in words and symbols. I suppose that all men feel in some degree this psychological compulsion to put in words their experience and their judgment of life. But in the case of the artist this often takes on the proportions of a major obsession. And it is perhaps even more the case in modern times—since the virus of romanticism entered into the blood of our race, and since—with growing knowledge and doubt, with growing sophistication—it has become so much more difficult to see our way clearly, to encompass experience in one comprehensive formula, to find some word of assurance and comfort for a soul distracted and torn asunder. The French in the nineteenth century called this the *mal du siècle*, the sickness of the age. But they were largely content to utter their doubt and despair without any strenuous effort to throw them off. In America today, where the occasions for doubt are perhaps even greater, but where there is still the determination to assert some faith, it is an undertaking even more difficult, more maddening. Thus George Webber was

trying to articulate something immense and terrible in life which he had always known and felt, and for which he thought he must now find some speech, or drown. And yet it seemed that this thing which was so immense could have no speech, that it burst through the limits of all recorded languages, and that it could never be

rounded, uttered, and contained in words. It was a feeling that
every man on earth held in the little tenement of his flesh and
spirit the whole ocean of human life and time, and that he must
drown in this ocean unless, somehow, he "got it out of him"—
unless he mapped and charted it, fenced and defined it, plumbed
it to its uttermost depths, and knew it to its smallest pockets upon
the remotest shores of the everlasting earth.

Or again, as Wolfe says of Eugene Gant, "This is the artist,
then—life's hungry man, the glutton of eternity, beauty's
miser, glory's slave," whose undertaking is "utterly to possess
and capture beauty." And in this he is driven by the fact that
he labors not merely for himself but for all men whose
tongue he is.

He is the tongue of his unuttered brothers, he is the language
of man's buried heart, he is man's music and life's great dis-
coverer, the eye that sees, the key that can unlock, the tongue that
will express the buried treasure in the hearts of men, that all men
know and that no man has a language for—and at the end, he is
his father's son, shaped from his father's earth of blood and sweat
and toil and bitter agony; he is at once the parent and the son of
life, and in him life and all man's nature are compact, he is most
like man in his very differences, he is what all men are and what
not one man in a million ever is; and he has all, knows all, sees
all that any man on earth can see and hear and know.

It is clear that this man's mission is to utter the unspoken
word of mankind upon the whole experience of life. And it
is furthermore clear that, in accomplishing this mission, he
holds himself responsible for all knowledge. He was drafted
from birth to the Faustian life. He must read all books, visit
all countries, possess all women, scan all faces, walk all streets
and mountain paths, live in all social levels. He is driven by
a relentless fury to crowd all life into one narrow span, lest
he should miss one least item of what must be taken into
account in the appraisal—one least hint of what might prove
the open sesame to the secret door.

That is his obligation and compulsion as the "pilgrim of eternity." And that might have been well enough if it were not that, over and above the poet and spokesman of the race, he is *himself*—condemned by the limitations of his ego to seek for the personal gratifications of fame and success. It is this which complicates the pattern and takes the story into so many dark places. Like other mortals this man is liable to psychic perversions that threaten to spoil whatever he undertakes in his pursuit of the ideal. He is the creature of his heredity and of environmental conditions that determine him to violence and frustration. I find here the artistic justification for the otherwise disproportionate attention given by Wolfe to his childhood. He wishes to show that his hero was given in childhood the bent that doomed him to so much suffering and disillusion, as well as the bent for artistic creation by which he triumphed in the end over evil and disorder. In *Look Homeward, Angel* Wolfe lays himself out to show how, in the perpetual conflict of temperaments, between the grasping materialism of Eugene's mother and the crazy inward brooding of his father, the children had their natures distorted and were wrought to a pitch of desperate neuroticism. Their family did not seem to fit into the pattern of life of their town, "because they had twisted the design of all orderly life, because there was in them a mad, original, disturbing quality which they did not suspect."

In *The Web and the Rock*, he makes even more of the contrast of temperaments; and his mother's family becomes the type of all that is dark and mad in human nature, while his father is made a symbol of that ideal world in which he takes refuge from the ruin and madness of the other. We are given pictures of slum life in Libya Hill—the horrible death in-life of slatternly pregnant women, of sneering, bullying, murderous, obscene gangster boys from a certain section of the town which has been settled by poor white trash from the back-country hills. And we have many tales of the uncles and aunts and grandparents on his mother's side—sunk in poverty, violence, superstition, pride and ignorance. Even as a boy he realizes that this is the same stock, and that he is of them by his mother's blood.

Bone of their bone, blood of their blood, flesh of their flesh, by however various and remote a web, he is of them, they are in him, he is theirs—has seen, known, felt, and has distilled into his blood every wild passion, criminal desire, and rending lust they have known. And the blood of the murdered men, the rivers of blood of the murdered men which has soaked down quietly in the wilderness . . . has stained his life, his flesh, his spirit, and is on his head as well as theirs! . . . Just as his father's life spoke to him of all things wild and new, of exultant prophecies of escape and victory, of triumph, flight, new lands, the golden cities—of all that was magic, strange, and glorious on earth—so did the life of his mother's people return him instantly to some dark, unfathomed place in nature, to all that was tainted by the slow-moldering fires of madness in his blood, some ineradicable poison of the blood and soul, brown, thick, and brooding, never to be cured or driven out of him, in which at length he must drown darkly, horribly, unassuaged, unsavable, and mad.

However correctly he has traced the causes, there is no doubt that Wolfe's hero is more than a little bent away from the normal in his psychological reactions. In *Look Homeward, Angel* he felt himself in school a hunted animal with all the herd against him. In college he was morbidly sensitive to the ridicule of upper classmen and fraternity men. He felt that his family disliked him, and he could not break away from home without words of extreme bitterness toward his mother. In *Of Time and the River,* his quarrelsomeness had grown—his resentment against those who looked down on him socially or who failed to appreciate his talent. The scorn he heaps on Professor Hatcher's class of playwrights is out of all proportion to the occasion—and so is the irony he directs at his Jewish pupils in the University, at the publishers Rawng and Wright, at some of his literary contemporaries like T. S. Eliot. He begins to have something like delusions of persecution. He feels that he will not be able to survive his contacts with the Jews—himself so tender and sensitive, the Jews so tough and unbreakable. Again, he feels a furious resentment at his family because they do not recognize him for a literary genius but seem to think he ought to do something more practical than writing books. He behaves very badly toward his friend Starwick when he finds that he has the love of Ann, and he talks to her in the most outrageous manner.

But it is in *The Web and the Rock* that this perversity rises to a climax, above all in his relations with Esther Jack. He is wantonly unfaithful to her, and unreasonably jealous and suspicious. He makes her the symbol of a great conspiracy of evil forces against him; he suspects her of having sold him out to his enemies and of laughing at him behind his back. He abuses her as a Jew and heaps humiliations upon her which it makes one writhe to think of. And all—in the last analysis—because he is in an agony of discouragement and wounded pride over his manuscript, which has not been snapped up by the publishers. He must lash out at someone, and he makes his nearest and dearest the victim of his personal peeve. That is one reason for his abusing her; and another is that, while she is the most precious thing he has, he is too perverse to keep it. He wants a great and faithful love, and at the same time he wants to be free to make love to all the world.[1]

All this, as I see it, is of the utmost importance to Wolfe's general theme; for it is these personal flaws and discouragements that in his own case make impossible the finding of happiness—entering the secret door—reaching the mystic goal

[1] The essential truthfulness of Wolfe's account of this affair will be but the more impressed on anyone who will read Aline Bernstein's account of it in *The Journey Down* (1938). Indeed, the chief difference between George's and Esther's side of the story so far as characterization is concerned is that Wolfe paints George much blacker than "Esther" does.

of his pilgrimage. And what is true for him is true for others. There was always some ugly emotional twist which prevented the people he knew from realizing the happiness or fineness which was rightly theirs and to which they were so close.

What was wrong with life? What got into people such as these to taint their essential quality, to twist and warp and mutilate their genuine and higher purposes? What were these perverse and evil demons of cruelty and destructiveness, of anguish, error and confusion that got into them, that seemed to goad them on, with a wicked and ruinous obstinacy, deliberately to do the things they did not want to do—the things that were so shamefully unworthy of their true character and their real desire?

Sometimes, in the effort to express his feeling about this perverse strain in life, the author gives utterance to views smacking of medieval superstition.

He could not find a tongue for his bewilderment, but he now felt with unutterable certitude the presence of a demon of perverse denial which was, and was everywhere, abroad throughout the universe, and at work forever in the hearts of men. It was the cunning, subtle cheat, the mocker of life, the scourger of time; and man, with the full glory and the tragic briefness of his days before him, bowed like a dull slave before the thief that looted him of all his joy, and held him sullen but submissive to its evil wizardry.

The golden harvest was there to be taken, but something prevented men from stretching out their hands and taking. They were a race

of famished half-men who wanted food and had not the courage to go beyond the husks, who sought for pleasure constantly and stained the night with the obscene glitter of a thousand weary amusements, who longed for joy and comradeship and yet with dull, deliberate intent, fouled their parties with horror, shame and loathing every time they met.

submissive loss

Thus speaks the voice of experience, of disillusion and despair; and it is a dominant note of all three of the earlier volumes. Is there no answer, no way out of this intolerable dilemma? Must not the spirit of man react instinctively somehow to throw off the weight of such a nightmare? Well, yes, to be sure. There are inevitable psychological reactions and adjustments; they go on making themselves whether one knows it or not, and whether or not one understands the psychic mechanism which is in operation. Most of the record is occupied with these spontaneous workings of the psyche going through the movements necessary for its survival. And sometimes the account takes almost the form of philosophical statements. Such philosophical attitudes become more noticeable in the later volumes, and it was reasonable to expect that in the final volume they would be set forth in terms more definite and firm.

To begin with, there is the process of romantic escape from what is too distasteful in actual experience. Eugene Gant as a boy, when thwarted or wounded by life, could make the usual excursions into the world of romance and fantasy. And on the pattern of the boys' books of the time, he would invent long tales of adventure, bravery and love in which he was the leading actor. "Lifted by his fantasy into a high interior world, he scored off briefly and entirely all the grim smudges of life: he existed nobly in a heroic world with lovely and virtuous creatures." Or, "Steeping himself in ancient myths, where the will and the deed were not thought darkly on, he spent himself, quilted in golden meadows, or in the green light of woods, in pagan love." The attraction of Francis Starwick for him was that he lived not in the world of real things but in the fictitious world of the imagination. Starwick brought him "a life forever good, forever warm and beautiful, forever flashing with the fires of passion, poetry and joy, forever filled with the swelling and triumphant confidence of youth, its belief in new lands, morning, and a shining city, its hope of voyages, its conviction of a fortunate good and happy life—an imperishable happiness and joy —that was impending, that would be here at any moment." In the same way George Webber's father's life spoke to him "exultant prophecies of escape and victory." In the contrast of mother and father themes, the mother stands here for what Freud calls reality—that is, the disagreeable and unavoidable in experience—while the father stands for escape from reality into all the realms of the imaginative and ideal.

As time goes on, however, Wolfe's hero more and more realizes that his satisfaction is not to be had outside of reality but within it. "And as all the strength and passion of his life turned more and more away from its childhood thoughts of aerial flight and escape into some magic and unvisited domain, it seemed to him that the magic and unvisited domain was the earth itself and all the life around him— that he must escape not out of life but into it." It is this impulse to find the ideal in the real which leads Eugene to turn from the fairy-like beauty of the life of the rich to seek his satisfactions in dark streets where poverty makes closer contact with the primary facts of earth.

Another form of psychic adjustment is that associated with the images of the rock (or city) and of the river of time. He has a passion for countless multitudes, a craving to know them all and to absorb them all into his being, and out of the entirety of human experience to distill the magic potion. It is a similar need to identify himself with the whole of life that leads him to brood so much on the river of time, flowing forever out of the immense and populous past, carrying all ages, all races, in solution in its waters; flowing steadily on into the future as it traces out the common destiny of men. His appetite is insatiable. He can be content with nothing less than the whole of this eternal river—to absorb it all into himself— to drown himself in it—to lose his personal identity in the vast anonymous flow of time. It is a titanic and impossible undertaking, and more than once the author records his failure.

What have we taken from you, protean and phantasmal shape of time? What have we remembered of your million images, of your billion weavings out of accident and number, of the mindless fury of your dateless days, the brutal stupefaction of your thousand streets and pavements? What have we seen and known that is ours forever?

Gigantic city, we have taken nothing—not even a handful of your trampled dust—we have made no image on your iron breast and left not even the print of a heel upon your stony-hearted pavements. The possession of all things, even the air we breathed, was held from us, and the river of life and time flowed through the grasp of our hands forever, and we held nothing for our hunger and desire except the proud and trembling moments, one by one. Over the trodden and forgotten words, the rust and dusty burials of yesterday, we were born again into a thousand lives and deaths, and we were left forever with only the substance of our waning flesh, and the hauntings of an accidental memory, with all its various freight of great and little things which passed and vanished instantly and could never be forgotten. . . .

His chief error was that of taking quantity for a measure of value, of mistaking multiplicity for quality and importance. There are intimations—as the story progresses—that Wolfe is coming to seek the solution not in the piling up of experience but in sorting it out. In his dreams Eugene Gant begins to strain toward some more classic view of life. "Even human grief, pain, and trouble took on a color of classical perfection, of tragic grandeur, and the tortured and distressful skein of human life, with all that is ugly, trivial, and disgusting in it, took on the logical pattern of design and ordered destiny." Order and design in place of bulk and variety. Selection and cultivation of a little of experience instead of frantic effort to trap it all. This is the note sounded again at the end of *The Web and the Rock*. Esther, deserted and half oblivious in the New York park, is thinking out her soul's message to George

Webber in the Munich hospital. She remembers words of his voicing the horror of his nightmare, and she has an answer for each.

"The horror of eight million faces!"
Remember eight—know one.
"The horror of two million books!"
Write one that has two thousand words of wisdom in it.
"Each window is a light, each light a room, each room a cell, each cell a person!"
All rooms, all windows, and all persons for your hunger? No. Return to one: fill all that room with light and glory, make it shine as no other room ever shone before, and all life living on this earth will share it with you.

Thomas Wolfe tells us that, as his editor was examining the manuscript of *The October Fair* (never published under that title), he found that the book described two complete and separate cycles. "The first of these was a movement which described a period of wandering and hunger in a man's youth. The second cycle described the period of greater certitude, and was dominated by the unity of a single passion." Well, the first of these periods is evidently that set forth in *The Web and the Rock,* as well as in the earlier novels about Eugene Gant. The period of greater certitude makes its appearance in the final volume. As we anticipated, the appetite for sheer quantity in experience somewhat gives way there before the impulse to selection; the cultivation of life takes on a phase less extensive and more intensive.

But there is one final and very important theme which I have not touched on—still another effort to adjust the psyche to the distresses and disillusionments of life. This is what we might call the theme of return to the past. It is a common psychological operation, and evidently one of the greatest importance to Thomas Wolfe. But the prominence he gives it in his work seems to me to point strongly to the influence of Marcel Proust. Proust's great series of novels, called in

English *Remembrance of Things Past,* has for its general title in French, *À la recherche du temps perdu,* literally, "the search after lost time." Proust's undertaking was to describe the process by which he explored back into the mists of childhood experience, and thereby discovered his own peculiar secret of happiness. It was to disentangle himself from the web of time—to break through into the state of pure time—time no longer flowing and destroying, but fixed in the imagination as an unchanging ideal thing. It was by a happy accident that he discovered how this might be done. And the trick by which it was done was that of associating a physical sensation in the present with a similar physical sensation in the remote past. And so, in some mysterious way, the happiness which he had always missed in actual experience, the sense of fulfillment, is attained in the mystic identity of the present moment with that of long ago.

Now, I doubt whether Wolfe would have accepted, even if he could understand them, the full implications of Proust's metaphysical theory, which is said to be derived from Bergson. It is a theory suited to an extreme neurotic temperament—a temperament disposing one to escape from experience into pure abstractions of thought. But there is a common psychological element in what Proust and Wolfe go through. It is found in the recall by means of present sensations or impressions of closely similar impressions received in extreme youth. And the unconscious motivation is the urge to give to the present the tone of hopefulness and security and liveness which attached to childhood experience, to substitute the good impressions of childhood for the weariness and disenchantment of maturity.

This theme appears in many incidents in both *The Web and the Rock* and *Of Time and the River.* Take, for example, the occasion when Eugene Gant, worn out by suffering and discouragement, is sitting in an old inn in the city of Dijon. A peacefulness settles down upon him as he quietly watches the

doings of the ancient tranquil city. Inside the hotel two wait-
ers are polishing silverware and talking together in a cozy
pleasant way. The younger waiter is awkward and violent in
his handling of the silver and it makes a loud jingling noise.
"Ah!" says the older waiter. "On fait la musique." (You are
making music.) Eugene's mind is carried back fifteen years.
"Suddenly he was a child, and it was noon, and he was waiting in his father's house to hear the slam of the iron gate, the
great body stride up the high porch steps, knowing his father
had come home again." He follows with attentive ear the
various homely noises in the town square in France. "And
presently there began the most lonely, lost and unforgettable
of all sounds on earth—the solid, liquid leather-shuffle of foot-
steps going home one way, as men had done when they came
home to lunch at noon some twenty years ago, in the green-
gold and summer of full June, before he had seen his father's
land, and when the kingdoms of this earth and the enchanted
city still blazed there in the legendary magic of his boyhood
vision."

It is clear from many similar incidents that Eugene Gant
the man is trying to take refuge from the tribulations and
frustrations of manhood in the mental world of the child.
"That was a good time then." It is another way of seeking his
mystical father, but in a sense it means the abandonment of
the quest. He wants to go back home again and give up his
manhood. But that he cannot do. And it is for the final volume to answer the question where he is to go if he can't go
back to the child.

Does "You Can't Go Home Again" imply an impossibility of return to childhood? See bottom 198

IX. THOMAS WOLFE

Discovery of Brotherhood

realist

"Close thy *Byron;* open thy *Goethe*."
—CARLYLE

sentimentalist

IX. THOMAS WOLFE

Discovery of Brotherhood

You Can't Go Home Again opens in April 1929, with George Webber back in New York and seeing Esther Jack every day. In the summer he returns to Libya Hill to attend the funeral of Aunt Maw. This year sees the publication of his first novel, *Home to Our Mountains* (corresponding to *Look Homeward, Angel*), and his final break with Esther Jack. He goes to live in a Brooklyn cellar and works desperately for half a decade on his second novel, meantime making intimate acquaintance with the underworld of poverty and ugliness. He forms a devoted friendship with Foxhall Edwards, a publisher's reader, whom he heartily admires for his character and honest intelligence, and who supports him with editorial advice and with his faith in Webber's genius. His greatness is publicly proclaimed by Lloyd McHarg, the most famous and popular of American writers. After the publication of his second book (corresponding to *Of Time and the River*), he visits Germany and is hailed as a true Dichter and the American novelist most loved by the cognoscenti there. But he comes away saddened by the malady of spirit from which the Germans are suffering and with which America herself is threatened. In spite of his deep fondness for Foxhall Edwards, whom he had considered his second father, he differs with him radically in his philosophy of life, and the need for independence leads him to "leave" his friend. But he does not do so without writing him a long letter of explanation, ending with his credo. Something tells him that he is going to die, and his credo makes the final chapter in the long chronicle.

In spite of enthralling incidents, amusing dialogues, and many of the most brilliant character sketches in English fiction, there is even less "plot" in this autobiographical record than in any of the earlier books—no more plot, really, than is indicated in the outline I have given. But the book is not less interesting, on the whole, than those which preceded it, and certainly not less important than the others for the author's thought. In the period covered, George Webber was steadily engaged in thinking out his own problems and those of American society in general, which were closely connected in his mind. He was finding things out for himself, and first of all he realized that he could not "devour the earth," as he had undertaken to do, but, growing up, he must accept his own limitations. He was no longer overwhelmed, as before, by Amount and Number; but instead of trying to swallow experience whole, he was learning to observe and classify phenomena and draw rational conclusions from them. At first he was shocked and outraged by the reception given his novel in Libya Hill, where he was considered to have betrayed his home, crucified his family, proved himself no true Southerner and no American. In his effort to throw off the sense of guilt which he could not help but feel, he lashed himself "into a fit of violent recrimination, in which all that was worst and weakest in him was coming out—distortion, prejudice, and self-pity." He came at length to think coolly of the matter. He realized that, while he had been too literal in his account of persons in his home town, he had not been literal enough in regard to himself—had not looked deep enough into his own motives, and had been too much inclined to play the spoiled genius.

He realized that, indeed, he could not go home again—he could not take refuge in any of the childish evasions to which he had been inclined, of which we have given some account.

He must take a new and forward direction, and defend himself against his atavistic yearnings (back to the ancestral cave, back to the mother's womb). He could not escape from the truth of life either in the nostalgia of childhood, or in romantic love, in fame, in Europe, in country life, in lyricism, estheticism, in party, or in any substitute for his lost father. He found that none of these would work for long. None of them would satisfy the spirit that was in him, which demanded something less illusory and less egotistic.

But this took time. And the last book is mainly a record of the process by which he was weaned from his two most persistent obsessions—love and fame. It is a novel and a work of the imagination by virtue of the brilliancy with which this process is dramatized without, one feels, any failure in autobiographical truth. First these passions must be gratified. Webber was not content with the success of his first novel. He recognized its many imperfections. He feared that it might prove, like so many first novels, a flash in the pan, and that genuine and solid fame might escape him. And so he struggled with toil and sweat and in desperate loneliness to "find the way"—the right and truthful and artistic way—in his second book. And it was not until after the publication and great success of this that his spirit was free from the selfish grip of this "last infirmity of noble mind."

In the meantime he had witnessed an impressive exhibition of the hollowness of fame, its insufficiency to meet the demands of the soul. He met in England the great and famous novelist who had publicly given him such enthusiastic praise. Lloyd McHarg had been spending some time in various European capitals fêted by prominent men in all walks of life, tasting the wine of literary glory. His love for companionship and excitement had led him on from one festive occasion to another, in which his lavish and generous spirit had been spent on many an unrewarding Babbitt, and he now seizes eagerly on Webber as a soul with whom he can have more

satisfying converse. He carries him off on a whirlwind automobile excursion across the face of England. But the strain
has been too much for him; his inexhaustible energies give
out. He suffers a formidable collapse, and soon gives up the
ill-considered project. But it is not the physical breakdown
that is most alarming. He is a man of extraordinary powers of
recuperation. It is the sense we have of spiritual disillusion.
The fruits of fame have proved but Dead Sea apples. He is
too great a spirit to be satisfied, even for a time, with this unnourishing food. It is in the desperate effort to find what his
soul craves beyond personal distinction and triumph that he
drives himself so desperately from one excitement to another.
Lloyd McHarg is a vivid presentment of one of the most attractive and picturesque figures in our literary world. There
is nothing mean or unsympathetic about it. But for George
Webber, it is made to symbolize the inadequacy of fame to
satisfy the deepest needs of the spirit.

The inadequacy of love was symbolized and dramatized in
a series of still more vivid and fascinating scenes all grouped
about a party given by Esther Jack and her husband. There
is no abatement in George's love for her, or none that he will
acknowledge to us or himself. But he has come to associate
her too certainly with a way of life which is false and oppressive in its social and moral implications, from the toils of
which he must at all cost free himself if he is to go on as an
artist in the pursuit of truth. It is a life luxurious and refined,
which brings with it all the gratifications of power and distinction. Esther's set is made up of hard-working and talented
people. Even the financiers are liberal-minded, condemning
the social crimes that are represented at the moment by the
execution of Sacco and Vanzetti, and favoring all progressive
movements in art and politics. They are charming and urbane, and even lovable in their way. But their livings are
derived from exploitation of the poor, from political corruption and economic oppression. Their luxuries and refine-

ments, their freedoms and indulgences, are had at the cost of cynical complaisance in the face of every betrayal and perversion. George's very love for Esther is made possible by a moral code on the part of her husband in which there is no place for heartening faith. The brilliant company in which they move is one in which adultery and sexual perversions are cultivated and smiled upon as the normal way of life. And the entire social and financial structure—symbolized by the huge apartment building in which they have their charming home—is based on foundations insecure of human slavery and trickery.

George Webber had not wished to attend the Jacks' party. It was not merely his social awkwardness that made him unhappy there. It was the spiritual nausea he suffered in the contemplation of this way of life, and his profound sense that as an artist he would be destroyed if he did not make a clean break with it all. "Could he write truthfully of life as he saw it, could he say the things he must, and at the same time belong to this world of which he would have to write? Were the two things possible? Was not this world of fashion and of privilege the deadliest enemy of art and truth?" So now his very ambition as a writer made it necessary for him to give up the worldly prizes for which he had striven and of which he had dreamed from boyhood on. "There had to be a higher devotion than all the devotions of this fond imprisonment. There had to be a larger world than this glittering fragment of a world with all its wealth and privilege. Throughout his whole youth and early manhood, this very world of beauty, ease, and luxury, of power, glory and security, had seemed the ultimate end of human ambition, the furthermost limit to which the aspirations of man could reach." But now "he had sensed how the hollow pyramid of a false social structure had been erected and sustained upon a base of mankind's blood and sweat and agony."

It will be seen how "socially conscious" Wolfe had become

with the realizing of his personal ambitions. And that is indeed the most remarkable feature of this final volume in comparison with those that went before. The emphasis has passed from the cloudy sentimental cravings of the ego to the clear dictates of the super-ego, from love and fame and power to the consciousness of brotherhood, the voice of the social conscience, and the aspirations of the citizen devoted to the common good. The Jacks' party takes place just before the stock-market crash of October 1929. Webber's years in Brooklyn were the years of greatest suffering among the poor and homeless. The business depression brings on the failure of the bank in Libya Hill, the bankruptcy of the city government, and the complete collapse of the crazy structure of greed and speculation in that booming town.

The mature and successful George Webber has become more sensitive to the social injustices of our world. He notes the way in which Rutherford Bland supports himself by usurious charges on money lent to negroes, some of whom in the course of years pay continuous tribute to him for a loan of five or ten dollars, long since spent. "The practice," Wolfe notes, "criminal as it was, was a common one, winked at by the local authorities, and but one of many similar practices by which the unscrupulous white men all over the South feathered their own nests at the expense of an oppressed and ignorant people." He gives a long and vivid account of the Federal Weight, Scales, and Computing Co., of which Randy Shepperton was an employee. He shows how they drive their salesmen to create a need where there is none and make sales to persons who cannot afford to buy; how the most successful of them are rewarded by a "week of play" at some resort at the company's expense, which is a kind of Roman orgy. He considers "what this tragic spectacle of business men at play meant in terms of the entire scheme of things and the plan of life that had produced it." And he sees how ruthlessly their faithful servants are thrown off on the world when a bankrupt and oversold public can no longer enable them to keep up their quota. He shows us homeless men in New York seeking a refuge in the foulness of the City Hall comfort station, competing for places in the W.C. as shelter from the wintry cold, while near at hand luxurious citadels of wealth and privilege rear themselves proudly in every direction. In London, he observes the oppression and contumely suffered by the unprotesting poor. In Berlin, he witnesses the reign of terror and distrust, the suppression of literature and free thought, and is told that there are plenty of Nazis at home, eager to tell us what we may read and believe, eager to denounce anyone whose independent mind leads him to opinions different from those of the mob.

He comes to realize that the old forms and systems are no longer adequate to realize the ideal of American democracy. But the businessmen of the nation have not realized this. They think that all they need do is start over again on their career of salesmanship, competition, expansion, speculation, and exploitation. They must be made to understand that they "can't go home again." They cannot return to the methods of selfish individualism and greed. There must be instead "a complete revision of the structure of society as we know it." The artist can no longer remain absorbed in his Sorrows of Werther. He must no longer think of himself as a special and superior breed, for "in order to belong to a rare and higher breed one must first develop the true power and talent of selfless immolation." He must give up his intense and passionate concern for his own petty interests and designs in favor of an equally intense and passionate concern "for the interests and designs of his fellow men and of all humanity." His function will be to maintain "the plain and searching light of truth" in a world where it is threatened with extinction.

It will be seen how completely in his social attitudes Wolfe has put himself in line with the other typical novelists of our times—with Dos Passos and Caldwell, with Farrell and Stein-beck. From a Byronic sentimentalist he has made himself a social-minded realist. From a frantic individualist, he has be-come a proponent of the collective conscience and aspiration. In the political alignment of our day, he has ranged himself, along with all our great literary figures, distinctly on the left.

It is true that the final chapters, in which his social phi-losophy is explicitly set forth, are among the thinnest and least satisfying of all his writing. Wolfe had no gift for intel-lectual abstractions. But some of this feebleness can be laid at the door of unavoidable haste. He was after all a man, if there ever was one, who heard "time's wingèd chariot hurrying near." Again, it is true that his motives in turning from an egocentric philosophy were obviously mixed, that something of rationalization enters into all his account of his personal reactions, and the old Adam (meanness and prejudice) was strong in him to the end. But only the saint is free from im-purities of motive, and conversion may be no less sincere for being late and difficult. Besides, it is as easy to rationalize a move to the right as a move to the left. And I see no more reason to doubt Wolfe's honesty than that of the others who took the same direction and professed the same faith.

What distinguishes him from the others is the decidedly romantic, transcendental and poetic tone of his social think-ing. He is as far as possible from economic materialism, from the kind of realism which puts its faith in data and the phys-ical "facts." It is the spiritual bankruptcy which he deplores, whether in the complacently prosperous or in those whose house of straws has collapsed. The scores of men in Libya Hill who committed suicide after the bubble burst did so be-cause they had no spiritual resources—had never had that within which would give a meaning to life and make it worth living after the loss of their flimsy fortunes.

The social malady in America he traces back to something in our make-up not unrelated to our idealism and our poetry of the heart. Throughout his work he returns again and again to that wistful seeking in the night which he considers so characteristic of American youth and manhood. He finds significant those groups of boys and men who stand about the corners on Saturday night, vaguely waiting, hoping vaguely for something, they know not what, to assuage the boredom of their lives and bring them excitement and satisfaction. It is the want of fulfillment for this unworded craving to which he attributes so much of the ruin of character and life which we see on every hand—so much of dissipation, corruption, frenzy and nameless evil. Our culture, he seems to say, has failed to provide the right and liberal pabulum for our lonely and hungry spirits; it is because of this that our little towns are "lost," with all the people in them. But this same craving and seeking is at the root, I think he means, of our best ideals —our democratic dream, which will not cease to hold us though all the old forms and systems should be destroyed. It is out of the heart that comes corruption and ruin, and it must be from the heart that will come restoration and regeneration.

Thus far I have done no more than outline the principal themes and thought-development in the series of Wolfe's novels. Having these in mind, no one should have any difficulty in following the line of his intentions. Every incident, every character can be accounted for in terms of these themes and their contrapuntal development. The only criticism that can fairly be made on the structure of these novels is that here and there details may be developed beyond what is necessary for the unfolding of the thought. This is autobiography before it is fiction, and the artist may be carried beyond measure and symmetry by his desire to work in every item of his actual experience. But apart from that, the form of the thing is as clear as that of a tone poem of Richard Strauss, an opera of Wagner, or a symphony of Tschaikowsky.

* * *

Few readers, to be sure, are greatly concerned with the architectonics of fiction. Most will be more interested in what I have said as a statement of Wolfe's thought than as a demonstration that his work has form. And I have not yet found time to comment on certain important features of his work which would amply make up for want of structural form even if it were marked and grievous—his power in the creation of characters and scenes, the extraordinary relish he takes in every phase of human experience, the force and beauty of his descriptions, and the lyrical splendor of feeling with which he records a poet's reactions to human life and destiny. I cannot possibly do justice to any one of these within the limits of this chapter; and once again, as in the case of Faulkner, I must reconcile myself to leaving some topics virtually untouched rather than give to Wolfe too dominant a position in comparison with the others. He certainly tops them all in range and stature; but there is hardly one of them who is not his superior in some point of human truth and artistry.

To begin with what is, after all, the main business of a novelist, he has an undoubted genius for the creation of characters and setting them in scenes that bring out their quality. There is in these four books the matter for dozens of novels. There are literally dozens of characters who, by their vivid colorfulness, their individuality, their drollness and eccentricity, make one think of Dickens, and who, by their fierce vitality, their tragic perverseness, the insuppressible force of life that is in them, go beyond Dickens and make one think of Shakespeare or Ben Jonson. They are all, it seems, extraordinary; and yet we believe in them, not as we believe in the creations of romance, but as we believe in verified freaks of nature. And they are not freaks. For we have seen their like; we recognize the motives and conditions that made them what they are. And if they carry their passions and peculiarities to fabulous lengths, we cannot doubt the truth of the words they utter, the special things they do which no one would think of inventing, and which carry the very accent of individual truth.

We do not question the thunderous tones of old Gant summoning his children from bed in the morning, or the way he makes the great fires roar in the stove. We do not doubt that Eliza Gant had a car in the shed which out of thrift she had never used nor even allowed to be driven. We can see the expression of scorn and disdain on the face of Ben confronted with the general stupidity of the world; we hear the irritation in his voice; we feel the greatness and tenderness of his spirit, the love that everyone has for him, and the way on a summer afternoon they crowd round the office where he sits announcing the baseball scores. We witness the marvels of salesmanship accomplished by brisk and stammering Luke, and his raging torrent of stammered indignation over the indignities suffered by his brother at the hands of the police. We know how Uncle Bascom Pentland winces at the obscenity of John Brill ("Oh, vile! vile! vile!"), but cannot help laughing at the jokes of that vulgarian. We know the many affectations of speech of Francis Starwick, his foppish way of saying, "Quite!" and the maddening way he has of praising all things French, with his silly phrase, "The whole thing's there!" We hear how Creasman the nurse expostulates with the drunken surgeon McGuire for taking so hard the infidelity of his mistress, a married woman—"Haven't you learned yet, with all you've seen of it, that a piece of tail is just a piece of tail, and that in the dark it doesn't matter whether it's brown, black, white, or yellow?" And we hear him answer drunkenly: "Creasman, you got a dirty tongue. . . . Don't like to hear a woman talk like that. . . . Never like to hear a dirty-talkin' woman."

No two of his characters are to be confused; no two of them speak alike, unless they are anonymous muckers of Brooklyn or Manhattan. The speech is differentiated by class and individual, with a thousand specialties of tone and idiom and dialect. There is the racy language in which Aunt Maw tells her stories of Zebulon County before the Civil War. There is the tone of the Irish boarding house in Boston; the tone of Old Wakefield defending the Grand Army Post against the upstart impudence of the American Legion; the tone of Daisy Purvis suggesting a change of dishes for breakfast or lamenting that 'is Grace, the Duke of Basingstoke, has been reduced by oppressive taxes to sell his estate in Gloucestershire, leaving him only his place in Devonshire, his place in Yawkshire, and his hunting preserve in Scotland. There is the tone in which Judge Bland refers to the leading citizens of Libya Hill —"as eminent a set of sons-of-bitches as were ever gathered together in the narrow confines of a single pullman car."

All of Wolfe's characters are remarkable—more than life-size—gargantuan in appetite, prodigious in suffering, furious in their passions, gigantic in physical stature, extreme and unmeasured in all things. It is partly the vigor of his writing that gives us this sense of dealing with a race of Brobdingnags —the way he plasters them with adjectives and superlatives. But if we are inclined to think it is verbal exaggeration, he confounds us with facts, with actual circumstance and idiosyncrasy, which bear him out in his extravagance.

And above all it is by their speech that his account of them is borne out. This has the indubitable ring of truth about it. This is not the invention of melodrama, but the actual speech of men and women. And it renders convincingly the sense men have of the intensity of their own feelings and the unparalleled greatness of their sufferings and wrongs. The torrent of complaint to which George's sister Helen gives vent on the station platform—every burden is laid upon her, and there is no peace to be had, no peace to be had in the world— this corresponds exactly to the lonely obsession of her sleepless nights, with their endless repetitions of fear and anguish. No one has rendered better than Wolfe the pitiless candor of speech between kindred and intimates when unrestrained by the code of reason and politeness—the violent recriminations and passionate self-justifications, the savage invective, the blind anger in which things are said which can never be taken back and scars inflicted that can never be healed. The quarrels between Eugene and Eliza Gant, between Eliza and her children, between George Webber and Esther Jack, are among the most convincing scenes of fiction.

And not less convincing are the moments of peace and assuagement, of wisdom and vision, that drop mysteriously upon them when their passions are spent and their nerves discharged and voided of their evil humors. Most touching is the scene where old Gant, near to death, in a moment of tranquillity, after eating part of a chicken prepared by his wife, proudly informs his children that "no one else can cook a chicken like your mother." It is small and belated amends for all the sorrow and shame he has caused her in his life, but it was between them at this point an act of high magnanimity. It is enough to bring tears to our eyes, and it makes us hear again "the still sad music of humanity."

One thing that saves the work of Wolfe from being depressing is his enormous gusto—the satisfaction he takes in every aspect of the human spectacle, in every appeal to the senses and the appetites. Zola or Huysmans cannot match him for discrimination and assiduous collection of smells. His specialty is the smells of childhood—good smells and bad, the smells of vegetation and food and industrial products—the smells that render for the child the qualities of things and bring him the most vivid sense of his vitality, his livingness —the smells associated with emotion and memory, nostalgic smells recalling things long past or promising fulfillments in the future—shameful and humiliating smells—the enchanting odor of wood-smoke and of burning leaves—the scents of spring and the parched odors of summer and the passionate invigorating smells of autumn, of cooling earth and mountain winds and sodden leaves. Rabelais cannot match him for celebration of the joys of the palate and the joys of the eye in contemplating things to eat. The icebox of the Pierces is a litany of fruits and meats and savory vegetables. Juicy beef-steaks and divine sauces march continually through his pages; sparkling wines and foaming beer and musty ale and heathery highballs are like refrains to his psalm of life. And not less the blond voluptuous bodies of women haunt his imagination.

In this appeal to the senses, it is not so much the thing itself as the idea of the thing that intrigues him. It is the thing as characteristic, as capable of being distinguished and being put in sounding and savory words. It is the precious thing as worthy of man's estate, the proper furniture of his abode, his due perquisite as a spiritual being and lord of the universe. And this applies, *a fortiori*, to landscapes and seasons, the beauty of nature and the physiognomy of the earth, all more lavishly presented than in any other contemporary novelist and in a vastly more extravagant vein of poetry. No one has written more eloquently of mountains, of summer sunrise in a garden, of French cities and the English countryside, and of the "grand and casual landscapes of America." No one has done greater justice to the sleepy back streets of small towns, the dreary lengths of lamplit city streets in winter, and to all the riot and intoxication, all the splendor and misery, of Manhattan and its manswarm. No one has better rendered the passion and romance of travel by train, the power and mystery of locomotives, the changing aspects of the country as you pass from one region to another, as from the glamorous and dreamy South into the magnetic and prevailing North. Wolfe's heroines love to lie awake all night in their pullman berths with curtains raised, spying out the marrowy and shameful secrets of towns as the train pauses at the station, thrilling with the mysteries of human nature in its furtive and nocturnal phases.

Nothing human is alien to him, and it is ever the emotional essence, the quality of the living experience, both as it is seen from without and as it is felt within, which he is eager to catch in the net of words. Above all, it is the intangibles of inner experience—the loneliness and wordless longing of men, the pathos and grandeur of the spirit, the long, long thoughts of youth, the beating of strong wings against the bars of our temporal cage. And then there are the long and wide views of the manswarm in its crowded haunts, across the continent and down the centuries, the sounding of the wells of memory, the visions of lost time and of the ever-flowing river of humanity.

Such are the themes on which he spends himself with tireless passion, directing upon them a furious and unremitting battery of words drawn from the literary arsenals of all the world. I have compared the structural form of his writing to the music of Wagner, Strauss and Tschaikowsky. These three composers come naturally to mind in connection with Wolfe, because in his verbal style he has much the same qualities of romantic declamation and exaggeration as they have in their music. I have sometimes referred to his writing as Southern rhetoric on the rampage. And I think it is not too fanciful to associate Wolfe's inclination to extravagant and ornamental writing with something in the tradition of Southern culture which one finds in authors like Edgar Poe and William Faulkner. The defeated and impoverished South is acutely conscious of its gentility and tarnished elegance, and often strives to compensate with these for what it lacks in fortune and efficiency. It sometimes makes one think of a poor countryman of proud lineage trying to dazzle his prosperous city cousin with graces and refinements never learned in store or bank. Both Wolfe and Faulkner have brought to the contemporary novel an outmoded romanticism of feeling and fancy. And in their styles one feels that they have raked the attics for cast-off finery.

Wolfe uses three or four times the requisite number of words for anything he wants to say. He makes the most prodigal use of adjectives, and not merely simple adjectives of description, referring to specific qualities like color, texture, temperature; but still more those adjectives that are intended solely to enlarge and exalt the subject in the realm of emotion. Everything is superlative, gigantic, unique, mysterious, magical, impossible, unutterable, intolerable, and of an extreme degree of intensity, whether of beauty or terror. The adjectives and phrases go regularly in pairs, or in long tumultuous series, with a high percentage of sonorous Latin words and words abstract and vague in connotation. It is an inflated style, in which everything is blown up to many times its natural size. It is a drunkenness of words. There is an excessive repetition of emotional words, as if the author were reciting an incantation, or trying to put the reader under a hypnotic spell.

Then pity is there, is there at once with its dark face and sudden knife, to stab us with an anguish that we cannot utter, to rend us with its agony of intolerable and wordless regret, to haunt us with the briefness of our days, and to tear our hearts with anguish and wild sorrow. . . . And oh! for beauty, that wild, strange song of magic, aching beauty, the intolerable, unutterable, ungraspable glory, power and beauty of this world, this earth, this life, that is, and is everywhere around us, that we have seen and known at ten thousand moments of our lives, that has broken the sinews of our lives asunder as we have lashed and driven savagely down the kaleidoscopic fury of the years in quest of it, unresting in our frenzied hope that some day we shall find it, hold it, fix it, make it ours forever—and that now haunts us strangely, sorrowfully, with its wild song and aching ecstasy as we lean upon the sills of evening in the city.

It is a style often tawdry and sophomoric, not even keeping to the natural rhythms of prose, but swollen into pentameters —flaunting the finery of Milton or Byron.

Or in the black dark of some forgotten winter's morning,/ child of the storm and brother to the dark,/ alone and wild and secret in the night/ as he leaned down against the wind's strong wall/ towards Niggertown,/ blocking his folded papers as he went/. . . . Deep as the tides of time and memory,/ deep as the tides of sleep the river runs/ . . . and presently, just for a few brief moments as it swept along/ below the magic and familiar hill,/ he caught a vision of the great white house/ set proudly far away up on the hill/ and screened with noble trees. . . ./ Even while he stared within his mother's flesh,/ she was an adolescent girl, orphaned of love,/ knowledged in grief and loss and bitterness,/ and strong in hopeful fortitude. . . . We reach for life with all these traps and nets of words,/ our frenzy mounts up with our impotence,/ we try to keep and hold some single thing/ with all this fecund barrenness of print,/ and the sum of it all is a few blown papers in the wind.

This lapse into blank verse—rolling iambs ranged in fives —became with Wolfe a habit, a kind of vice. I do not suppose it was a conscious trick, and that he worked it like an organ stop. He simply fell into this strain whenever he felt the mounting sense of the poetry of his thought. I am not sure that I know just why this mixing of verse rhythms with prose is so offensive to an ear tuned either to fine poetry or to fine prose. I know of only one first-class prose writer who is guilty of the practice. Thomas De Quincey sometimes indulges in it in his most sentimental moods. And even with De Quincey it is a blemish. Wolfe has been much influenced by De Quincey, as anyone can see who will compare, say, the peroration of his sketch, "Death the Proud Brother" (in the volume, *From Death to Morning*), with various passages in De Quincey's *Confessions, The English Mail Coach,* and his chapter called "The Affliction of Childhood." There are the same elaborate apostrophes to abstractions like Death and Sleep, the same extended parallelism and musical repetition of phrases, and the same passages in meter. Or rather not the same. For Wolfe has not De Quincey's ear for the niceties of rhythm and sound. He is much further from the classical sources of De Quincey's labored eloquence. And what in

De Quincey is a venial offense often in Wolfe comes very near to being a mortal sin.

I do not think the purist's objection to the confusion of prose and verse is merely conventional or pedantic. To begin with, there is the incongruity growing out of conflicting ranges of association. The use of meter in prose writing is like wearing a boiled shirt with tennis shorts or sporting a sweatshirt at a formal dinner. And then there is the tendency to pad the phrase in order to round out the pentameter, serving to reinforce the already too strong drive toward lushness and redundancy. With that there is the disposition to play up emotion at the cost of sense, landing our writer in sentimental moonshine. There is the temptation to windiness and fustian. There is danger that the pseudo-poetry will drug the senses and blunt one's feeling for the subtle and varied rhythms of prose. Altogether it is a hazardous and dubious indulgence.

However, I do not wish to lay too much stress on this matter nor browbeat any reader who may happen to enjoy what so upsets me. I do not mean to say that, on the whole, this writing does not carry one along with it. There is in Wolfe a power of feeling and imagination that overrides a hundred faults. And in any case, the heart of man is naturally at home with bigness and inflation; the heart of man is windy and romantic, doting on words that flatter and bamboozle.

It is a mad and frenzied style. And the hero of these pages is a mad and frenzied man. He tells us so himself a hundred times, and often we wonder whether he is not telling the literal truth about Thomas Wolfe. There is more than a hint of paranoia in the behavior of Eugene Gant and George Webber; and we wonder whether, if Wolfe had lived, these symptoms might have appeared in aggravated form. At least, we did so wonder until the final book appeared, with its assurance that sanity at length had gained the upper hand. The emotional unbalance of adolescence was unduly prolonged

into the period of manhood. But with success in his vast undertakings, the fever abated and something like calmness
supervened. And with greater calmness there was a notable
abatement of lyrical frenzy in the style.

But even in the earlier volumes, our judgment of the work
was not too heavily affected by the madness of its manner.
That it was far from a model of classic reason and order we
must admit. But that it was thereby less human and representative—no. Madness is but the final term of the contradictions and propensities common to us all. Madness is the breaking point of human nature driven to distraction between its
ideals and its limitations. It is in a sense the most human of
our states of mind, for it is the gauge of our discontent with
reality. This is a romantic point of view, and Wolfe is the
most romantic of realists. That is why, to many readers, he
will seem the most satisfying of the eight authors of our
group. He has more to say than any of them on what man is
like in his heart.

We may be glad indeed that in *You Can't Go Home Again*
Wolfe came out of his period of *Sturm und Drang*. But it
would have been matter for regret if he had never passed
through that period nor left his cloudy luminous record of it.
It is a pity that we can look for nothing more from his fervid
and magical pen. But we have just begun to enjoy what he
left us when he died. We have scarcely begun to assimilate it.
He is still very much a writer of the moment. And it will be
long before he becomes that thing of the past, a specimen in
the literary museum.

X. ERSKINE CALDWELL

The Comic Catharsis

"And if I laugh at any mortal thing,
'Tis that I cannot weep ..."
— BYRON

X. ERSKINE CALDWELL

The Comic Catharsis

Erskine Caldwell is probably the best example we have of the artistic imagination working consistently in matter of concern to the social conscience, and yet not subdued, like the dyer's hand, to what it works in. By this I mean that, dealing consistently with data of the most obvious economic and sociological significance, he does not treat it in the manner of sociological treatise or reformist propaganda, but keeps—in his novels and short stories—within the strict limits of esthetic presentation. And the result is, curiously enough, that he is the cause of bewilderment and scandal to many serious and cultivated readers. For intellectual cultivation and moral seriousness do not necessarily mean a capacity to enjoy works of the imagination on the esthetic level. The enjoyment of art is natural enough to men in general, cultivated or uncultivated; but a certain measure of cultivation is only too likely to confuse a reader with other than esthetic concerns, and moral seriousness may lead a man to attribute frivolity and corruptness to a work in which matter of conscience is treated artistically.

The human spirit, on its moral and practical side, is given to self-distrust, anxiety and dread. It dreads unsettlement, distraction from its strenuous aims, and division of its forces. This sort of fear is natural enough, and grounded in experience of our own limitations. We know that our energies are limited, and we fear that anything short of a total devotion of them to our practical aims may lead to weakness and ineffectualness in action. And in our concern that right should prevail or that we should be successful in our endeavors, we are likely to forget that the narrowest view of any subject is not the most correct view or that most likely to promote success. We forget that our very concept of rightness is based in the notion of value, and that in the notion of value there is an appreciable tinge of the esthetic. Value is attributed to that which yields satisfactions to human beings; and satisfaction is as clearly an esthetic concept as it is a moral one.

We have no reason to conclude that puritanism is the code most likely to promote the general well-being of the race or even to insure its survival. In any case, it would be a dreary world in which men's imagination was confined within the strait-jacket of puritanism. There is some reason to think that the spirit is better for an occasional holiday. If nothing else, this brings a certain relaxation to the strained nerves. Our psyche is a mechanism of great complexity and varied needs. It craves exercise of various kinds. Even in matters of conscience, the esthetic and the scientific approaches may be purgative and salutary to the spirit—calming it, stabilizing it, raising it above the anxiety and nervousness of the puritan attitude. More than that, they may be broadening—the esthetic and the scientific attitudes; they may lead to discriminations and refinements, to wise attenuations and humane indulgences. Given a spirit of some gravity and depth, every gain in breadth and imagination is in the end an ethical gain, an enlargement of moral wisdom.

The inexperienced or unimaginative reader may at first blush question the social seriousness of Erskine Caldwell in such novels as *Tobacco Road,* such tales as those included in the volume, *Kneel to the Rising Sun.* He may take him to be a cynical soul, one that delights in the miseries and degradations of human nature. And that, because the life of poverty and humiliation is presented in the manner of fiction, without expository comment, in speech and action, pointed up with the resources of humor and irony and imaginative high lighting. For such a reader it is important to explain that Caldwell is the author of several volumes of sociological studies of the utmost earnestness based on careful personal observation, notable for their plain matter-of-factness in reporting conditions, for the obvious concern with which the writer views the unfortunate conditions reported, and his modest but serious effort to suggest means of ameliorating these conditions. In 1935 he published *Some American People,* based on leisurely travel through the Pacific Northwest, the Middle West, including Detroit, and through certain counties in Georgia, and on numerous interviews with persons in distress mainly as a result of unemployment. In 1937 he published *You Have Seen Their Faces,* with some sixty or seventy odd photographs by Margaret Bourke-White, now Caldwell's wife. The pictures represent typical men, women and children from the poorer agricultural regions of the South, whites and negroes, seen in their homes, in the fields, in church, in school, in the chain-gang. Each picture is accompanied by some characteristic sentiment or statement about himself from the person represented. There are, also, serious essays on the history and present state of tenant farming and share-cropping, and the economic and social condition of the people involved.

The ordinary comfortable reader, unacquainted with government reports and other statistical studies, will be amazed and shocked at the desperate conditions reported by Caldwell even in those deepest years of the long depression, and above all with the almost universal state of hopeless misery prevailing throughout large regions in Georgia, Alabama, Mississippi, Louisiana, Arkansas and Tennessee. If the reader's patriotism requires him to assume that extreme injustice and bestial living are not possible under our system of government, he may be inclined to discount some of the plain facts reported by Caldwell, and still more to question the connection he draws between the facts and certain of our economic and industrial arrangements. Caldwell does not make any such comparisons; but one is led to wonder whether, under the system of tenant farming in the South either whites or negroes are much better off economically, politically, or morally than peasants in Poland, Russia, Yugoslavia or even China, at least in time of peace. One wonders whether the condition of the unemployed workman and the homeless girl turned prostitute in Detroit (with a municipal permit) is so much better than that of similar groups in London, Marseilles, Birmingham or Budapest. Such thoughts are highly distressing to a patriotic American, and the easiest way to deal with them is to deny the facts, to assume that they are grossly exaggerated, or to attribute them not to any defect in our social and industrial arrangements but to the natural shiftlessness and depravity of shiftless and depraved people.

There will be ways for the reader to break the force of the facts presented by Caldwell. But even so, the average open-minded person cannot fail to be impressed either by the facts or by the serious intentions of an author who has taken the pains to inform himself so widely and to set down what he has observed in so straightforward and matter-of-fact a manner. He will realize that he is dealing here not with an irresponsible sensation-monger and spinner of shocking tales. And then if he will look into the studies of federal officials and the staid publications of Southern University presses, he will realize that what Caldwell is dealing with is a set of conditions having their roots in a long and tragic industrial history. He will come back to Caldwell's pamphlets and ponder his general assertions—that the plantation system was one which resulted in the rapid impoverishment of the soil over a region larger than Europe; that the share-cropping system was one in which a small class of owners enriched themselves at the expense of millions of men who could never make enough from their toil in the cotton fields to free themselves from debt; that in vast sections the owners regularly forced the white share-croppers to give up the land and replaced them with negroes who could be more easily cheated and exploited and maintained in a state of virtual serfdom; that the system of tenant farming represents a still more hopeless outlook than that of share-cropping, a still lower level of subsistence and decent living.

The chief theme of Caldwell's writing is the agony of the impoverished land, which has now so nearly reached a state of complete exhaustion in large sections of the old South that it is only a matter of time (he thinks) when the dust storms will cross the Mississippi and extend the desert to the east. That is the material basis for the social conditions which he sets forth in his stories. But, of course, it is the people who interest him as a student of human nature; and with the people, it is not so much their material sufferings as the moral degradation which follows steadily on the decline of their material well-being. It is the illiteracy passed on from generation to generation of those who cannot find time to go to school or have not clothes to wear to school. It is the benighted ignorance of people without books or newspapers, often without even a church, with little more than the superstitions and traditional error of bygone ages to guide them in the conduct of life. It is a state of poverty which leads parents to marry off their twelve-year-old daughters in order to have one less mouth to feed; the isolation which makes incest as common as marriage. It is the diseases caused by malnutrition and excessive childbirth which turn women into sickly slatterns. It is the dull indifference to others' sufferings, the want of imagination and sympathy, engendered by a life obsessed by the constant craving for food. It is the shiftlessness and improvidence and irresponsibility wrought by habitual want of hope.

This is not the exclusive subject matter of Caldwell's stories. But it is the central and dominant theme. The pitiful state of the white agricultural laborer in Georgia is what possesses his imagination above all other subjects. And it is clear enough that it has taken deep hold on the moral feelings of this son of a Presbyterian minister. He might have dealt with this matter as an economist, as a sociologist, as a social reformer—as the John the Baptist of some gospel of social reorganization. He has, I think, the seriousness for any of these ways of dealing with his subject. But it so happened, by some chance of birth or circumstance, that this man is by bent an artist rather than a scientist or propagandist. As a student at the University of Virginia, as a mill hand, a farm laborer, a cook, it was not for sociology that he was preparing himself; it was for a still more serious endeavor, as it must have seemed to one of his temperament—that of molding the stuff of life as he knew it in the shapely and significant forms that gratify the esthetic sense. He was one destined to follow in the steps of Chaucer and Dickens, of Balzac and Gorky.

We say, in a general way, that the artist is one interested in beauty and skillful in the representation of beautiful things. But that—as beauty is frequently understood—is a very limited definition and leaves out of account a large part of the action of the esthetic faculty. The artist is one interested in shape and color and quality and in the representation in some medium of whatever is characteristic in shape and color and quality. He appeals to our own interest in the *characteristic* and the pleasure we take in its representation. And so it comes about that anything in human nature may be the subject of artistic representation provided it can be shown as characteristic; and that the reader esthetically disposed can take a positive pleasure in the skillful representation of anything characteristic in human nature, provided only that his pleasure is not inhibited by some more powerful emotion. The human spirit is many-sided, and we are fortunately capable of taking esthetic pleasure in subjects which, on some other view of them, are painful or disgusting. This is a happy provision of nature, since it makes it possible to reap a benefit from circumstances which otherwise might be a total loss to us as human beings. Thus it comes about that a spirit as serious and feeling as Erskine Caldwell's may take a positive pleasure, on the esthetic side, in the representation of characters and situations which are abhorrent to him as a moralist or a man of feeling.

Caldwell's subject in *Tobacco Road* (1932) is a Georgia farmer whose dominant instinct and passion is to grow cotton. He is, that is, a potentially useful and productive member of the community. He is living on land once owned by his grandfather, in a tumble-down shack whose present owner has retired to Atlanta and left it with all other buildings on the land to be occupied without rent by the families established there as long as it will stand up. The land was once fertile, but was long since worked out. Lester Jeeter's father planted exclusively cotton and completed the exhaustion of the soil; the land he and his father lost parcel by parcel as it was sold to meet their debts. The present Jeeter owns nothing whatever but a change of clothing, a bed, and a few utensils. He has long since been unable to secure credit at the store or the bank; and for several years he has not planted even a small patch of cotton, not being able to get either seed or fertilizer. He and his family are slowly starving to death; but, being deeply religious, he cherishes the hope that God will somehow come to his relief before it is too late.

Jeeter's wife has borne him many children, but only three are left. Some have died, and most of them, at an early age, have abandoned the farm to marry or seek employment in the mills. The Jeeters cannot read or write; they have no means of locomotion but a broken-down car whose tires will not hold up the distance to the nearest town. They have no communication with the children who have left them, and have only the remotest notion how many grandchildren they may have scattered about the country. Jeeter's wife has long suffered from pellagra; she is a languid drudge; her sole preoccupations are a little food, snuff (which cannot be had), and a proper dress to be laid out in when she dies—of this she has small hope or prospect. They have one daughter, a young girl whom they cannot marry because her hare-lip makes her so repellent. Her father has long meant to take her to town and have the hare-lip sewed up; but with no money and less enterprise, he has always postponed it for something more urgent. The still younger Pearl has already been married; her husband earns a living shoveling coal for the railway. But Pearl is not old enough to be fit for matrimony; she is a frightened little animal, who cannot be persuaded to sleep with her husband or to speak a word to him. In the Jeeter household there is also a grandmother, so old and decrepit that no one ever has anything to say to her except to scold her. Everyone resents her existence, and they give her nothing to eat out of their scanty store. She lives on odds and ends; and she is so hungry that she regularly gathers wood and lights the fire three times a day in hopes there may be something to cook. Then finally there is the son Dude, who spends his time bouncing a ball against the side of the house to the evident damage of that rickety structure.

The moral status of these people is hardly recognizable as human. They do possess language; they wear clothes; they handle implements; they can do the manual work of men; and they believe in "God." That is about all there is to distinguish them from other mammals. Their most distinctive traits, as human beings, are their extreme ignorance and incompetence and their shocking moral callousness. And yet there is nothing to suggest that they are naturally depraved—if such a thing is conceivable—or even that they are naturally shiftless and improvident. Everything distinctively human in sentiment has been withered away by the unremitting pains of hunger. And their shiftlessness is too natural a growth of conditions so utterly hopeless. It is true that Jeeter might have moved to town and become a mill hand. He might have secured for himself and family that measure of humanity which is possible under such conditions. But his not doing so is the result of his one virtue—his deep attachment to the land, his instinctive craving to be productive.

Now, the Jeeters are representative of conditions widely prevailing in the agricultural backwaters of Georgia and elsewhere in the South. Here is matter of the highest sociological and moral interest. And the esthetic problem is this: what angle of approach to take, what tone to assume, and how dispose the subject matter so as to distill from this painful stuff the esthetic pleasure derived from the skillful representation of the characteristic in human nature. There will be several possible solutions of this problem according to the gifts and temper of the author. Caldwell's solution is something like this. He will choose a succession of incidents, characteristic and familiar, but such as to bring out in high relief the childish naïveté of these people. By any civilized standard their behavior is outrageous in the extreme. At every turn they violate our notions of decency and good sense. They are like animals of some inferior species, or like little children not yet trained in the ways of adults. But they are dressed and labeled men; they have the stature and responsibilities of adults. If we judged them strictly as men, we should have no choice but to be severe. But what prevents us from judging them so is their utter helplessness and ignorance, their incredible innocence, their total lack of awareness that their behavior is shocking.

There is an element of paradox and incongruity here, and

there is an element of surprise, which—as the psychologist
will tell us—is of the essence of comedy. Indeed, these characters fit in rather well with the special theory of the comic
developed by Henri Bergson in his famous treatise on Laughter. Bergson holds that the comic effect results where human
beings, who are supposed to act like human beings, with intelligence and the flexibility of free agents, exhibit instead
the wooden and automatic movements of puppets. We take
them for human; we look for the human reaction; we are
all prepared for that; we are caught with sudden surprise by
movements not proper to human beings; the shock of this
recognition, this absurdity, releases some nervous spring
within us, and we laugh.

There are many kinds and degrees of comic effect, and
the reaction varies with the other emotional elements present in the experience. There are absurdities of action which
we do not need to take seriously since the moral sense is not
deeply involved; and we can laugh at these with a heartiness
not dampened by any feeling of the gravity of the subject.
Where subjects of grave importance are concerned, our
laughter may be checked or minimized. Not many readers
will laugh very heartily over the absurdities of the Jeeters.
The play taken from *Tobacco Road* introduces many circumstances which we do not feel to have a moral bearing, like
Jeeter's childish shrinking from the touch of cold water, his
disinclination to washing. So that one laughs more over the
play than over the novel. The Jeeters are not funny in quite
the same way as Mr. Micawber or Sairy Gamp or Tom Saw-
yer or Tartarin. The moral seriousness of the situation is
too near the surface for us to laugh. But the essence of the
comic is there, and it is what saves the day. It is our defense
against the intolerable degradation of human nature. It furnishes a sorely needed psychological relief. And it is what
keeps this sociological matter within the limits of imaginative
art.

It is very hard to draw the line between the tolerable and the intolerable in the esthetic representation of degraded types. It is doubtless in the last analysis a subjective matter, depending on the point in the reader's make-up where re-actions of disgust come in to inhibit all pleasurable response. There are two early novels of Caldwell, *The Bastard* and *Poor Fool* (both 1930), in which, I must acknowledge, the accumulation of horrors is so great, and the elements of re-lief so slight, or non-existent, that the net result for me as a reader is much more displeasing than pleasing. I have the im-pression, here, of a beginning writer exploiting his knowledge of the underworld and rather straining his imagination to pro-duce a sensational effect. Prizing Caldwell as I do, and wish-ing to put him in the best light with the intelligent reading public, I find myself inclined to soft-pedal these early efforts, hoping that only specialists will come upon them, or only persons already favorably disposed toward the author from the riper products of his genius. Brutal criminality so holds the center of the stage in these books, and even perversion, that the comic effect is hardly to be discerned. And while many of the characters may be regarded as mentally sub-normal, as well as illiterate, there is not the same suggestion about them of childish innocence, let alone sweetness of dis-position, which lends a wistful charm to the mellower crea-tions of the author's maturity. And there is not the same provision of lighter incident to reduce the strain of the cruel and shocking.

In *Tobacco Road* a large part of the story is made up of misadventures with an automobile. What particularly im-presses the reader is the criminal waste of money where money is so tragically needed; and that becomes a symbol of the childish incompetence of this whole outfit. But along with this the automobile episodes are so contrived as to bring in every other aspect of their topsy-turvy life, and mainly in forms that are consistent with the comic spirit. Sister Bessie, the preacher woman, has cast her eyes on Dude, and the Lord directs her to make him the successor to her late husband as her partner in the gospel business. Sister Bessie is not pleasant to look on; she is not of a suitable age for Dude; Dude has no present inclination to matrimony or to the gospel business. The whole idea is essentially immoral. But neither Sister Bessie nor Lester Jeeter has the slightest notion that there is anything wrong about it. Their type of religion and their social code are not such as to admit these niceties of sentiment. Sister Bessie lives in a shack as ruinous as the Jeeters'; but she has a banking account of eight hundred dollars, left her by her late husband. And that is a great attraction to the Jeeters. This eight hundred dollars wisely disposed would go a long way toward lifting these people out of the bog in which they are sinking. But the sole idea of Sister Bessie is to buy herself a fine new car in which she and Dude can tour the country and spread the gospel abroad. This, under all the circumstances, is an idea as criminal as it is cockeyed.

None of these innocents has the remotest idea of the values of anything more than a jar of snuff, nor of the precautions one takes in bargaining not to be cheated by the other party. It does not occur to Sister Bessie that she might spend part of her fortune on a car and keep the rest for incidentals, like sewing up Ellie May's hare-lip or stocking the Jeeters' larder or providing Lester with cotton-seed and guano for the summer's crop. (This doesn't occur to Lester either.) She marches straight into the dealers'; they ask her what priced car she wants, and she says an eight hundred dollar car. Within five minutes they have sold her a car which, for aught we know, cost them no more than three hundred dollars, and with insufficient oil to run any distance. Such a thing as oil is beyond their range of vision. Neither she nor Dude knows anything about driving, or that there is anything that should be known. Dude's sole concern is for the noise he can make blowing the horn. Within two days they have broken the back spring, smashed the right front fender, torn off the left front headlight, burned out the bearings, ruined the upholstery carrying firewood to town, and killed two persons—a negro driving his cart, and grandmother run over in a heedless maneuver. They are less disturbed by the deaths of the negro and grandmother than by the damage to the upholstery.

The moral obliquities of these people are on all fours with their mental defectiveness. And their mental defectiveness is that of a race of people who have never been able to sign their own names or read a newspaper, whose cultural heritage is that appropriate to men without land, without money, and without experience of any of the simplest amenities of life.

XI. ERSKINE CALDWELL

Substitutes and Compensations

"Extremes meet; and qualities display themselves by the most contradictory appearances. Any inclination, in consequence of being generally suppressed, vents itself the more violently when an opportunity presents itself."

—Hazlitt

XI. ERSKINE CALDWELL

Substitutes and Compensations

In *Tobacco Road* the mentality of the characters is not merely defective. It is confused and topsy-turvy. They do not associate ideas in the manner of civilized beings. And that is one reason why we are both amused and scandalized by the peculiar tie-up in them between piety and shameless conduct.

In *Journeyman* (1938) Caldwell has given us a glimpse of the type of religion that flourishes among the more ignorant of the poor whites. The central character is one Semon Dye, an itinerant preacher, who is making a few days' stay with Clay Horey, a slightly more prosperous Jeeter. Semon Dye is a big lanky ruffian with a gift for words and a dynamic personality, who first charms people by his wit and wisdom and then rules them with a tyrannous will. His being a forceful and sincere preacher does not exempt him from the natural proclivities of a man. He can drink corn liquor with the best. With women he has had a wide and uniformly successful career. He is well along in years, but his day is not yet done. "My day is a long way from being over. But when my day is done, it's going to have been a long one." His will brooks no opposition; and when he cannot have it peacefully he imposes it at the point of a gun. He shoots the negro man who comes to protest against his seducing his yaller girl. He wins Horey's car with loaded dice, and then wins Horey's young wife Dene. And all this while he maintains his intention of preaching to the people of this district on Sunday.

Sunday afternoon they gather in great numbers at the

schoolhouse; and he holds forth all the afternoon and evening. He takes the greatest pride in his gifts as a preacher. His aim is to make every man and woman "come through," and also to take up a generous collection. "Coming through" is the final stage in a series of convulsive seizures in which one thrashes round on the floor, tears one's clothes, loses consciousness, and generally comports oneself like an epileptic. It appears to be a means of throwing out the devil, cleansing oneself of sin, and attaining a state of holiness. It offers intense and gratifying excitements to people on the lower and more brutal cultural levels, and serves to compensate them for the normal boredoms and deprivations of their starved lives.

Semon Dye on this occasion has a very large measure of success. All but one of the company come through, including the preacher himself. But one person holds out, and that, the one he is most concerned to bring to God—the prostitute Lorene. She is, he considers, the worst sinner in the schoolhouse and most in need of his ministrations. And when he comes to after his own paroxysm and finds that he has not been successful in this supreme instance, he regards the whole thing as a failure. He has met a will that is stronger than his. He is so deeply moved by his unsuccess that he even forgets to take up the collection. He spends the night at Horey's and the next day drives off in Horey's car with Lorene. He has an understanding with her by which he will go fifty-fifty with her on her earnings "putting out."

The reader accustomed to some reasonable logic in religion, some association between religious faith and moral conduct, will be shocked and perhaps incredulous, and may be inclined to think that Caldwell has made this all up out of whole cloth. But the phenomena he is here presenting are too well and widely known to admit of that conclusion. That he has selected and arranged things dramatically so as to point up his idea, that he has rounded them out and developed their inherent logic, is no doubt true. But the fact remains that, on certain cultural levels, there is a curious discontinuity between religion and morals, in spite of the religious emphasis on the concept of sin. Caldwell does not suggest that Semon Dye is a fakir or a hypocrite—that he takes no stock himself in sin and hell fire. The point is that he trades upon them like any commercial exploiter. They are his stock in trade; and his success in putting them across is the chief source of his personal pride. But it does not follow that he is a good man himself, or that he has a genuine abhorrence for sin. On the contrary. He is going to preach to the people of Rocky Comfort. He is confident that they are sinful, and the sinfuller they are, the better he likes it. He is superior to the settled preachers with parishes. "I'm a traveling, ranging, journeyman preacher, and I know just about every sin there is in Georgia. And then some!" Sin is the means by which he works these people up into a lather of fear and delight. They are afraid of hell fire, but they get a great kick out of his allusions to sin, above all the sins of the flesh, and his suggestive anecdotes in illustration of the theme. It is all a part of the orgiastic excitement which culminates in the "coming through." They will feel purified and assuaged on the following day, but it is not so certain that their morals will be improved.

As for himself, it never occurs to him to carry over his religion into his personal conduct. He seems to enjoy special exemptions as a man of God. "I'm Semon Dye. The Lord don't have to bother about me. He sort of gives me a free rein." And other people take him largely at his own valuation. There is something demonic about him that lifts him above the ranks of common men. His personal charm is so great, he offers so much relief from the monotony of life, that even those who suffer most at his hands are sorry to see him go. He is to Rocky Comfort what a poet is to New York or Paris. "Somehow I sort of hate to see Semon go away now and leave us," thinks Horey. "Semon was a sort of lowdown scoundrel, taking all in all, but he had a way with him just the same. I couldn't put up with a rascal like him very long, because I'd sooner or later go get my shotgun and blast away at him. But it does sort of leave a hollow feeling inside of me to know he ain't here no longer."

Such a tribute from Horey has something pathetic as well as something funny about it. It makes one feel not merely how benighted these people are, but how terribly boresome a life it is that craves to be relieved in ways like this. Religion is but one of the means by which these people seek diversion, make up for the meagerness of their lives, and violently discharge their pent-up nervous energies.

Another classic indulgence of the poor white is the lynching of negroes. This is Caldwell's subject in the most recent of his novels, *Trouble in July* (1940). When Sheriff Jeff McCurtain hears of the search for Sonny Clark charged with rape of a white girl, he is of two minds whether to try to prevent a lynching or to go fishing for several days till the trouble is over—so he may "keep this lynching politically clean." But he is ordered by Judge Ben Allen, the political boss, to check the mob—Judge Allen has been telephoning round and has decided it is politically expedient at this time to have no lawbreaking. Meantime, Jeff gets concerned over possible harm to another negro whom he had in the jail on some minor charge and whom the mob has taken as a hostage; if they cannot catch Sonny Clark they will string up Sam Brinson. Sam Brinson is a man whom Jeff regards as a special friend of his, even if he is a nigger, and he starts out on an earnest search for him. In the meantime it has been made perfectly plain to the reader that Sonny Clark is entirely innocent of the charge against him; he is a well-meaning kid; the white girl Katy had taken a fancy to him, and Mrs. Narcissa Calhoun, fanatical nigger-hater, had come up at a critical moment and drawn the wrong conclusion. The case is so clear that even Katy's steady will not believe a word of the charge; he tells her she is nothing but a cotton-field slut, and she ought to be ashamed to let people lynch a little nigger boy that's as innocent as the day is long.

But even if Katy were willing, it is too late to stem the tide of passions that have been roused in the mob. Katy's father is a man who has killed more than one nigger, and white man too; and the whole mob are driven on by sadistic instincts that fiercely crave expression. There are many obscure impulses which mark the negro as the natural victim of their savagery. The white men's fear of the negro raper is in part an oblique reflection of their own craving for negro women. Their own offenses against the negro can be given a kind of vicarious atonement through the crucifixion of the black man. There is doubtless a kind of perverse religiosity involved. The negro becomes a physical symbol for men's consciousness of sin. The puritan fanatic, Narcissa Calhoun, is circulating a monster petition to send all negroes to Africa where they came from. This involvement of nigger-hating with religious fanaticism is a theme of other Southern writers; it is prominently featured in Faulkner's *Light in August*.

Above all, with the white man who is nearest to the negro in economic and cultural status, there is the powerful urge to establish and maintain a superiority which there is little to confirm but the difference of color. The negro is an economic competitor with the impoverished white; he is capable of enduring poverty with more good nature; and sometimes it is the humiliating experience of a white man in the country store to see a nigger with more money to spend than himself. This had happened to one of the men in Caldwell's story, and it made him feel "it was getting about time to clamp down on a nigger again. . . . Hell, this is a white man's country! Ain't no nigger going to flash a bigger roll of money than I can, and me not do nothing about it. It ain't right." But more than all these psychic inducements to victimize a negro is the simple need for animal excitement strong enough to make up to these poor creatures for boredom and deprivation, for their almost total want of civilized pleasures and diversions, for empty bellies and the threadbare poverty of their emotional life.

These men have no grudge against Sonny Clark; many of them, like Jeff, are fond of individual negroes. They have themselves no disposition to spare the purity of white women; no reason to think of Katy Barlow as anything but a perverse little chippy. But all that is beside the point. The emotional drive is beyond reason. They must have blood; and when once they have strung up Sonny and riddled his body with bullets, when now Katy has a change of heart and confesses that her charges were baseless, they cannot stay the force of their passion till they have stoned to death the white woman whose honor they had set out to avenge.

I will not stop to note the strain of comedy that runs through the gruesome incidents of this story, or discuss the esthetics of the case; but instead pursue a little further the law of psychic compensation which operates so regularly in Caldwell's fables. In *God's Little Acre* (1934) there are two main examples of this psychic phenomenon, objectified in the two leading persons of the story. The one is Ty Ty, a Georgia farmer, and the other is Will Thompson, his son-in-law, a weaver in a South Carolina factory town. Ty Ty is possessed by the fantastic notion that there is gold on his land, where he lives with his family and his negro dependents; and he and his sons have spent all their time for years in a frenzied digging in the sand. They live in a shack in extreme indigence, though the land is good enough if they would work it, and all their toil is labor lost. As his son-in-law tells him, "You can raise more cotton on this land in a year than you can find gold in a lifetime." But the search for gold is more exciting; it is a perpetual fever in the blood. It sheds a transcendental glamour over lives otherwise so dull and drab.

In Will Thompson is dramatized the most common and powerful of all psychological mechanisms for supplying excitement and value to a life deprived of normal gratifications. Sexual indulgence is normal enough, to be sure, and calls for no fancy explanation; but when it takes the uncontrolled and extravagant course that it does with Will Thompson, with such an accompaniment of imaginative fireworks, so much of ritual and ostentation, we cannot but feel that it stands for more than itself, expresses more than itself—that all the frustrated urges of flesh are being poured through this one narrow bottleneck, all hungers of flesh and spirit finding their satisfaction here, finding in the lurid intoxication of sex their one supreme, their one available and adequate symbol.

And this impression is borne out by the way in which the other characters respond to the reckless anarchism of Will's behavior. They all of them share, at least vicariously, in the ritual of his loves. Ty Ty is an old and widowed man; but still for him the sexual act is a matter of passionate and sympathetic interest. It is a matter of pride to him that his daughters and daughter-in-law are women of such great beauty. He is forever celebrating in most open fashion their bodily attractions, and without offending the women themselves. But it is the younger man who becomes the effective instrument of his senile lusts. It is not enough for Will to have married his daughter Rosamund; in the course of this brief story he must also mate with his unmarried daughter, Darling Jill, and with his daughter-in-law, Griselda. However grieved Will's wife may be at his infidelities, she cannot hold them against either him or the other women. Griselda and Darling Jill find that he is the one man, besides their father, who treats them as they like to be treated, with a kind of sacred and religious rage. And the father reflects that Will Thompson comes as near understanding the secrets of mind and body as he himself.

The sexual life of Will Thompson is obscurely bound up with his vocation. He is a weaver out of work, because the strikers have not the courage to go into the mill, turn on the power, and run it for themselves. He is filled with a burning desire to turn on the power at the mill, and in the end he loses his life when in carrying out this aim he is shot by the guards. His life follows a ritual of tearing and building. His turning on the power is prefaced by tearing his shirt to shreds; the weaving perhaps, in his unconscious mind, takes the form of repair and restitution. Before going to bed with Griselda he makes a speech, declaring that he will tear her clothes to pieces and look at her as God intended. His whole body becomes an almighty and omnipotent phallus, his mouth the instrument of the phantasy he is enacting. He becomes a god. The men have decided to arbitrate the strike, but he says they can turn the power on and run the damn mill themselves—he is as strong as God Almighty now.[1]

Under any circumstances there is something formidable and demonic in the spectacle of sexual impulse on the rampage. And when, as here, it overrides serenely all social bars and limits, it becomes positively alarming. Even Ty Ty acknowledges that the death of Will was a fortunate thing, since after all there were wives and husbands to be considered, and Griselda and Jill "would have made a mess that

[1] For much of my interpretation here and in the third paragraph below I am indebted to a highly suggestive article by Dr. Lawrence S. Kubie, the distinguished psychiatrist and psychoanalyst, in the *Saturday Review of Literature*, November 24, 1934. I must note, however, that Dr. Kubie confines himself to a study of the action of this story as an example of adult distortion of infantile impulses, indicative of pathological states in all the persons concerned. He does not, I think, suggest the specific cause or occasion for the development of these psychological disorders, and makes no direct connection between them and poverty or deprivation, though many of the points he makes might suggest this connection to one familiar with the whole of Caldwell's work.

the law doesn't allow." Given the jealous nature of men and women, such a course of action threatens the peaceful living which is Ty Ty's great concern. But for all that, there was something about Will that all the characters admired; there was something dazzling about his lunatic exaltation. He was the carrier and symbol of a Power to which they all did homage, as he was the means by which they all gave vent to the stifled cravings of their being.

Even the reader's imagination may be impressed. And that is no doubt the reason why this book became the object of prosecution on the part of those gentlemen who run societies for the suppression of vice. They are in general simple-minded gentry, incapable of distinguishing between incitements to vice in the young and childish and the kind of literature that makes its unprovocative appeal to the mind of maturity and to that alone. The representatives of literature came promptly to the defense of Caldwell, and by good fortune the ruling of the court was made by a man of judgment and intellectual cultivation. He justly pointed out that what we have here is an instance of serious realistic writing, and defended the autonomy of art against the assaults of anxious and unimaginative moralism.

He wisely refrained from going into the finer points of the question. It would take a psychological expert to trace the obscure ways in which the theme of sexuality is associated in this book with that of poverty and deprivation. Throughout, the theme of food-getting constantly recurs in the form of eating, biting, grabbing, sucking, licking. Nursing and normal intercourse become confused. The confusion of woman's function transforms men psychologically into fierce children. The women all become types of the mother, but no actual mothers are portrayed. The maternal rôle is twisted toward perversion and prostitution.

How much of this is conscious on the part of the author we can only guess. We should, I think, do wrong to underestimate the subtlety of Caldwell and his awareness of modern psychological trends. In the case of religious fanaticism, he certainly is deliberate in showing how hunger of the spirit battens on the same conditions as belly-hunger.[2] Of the sexual element in orgiastic religion he is certainly well aware. It is only reasonable to assume that, in *God's Little Acre,* he means to exhibit among other things the sexual instinct as it manifests itself in cultural conditions rooted in poverty. Sexual indulgence is there a substitute for the pleasures of feeding; and sexual hunger is, more than that, a form of spiritual hunger. It is shown running amok and fertile in social effects that frighten and dismay. But it has, for all that, its splendor and exaltation. For it is in part the manifestation of normal instinct, an evidence of vitality; and beyond that, it testifies to the presence of that spiritual hunger which it is easy to divert and drive into devious ways but which it is very difficult indeed to quite suppress and eradicate.

Hardest of all for the hunters of vice to bear is, perhaps, the spirit of comedy that presides over the conduct of this display. For persons of their mentality do not appreciate comedy. They have no inkling of its value as intellectual criticism; nor yet of the aid and comfort it gives to thoughtful men in supporting the else intolerable absurdities and paradoxes of human nature. The most constant of comic paradoxes in Caldwell is the utter innocence of his characters in the perpetration of outrageous acts. They know not what they do. For the most part moral depravity in his stories is the exact counterpart of mental obliquity. We might call it the obliquity of the folk mind; for it seems to represent the natural complexion of mind of the whole community on a given cultural level. Ty Ty mentions in company intimate details of his women's beauty with the completest absence of any sense that he is violating the proprieties.

[2] See *Some American People,* p. 263; *You Have Seen Their Faces,* p. 142.

There is often in Caldwell's characters a callousness in the treatment of other people which suggests a virtual unawareness of the others as human beings. Someone suggests to Ty Ty that albinos have a gift for locating gold and that there is somewhere in the county such an albino. He sets out at once and captures the albino with the help of a lasso. He takes the young fellow away from his wife, brings him home by force and keeps him prisoner in the barn. He shows him off to his friends in the kitchen as if he were some strange animal, discussing his merits as a gold-finder as if he could not hear or care what was said about him. When the albino boy begins gazing with wonder at the beauty of Darling Jill, Ty Ty for the first time realizes that he is a person like another.

This same callousness toward others is shown by the characters in *Tobacco Road,* where it is obviously associated with a state of chronic hunger. All the people in this story are so constantly concerned with the craving of their own stomachs that they have no imagination left for others' sufferings. If they do not worry about grandma or the nigger killed by the car, it is because they have never properly taken in the existence of other beings as real as themselves. In Caldwell's short stories the most cold-blooded cruelty is exercised against niggers or women by men who have never learned that women or niggers have serious claims on white men. The man who is most forward in shouting prayers in the church will not give his negro tenants enough fat-bacon to flavor their corn-bread or pay them compensation for the accident that cripples them for life. The Ex-Governor takes for granted that the young daughter of his white tenant is his for the asking, with or without her parents' consent, and that he need not even wait for the license to "handsel" her. He is mighty surprised and hurt when she lights into him like a hellcat, and "pretty near bites the daylights out of him." The girl's father was relieved, for he was not sure that her mother would approve of the Governor's project, but his reaction was not one of moral indignation. He was carried away by the joke of Daisy's getting the best of the Governor. He sat down in his chair on the porch. "He leaned back and started to laugh. He could not wait for his wife any longer. He leaned back and laughed until he slid out of his chair." [3]

The absurdity often lies in the contrast between a man's shrewdness and his stupidity. The most benighted general state of mind may coexist with the utmost cunning in the calculation of one's own interest. We call it animal cunning, and in a human being it is shocking and ridiculous. Or it may be the contrast of an office that calls for courage and responsibility with a cowardly or irresponsible character in the incumbent. Caldwell is fond of sheriffs who run away from danger or have more regard for community prejudice than for their oath of office. His young men may combine a complete want of sexual morals with the shyness of the chaste. They will spend an afternoon on a girl's porch vainly trying to get up courage to propose to her, and then ride over to the neighboring town to pick up a chippy. When one of them marries, he spends the day of the honeymoon playing pool, and he wakes up in the morning scared to death to find himself in bed with his wife. "What in hell am I doing sleeping in bed with a white girl?"

Strange flowers of humanity push up through this dunghill soil of cultural degradation. The negro Jesse, struggling against the wiregrass in his cotton, amidst the intolerable heat of the dry season, cannot bear to witness the suffering of his donkey; he shoots the animal and goes on sharpening the blade of his hoe. Another negro gives himself up to the law for shooting his daughter; he could not stand hear-

---

[3] References in this paragraph are to "A Knife to Cut Corn Bread With" and "A Small Day," both in *Southways*. In the two following paragraphs reference is made to the following tales in *Kneel to the Rising Sun*: "The Sheriff," "Candyman Beechum," "A Day's Wooing," "Honeymoon," "The Growing Season," and "Daughter."

ing her say she was hungry after his landlord on some pretext had taken away his share of the crop. The moral sense of the town asserts itself, and the sheriff goes home so as not to keep the men from freeing the negro.

There is no more self-consciousness about their humanity than about their inhumanity and meanness. The tale is told in the same dry manner. Behavior has the same air of being automatic and inevitable, the outcome of economic pressures and conforming to a primitive code. The characters have the same innocence, the same naïveté. Naïveté is the best single word for describing these people, and the best way to characterize Caldwell as a storyteller is to say that he is an accomplished master of the *naïve* style. His manner is plain and straightforward and without a touch of facetiousness or of verbal irony. There is an almost unfailing irony in the representation of character and action. But it is in the conception, in the arrangement of the elements, not in the phrasing or the moral tone. The story is told simply, and for the most part in terms suitable to the characters concerned. There is no elaborate attempt at dialect, but a modified colloquialism that gives the bloom and accent of the local idiom. There is no far-fetched rendering of the idiosyncrasy of thought; but within measure the author follows the rhetoric of the characters' minds, their manner of associating ideas, their way of regarding things. It is all done with deftness and precision, without heavy emphasis, but with a soft-fingered sureness in the disposition of "values." And so, without interference, the characters expose themselves in all their simplicity, perverseness and absurdity.

Caldwell is fond of having his story told from the point of view of young boys, incapable of judging or of quite fully understanding the import of what they recount, thus adding another irony, and a kind of innocence too, to the chronicle of adult folly. He has a tender regard for the sensibility and the opening minds of children, who represent a healthier state of mind than most of the adults he pictures, and a happier view of human nature. Some of the most charming of all his tales are those which open the early volume, *American Earth,* involving a young Southern boy of good family whose sentiments have not been hardened by adult suggestion. There is the story of the aunt who had come South to visit with the boy's family, and who wishes to train him in the tradition of the Southern gentleman. Under her direction he is trying to learn to shoot rabbits, though it goes against the grain to kill an animal of which he is so fond. Fortunately he misses his rabbit with his gun but frightens it so that he can take it with his hands. He brings it home alive and feeds it lettuce, leaving it free to come and go, much to his aunt's disgust. But his father is on his side in the matter, and his mother looks at him as if he had done the right thing after all.

But the author is fond (as an author) of whatever will lend itself to his special gifts for storytelling, will shape itself up significantly for the imagination. For Caldwell nothing is more fascinating than a certain simplicity of mind, whether it goes with a good or a mean disposition; and perhaps it makes more diverting patterns where the disposition is mean. That is something which the moralist in us is reluctant to acknowledge, that in human nature it takes an admixture of the ugly to make the most interesting patterns for the artistic imagination. The moralist shrinks from the mention of evil save in terms of abhorrence, and the puritan of today is inclined to deprecate any disposition to play it up as a subject of art. But the artist insists on the free play of his imagination. Prudence may support the puritan; but in the long run wisdom is on the side of the artist. Wisdom knows that evil will not be done away by ignoring it; that our passion for truth demands the recognition of evil, the examination of it. And wisdom knows that the most innocent of ways to deal with evil is the way of art, and one of the subtlest and most illuminating. Puritan prudence would have confined Caldwell to the way of the sociologist and reformer. But he is obviously more of an artist than he is of a sociologist; and his art is the means by which he gives life and body to what he knows of human nature. Without it, the world would be the poorer by so much of valuable knowledge and insight. Not to speak of the loss of many capital stories!

XII. JOHN P. MARQUAND

The Moonlight of Culture

"The soul doubtless is immortal—where
a soul can be discerned."
—Browning

XII. JOHN P. MARQUAND

The Moonlight of Culture

And now let us turn to a bird of very different feather.
John P. Marquand is a writer of the moment who has introduced us to a world as different as possible from either the
bruisers and bohemians of Hemingway or the Georgia poor
whites of Caldwell. His people are New England bluebloods.
There is nothing brutal or shocking in his subject matter.
He is a skillful and versatile artist. He writes like a man of
the world, with an irony mild in seeming, however blasting
it may be in final effect.

Marquand is not a recent arrival among contemporary
writers. His first title, *The Unspeakable Gentleman,* dates
from 1922, the year following Dos Pássos' *Three Soldiers,*
and three years earlier than Hemingway's *In Our Time.*
Before *The Late George Apley,* he had already published
nine works of fiction, several of them most entertaining and
successful. Of these I shall have very little to say. *Thank
You, Mr. Moto* (1936) is a smart and clever mystery story. It
weaves an intriguing plot round the experiences of a blasé
American lawyer living in Peking. He has fallen in love
with the cultivated life and passive philosophy of the Orient;
his most characteristic remark in any situation is this: "Well,
it doesn't matter." That, he thinks, is the summit of human
wisdom. Mr. Moto is a Japanese agent who knows his way
round in the complicated world of oriental politics, and who
saves the life of our hero when he has incurred the enmity
of a sinister and mysteriously powerful Chinese bandit.

There is, naturally, an American girl in the story; and it is natural enough, according to the code of romance, that in the end the hero should give up saying, on every occasion, "Well, it doesn't matter."

That, I think, is all that need be said about this book, except that the story is related with great skill, that the reader is led along from incident to incident in an entirely painless manner, and puts down the book with the feeling that he has stayed a long while in China at the least possible cost of trouble and money.

This is the kind of book that you read for your entertainment in moments of relaxation, and no one would think of making a critical study of Marquand if he had nothing more serious to offer. In his *Wickford Point* the leading man is a novelist much like the author of *Thank You, Mr. Moto*. He can write stories to order and fix them up to suit the demands of his editor, who knows what truth is like in the "half world of the editorial imagination." He is a professional writer for the market, and he always has a ten dollar bill in his pocket for his impecunious relatives. He is a Harvard graduate and he knows how to write. I suppose the success of books like *Thank You, Mr. Moto* made it financially possible for Marquand to undertake the more serious work of *The Late George Apley* (1937). The Pulitzer award to *The Late George Apley* led many people to read *Wickford Point* (1939), and so to perceive that it is a very good story as well as being a delicate and telling satire on certain phases of New England society. Marquand is now so well established in the estimation of critics and discerning readers that, if he has anything else to say, he will be sure to get a hearing. I don't know what more he can have to say; but what he has said already is arresting enough to give him a very respectable rank in American letters.

I will begin with *Wickford Point* and leave the place of honor in my discussion to *The Late George Apley*. For while

Wickford Point is the better story and enables the novelist to display more virtuosity in both narrative and characterization, the subject of *The Late George Apley* is probably more important, and that book is more likely to stand as the prime example of Marquand's art.

The subject of *Wickford Point* is the decadence and futility of New England people whose sole source of distinction is the intellectual accomplishments of their ancestors. This is an important matter in New England, where so many people borrow so much of their importance from the waning reputation of the old worthies, where there is often so little present occasion for the pride and self-complacency with which they regard themselves, the bland provincialism with which they look down their noses at people from Memphis or Milwaukee. The Brills of Wickford Point have their vogue in the world because their grandfather was the poet of that name who was called the Sage of Wickford Point. He was a very mediocre nature poet whom nobody reads any more except Aunt Sarah, and a rather stuffy old fellow. But he had been associated with men like Emerson and Hawthorne, and his descendants are invested with an intellectual aura and a social quality which they do nothing to sustain. Some member of the family who prospered in business has had the foresight to establish a trust fund for the maintenance of the old place at Wickford Point. Otherwise they would all have gone to the dogs long since.

As it is, Cousin Clothilde can sit enthroned in the living room, with her languid head propped against a pillow, can cadge cigarettes off of anyone who comes, send her cousin Jim to town for gin and ice cream from time to time, can wander on from topic to topic in a vague languid amusing fashion, and can keep together a household of persons even less competent than herself. Every month her bank account is overdrawn, presumably through some error in the bank, and she always owes money to Josie in the kitchen and to the college boy who mows the lawn. Besides Clothilde, there is her husband—her second—who is always off somewhere hoping to get in touch with someone who knows someone who might be influential in getting him a commission from Ford or somebody to do a mural. There is Cousin Harry, Harvard graduate, who relies entirely on his connections with people of the best family to secure some job for him, but has not the ability to keep any job he gets. He is the most insufferable snob of the lot. There is Cousin Sid, whose digestion is bad and who toys through the years with a variety of quasi-scientific projects. There is Cousin Mary, who would like to be noticed and loved, but who is doomed to be ignored so long as her sister Bella is anywhere near.

And then there is Bella, the beauty of the family. She is the leading woman of this story and is shown at full length. The legend with her is that she is not understood. She feels that she is different from everybody else, and it makes her lonely. She is always complaining to her Cousin Jim that she can't stand the situation in the family; that nobody ever does anything about anything. At the time the story begins, she has been married to the writer Joe Stowe and divorced from him. And it is not clear whether she will take up with her cousin, Jim Calder, another writer; or with a flashy New York broker; whether she will break up the marriage of the wealthy mooncalf, Avery Gifford, whom she has earlier thrown over for Joe Stowe; or whether she will get Joe Stowe to marry her again. He has made a great hit with his writing since their divorce and is on easy street financially. What she does in the end is to cut her sister Mary out with the Harvard professor, Allen Southby. Southby has fallen in love with Wickford Point and is glad to take Bella with the lot. Like all the men, he considers that she is lonely and rare and misunderstood, and that no man can have a more blessed assignment than to make her happy. We don't know how it will turn out, but we don't much care.

There are many fascinating characters. But, along with Bella, the pivotal characters are Allen Southby and Jim Calder. Southby is a typical little academic pundit and pussy-cat, who has written a successful book of criticism and—poor dear —would like to write a novel. Unfortunately he can't write. He is the kind of college don who smokes a pipe and drinks musty ale, has a cozy apartment wainscoted in pine, and goes in for old pewter. Instead of blood his veins run with some pale liquor, the essence of books. He comes from Minnesota and is after culture and tradition. He wants to write a novel about Wickford Point, which to his conventional mind is the essence of culture and tradition. When Bella agrees to marry him and settle down at Wickford Point, his cup runneth over. He has found the shadow of that great reality of which Emerson and Byron are the substance.

His opposite is Jim Calder. He has been brought up at Wickford Point and is fond of the old sweet place. But he is fed up on its pretensions and futilities, and his strongest instinct is to free himself from its stultifying tyranny. Perhaps it is Bella who for years stands in the way of his emancipation. And when she has shown him fully what she is as a representative of the bogus tradition of fineness, it is a business woman from New York—a straight-shooting and clear-seeing person without involvements in the sentimental tradition— who pries him loose.

So they both have what they want. The academic pussy-cat who cannot write—the exile from Minnesota—can bask in the . . . in the moonlight of so-called culture. The true man of talent can get out into the sunlight of reality and do his work in a world where life is still going on.

I shall have but a word to say of the technical artistry displayed in this book. One of its great achievements is the way in which the author weaves together into one pattern the Wickford Point of the present with that of the past—bringing out many a subtle note of likeness and contrast and investing the whole with atmospheric depth and glamour. Another kindred achievement is the skill with which he handles the cut-back so as to bring into the story of the present moment all that we need know of the earlier history of Bella and others. Many an amusing anecdote is woven into the fabric of the story. The characterization is handled with deftness and with admirable indirection. The dialogue is very good in its mildly comic way. Many of the lines would go well on the stage. Indeed, if one occasionally is tempted to characterize the whole thing as light-weight, it is partly because the man is so smart, so clever, so up-to-the-minute. You think, what a fellow he would be in the drawing room, and you wonder whether it is possible for genius to be so good in the drawing room. I will give you one instance of his stagey cleverness in dialogue. Pat Leighton has come up from New York to see Wickford Point and to pry Jim Calder loose. Cousin Bella is jealous and catty, and it is up to Pat to hold her own.

Bella had opened her compact again, and now she dabbed her lipstick across her lips and looked down at the little mirror and then up at Pat.

"All the women here are trying to catch the men," she said.

She spoke casually but the room was quiet after she finished. She put some more red on her lips, but her eyes never left Pat's face.

"Yes," Pat answered, "that's true. I hadn't thought of that."

"I don't see why people don't understand," Bella said, "that men don't like to be pursued. It's biologically wrong and it never does any good, and besides it's frightfully inartistic. Don't you think so?"

"Yes," Pat answered, "I suppose it is."

Bella closed her compact again and shrugged her shoulders. . . . "No man with the guts of a guinea pig likes it," she said. "If you have to run after a man it simply means that he's getting tired of you—and it's so damned silly not to see it. There's something about Jim that makes all the girls run after him. Isn't that true, Pat?"

I have never seen Pat Leighton lose her temper, and she did not lose it then.

"Have you ever tried?" she asked.

Bella gave a light, amused laugh.

"Why, darling," she said, "I've never had to try. I do hope you're not taking anything I've said personally."

"No," said Pat, "I'm not taking it at all."

"Because I never meant such a thing, of course," Bella said.

"Of course you didn't," Pat answered. "It would look so like personal pique, wouldn't it? And you're always so nice about such things, Bella."

"Well, darling," said Bella. "I'm so glad you didn't misunderstand me. You're always such a determined person—so executive."

"Yes," Pat answered, "I suppose I am."

"I know you are, dear," said Bella. "Everybody says so. Well, I must be running upstairs. Jim, there's something I want to tell you, if you're not busy, darling."

"Never mind it now," I said.

"Well," said Bella, "I'll see you later, darling."

"Not if I see you first, honey bee," I said.

I have expressed the view that *The Late George Apley* is more likely to stand as the prime example of Marquand's work. And that in spite of the fact that *Wickford Point* is more amusing, is a better story, and is in many ways a finer example of the author's craftsmanship. The reason is twofold. First, the subject is on the whole more important. And, secondly, there is a certain monumental simplicity about the portrait of George Apley that compensates for the want of story interest. The futile heirs to a literary tradition are, no doubt, a sufficiently common subject of observation in the New England states. But George Apley represents something more common both there and elsewhere, and a much more solid and influential element in American society. These people depend upon nothing rarer than the possession of great wealth over several generations. There is, to be sure, a special local color to the Apleys derived from the fact that their wealth was made in Massachusetts and not in Illinois or Montana; but this difference is a fleeting one. Much the same phenomena develop anywhere in the country—one might almost say, in the world; and with a little change in minor details, this might be the picture of a man of inherited wealth in Philadelphia or in Baltimore.

George Apley was the head of a family of English extraction who had first settled in Massachusetts in 1636, and had enjoyed substantial prosperity from the beginning. They had been merchants, traders by sea, manufacturers, bankers and lawyers for three centuries. They had been Harvard men since the time of John Apley, who graduated in the class of 1662. Some of them had been rather relentless in their business methods, but never had anyone questioned their uprightness or probity. The main source of their income during the life of George Apley was the textile mills at Apley Falls, admirably managed by his Uncle William. There had never been any labor trouble at Apley Mills. In the days before the Civil War, Southern newspaper writers declared that "a slave on the average Southern plantation had better food, care, and greater prospects of happiness than the workers in the Apley Mills." But there were no labor troubles, because, as George Apley wrote in a memorandum to his son, "there were no such things as unsound ideas, and no desire for shoddy luxuries. There was no desire for luxuries because there were none, and I wish it were the same today." In his own lifetime there was some effort to unionize the Apley Mills, but this was prevented by the good management of Uncle William. "It was William Apley who arranged for the arrest and expulsion not only of these agitators [the union organizers], but of a certain subversive group within the Mills, whose names had been placed before him." Thus delicately does George Apley allude to the institution known as the blacklist.

One thing that distinguished the Apleys from the vulgar

rich was their frugality and freedom from ostentation and luxury. When, as an old man, George Apley had been visiting his son John in New York, and took the train back to Boston, it was the son who arranged for his father to sit in a parlor car, for the first time in his life; and the father protested against this unnecessary expense. As a little boy he received a letter from his father enclosing the gift of ten cents and celebrating the delights of economic spending. "Here is your ten-cent piece and do not forget that this is a good deal of money. Think of it this way: it can buy ten lead pencils or two tops and a string, or enough candy to make you very ill. Please try to think carefully exactly what you want, before you spend it, because there is no satisfaction as great as spending wisely, and few annoyances as great as feeling that money has been wasted."

This does not mean that the Apleys were stingy. They were very lavish with that part of their income which they did not turn back into business. An early ship-owner and trader endowed the Apley Sailors' Home to the tune of two hundred thousand dollars, thereby making up for any exploitation to which he may have subjected the seamen who enabled him to make his fortune. Our George Apley was a very prudent investor; he did not suffer great reverses in the depression that followed the War; and he was able to be of the greatest assistance to those of his kin and class who had not been as wise as he. Giving away money was one way of extending one's power and declaring one's virtue. When his cousin John Apley disgraced the family by divorcing his wife and marrying another woman, George had the satisfaction of putting on the screws financially. The only satisfaction that John had in the matter was the thought that he would never have to speak to George again. George Apley took most seriously his public obligations as a man of wealth. He accepted without question the conventional view that every rich man should collect something for the sake of the community. He did not care for oriental bronzes himself, but he went to great pains to build up a choice collection of these objects.

The two strongest motives of an Apley's life were his New England conscience and his pride of family. His conscience took the form of doing what he was supposed to do. The standard of behavior was social convention. As George Apley wrote his son: "As time goes on it will become more and more evident that you are a part of a society whose dictates you must obey within certain prescribed limits and in every walk of life we must give way to the common will. Yes, there are certain things one does and others one does not do." He is referring to his son's desire to be excused from spending his vacation at their extremely boresome and stodgy summer resort and instead allowed to visit a friend at Bar Harbor. "One of the things which you and I must not do," says his father, "is to neglect our duties at Pequod Island." As a matter of fact, the father is as much bored as the son with his supposed duties at Pequod Island, but he has formed the habit of not questioning them. "There are certain duties one cannot escape," he continues. "I do not know just why. I consider this quite often without arriving at any just rationalization." There his pen slips. He doesn't mean rationalization; but rationalization is the best way of dealing with something as little amenable to reason as his subjection to habit and convention.

When it is looked into, it would seem that every duty of the individual is referred back to some dictate of society; and society is another name for the pride of family and class. The chief care of George's parents during his Harvard days was that he should see the right people; and the right people were simply those whose wealth and family connections would make them sure of election to the right clubs. The same preoccupation dominated his feeling about his son's college career. He tells him that his first object must be to "make" the Club, and that everything else, including his studies, should be secondary to this. He hopes very much that John will not do anything that will give him the reputation of being peculiar. During the World War, George Apley becomes a patriotic fire-eater, and he regrets that his son, who is in the army in Texas, should hold views which the father considers "pacifistic." He reminds him that his name is up for the Province Club in Boston, and that such things might damage his prospects of election.

Marriage is the one act in which the individual is most bound to sink his personal feelings and seek the interest of the family. That means at all costs marrying into your own class; and in Boston your own class is taken in a very strict and limited sense. George Apley, while a Harvard student, entertained a strong, high-minded love for a girl named Mary Monahan. She was an intelligent, sensitive girl of fine character and natural good breeding; but she came of an Irish-Catholic family without wealth or social standing; and it goes without saying that he gave her up to marry the woman whom his parents considered suitable. His wife was a good deal of an invalid and remained heavily dependent on her parents all her life. His married life was uneventful, but clearly it was a bore from the beginning, and all it brought him was more duties and obligations. The only sentimental indulgence recorded of him was bird-hunting excursions with a married woman who shared his interest in natural history. No one ever thought for a moment that this relation was anything but platonic.

In connection with this type of Boston marriage, and the elaborate preparations made for the great sacrifice, Apley's biographer remarks naïvely that many Boston men fail to survive the excitement of the occasion. "The writer can recall, without mentioning names . . . several persons with the very best background who have disappeared from Boston on the eve of matrimony. Most of these have re-established their position at some time later, but two, to the writer's certain knowledge, have never been heard of since." George Apley did not often question the wisdom of the social dispensation of which he was a victim, though he did seem to realize dimly that it might be too much for some people. Writing to his son, with Mary Monahan in mind, he says: "You are reaching a time when you will find out what my own father pointed out to me at a very trying time in my own career: that family is more important than the individual, that a family must be solid before the world, no matter what the faults may be of a single member, that a family has a heritage to hand down which must be protected." And then he goes on to say: "Several individuals in my own generation have been sent to the South and West, where they are probably making new lives for themselves, but here their names are no longer mentioned." It is worth noting, by the way, that George Apley was always conscious of awkwardness and constraint in his relation to his children. And this seems to be typical of the Apleys. There was too great a burden of conscience upon them to admit of their indulging their affections naturally.

This does not mean that the Apleys were not persons of normal feeling. The emotional force which could not find expression in private life was sublimated in various ways. With George Apley it took the form of making him a fanatic on the subject of the Germans. He early made up his mind that, in the World War, Germany was synonymous with evil and the Allies synonymous with righteousness, and he was among the most active in developing the state of mind which brought the United States into the War. "When the *Lusitania* was sunk on May 7, 1915, he breathed a sigh of relief, for it was his opinion that his country would at last stand for the right." He was active in securing the dismissal of the conductor of the Symphony Orchestra, who was guilty of sympathizing with his fatherland. He was deeply concerned over the political menace of the Catholic Church. He observed how many tracts of land had been bought by the Church for schools and orphan asylums, all of them on rising ground, chosen, as it seemed to him, with amazing shrewdness from a military point of view. Though himself a Unitarian, his emotional trend was shown in his great enthusiasm for the revivalist Billy Sunday, to whom he made a contribution of five thousand dollars on condition that it should remain anonymous. After we went to war, he was active in many patriotic ways. He offered to furnish names of members of the Province Club who had shown their want of patriotism by advocating Peace without Victory. At his country place of Hillcrest he had the entire lawn plowed up for vegetables to help win the war, though plenty of fields were available for the purpose.

But the most dramatic manifestation of his emotional state, as well as his public spirit, was his effort to assist a certain reformer in his campaign to clean up vice in Boston. This brought Apley into disfavor with the politicians and the police, and he was framed. He was arrested by two policemen in a hotel room with some women of loose character; and while his innocence was absolute, things looked very black for him. At this critical juncture, when he was threatened with public disgrace, who should step in to save him but Mary Monahan, the pure flame of his Harvard days! Her husband was connected with politics, and the whole thing was arranged most satisfactorily to all concerned. Apley gave a sum for the upkeep of a South Boston gymnasium. The two detectives who arrested him voluntarily withdrew from the police force, and were given positions as watchmen at the Apley Mills. And, in the whole transaction, George Apley was simple-minded enough not to realize that he was compromising with the forces of corruption.

The social philosophy of George Apley was that of a man of inherited wealth, whose chief fetish is the conservation of what he has. He was not himself a money-maker nor a contributor to the production of wealth. But he took over almost unmodified the individualistic political economy which suited the great industrialists of the nineteenth century. He relied solely on the judgment of competitive business to correct the evils to which competitive business had given rise. The social measures undertaken under Hoover and Roosevelt were all to him so much socialistic nonsense. His views on the Sacco-Vanzetti case were those of President Lowell.

Well, the proof of the pudding is in the eating. The final test of a way of life is the quality of the living. George Apley had sacrificed his life on the altar of class and convention and the pride of the Boston brahmin. He had the satisfaction of knowing that he had always conducted himself truthfully, honorably and conscientiously. He could not tell himself that he was happy or even greatly interested in life. And he had many moments of doubt as to whether his way of life was rewarding. He had never allowed himself to get away from the confines of the Boston point of view or to judge anything independently. On a summer excursion in France, it seemed to him Boston had been with him all the while. Looking up a certain fascinating road in a French village, "I wished," he wrote, "that I might be walking up it to see something by myself and for myself without guidance and without advice. I wonder will I walk up any road alone?"

The wild place in the woods where he camped with a friend was soon turned into a family resort, well regulated according to the primmest Boston standards. One of the women insisted on getting them up every morning at six-thirty. Professor Speyer read aloud in the sylvan shade from good books. Boston propriety reduced all the women to frumps; they all wore the same uniform—flannel shirtwaist, khaki skirt, black cotton stockings and black sneakers. "I had thought on first coming to Pequod Island," writes Apley in a plaintive mood, "that we might get away for a while from certain things, that we might have a moment's breathing space, a respite from what we know so well and love so much. I suppose that this was rather too much to hope for. It sometimes seems to me that Boston has come to Pequod Island." He wonders whether their world is not a trifle narrow. "Do you suppose that it moves without any relation to anything else? That it is broken off from some greater planet like the moon? We talk of life, we talk of art, but do we actually know anything about either? Have any of us really lived?"

His children are even more conscious of the barrenness and emptiness of this way of life. And to the great distress of their father, they both make their escape from it. The daughter marries a newspaperman, and when he refuses to take a decorative position in the Apley Mills, goes to live with him somewhere in the wilds of Pennsylvania. The son gives up his clubs and all the prestige of his Boston connection and takes a place in a New York law office. And he flouts the Boston conventions by marrying a divorcee. It is their way of passing judgment on the futility of the Apley manner of life—their way of saying, Man shall not live by bread alone. I will not say, Boston brown bread! For that is a sweet and succulent mouthful compared with the thin wafer of pride and propriety on which their father had vainly tried to nourish himself.

I have included Marquand in my group of representative novelists mainly because of the feat he has performed of recovering New England as a subject for serious fiction. I may have been moved, too, by the wish to relieve the heaviness of a book that deals mainly with writers like Dos Passos and Farrell; and I feel that I am justified by the sheer artistry of these novels. But I admit that he does have a little the air of being out of place in this exhibit, and that because of what we may call a want of intensity in his art. He is the one among all these writers who might be felt to have picked his subjects not so much for their importance as for their smartness, for the scope they give to the author's cleverness. I do not mean to imply that the Apleys or even the Brills are not important social phenomena. What I mean is that Marquand leaves us a trifle uncertain at how deep a level of his consciousness these subjects have taken root. This is not a question of intellectual so much as it is of emotional concern. My review of the subject matter is sufficient to show that all the elements for intellectual appreciation are present. And yet somehow one feels that, in each case, the author has said to himself not: Here is something I have got to get out of my system; but rather: Here is a damn good subject for comic treatment.

It is very hard to put one's finger on the features in the work which correspond to this effect of emotional indifference to the theme. It is like temperature, and the only available thermometer is the reader's feeling. But we might take note of one point of technique which may have a bearing on this matter. The account of George Apley is given by a friend and admirer, a fellow member of the exclusive Berkeley Club, who is almost completely oblivious of the author's view of his subject. It was he who read the obituary notice of Apley at the annual meeting of the Berkeley Club, and his biography was undertaken on the request of Apley's son, who would like a franker, less conventional notice of his father. He thinks his father would like this in the interest of truth, which he prized in his way, "though he naturally did keep up his façade."

The biographer is rather shocked by John Apley's using the word "guts" in this or any connection, and wonders what the young man can find wrong with Harvard and Groton education. He tries to tell the truth as the son requests, but he almost always misses the point. He is aware that Boston is criticized for its snobbish self-complacency, and in the very act of repudiating the charge he manages to give a fine exemplification of it. "To us who know it and are a part of it there is nothing so unnatural in the preoccupation of a Bostonian with his environment; for order—so lamentably lacking in other cities—tends to make him so completely at home and so contented with his social group that he is unhappy in any other." The perfunctory reception of strangers is "due neither to pride in family nor to pride in intellectual attainments. . . . It is the intense congeniality of our own society which has its inception in a unique community of ideas resulting in a common attitude toward life." Precisely! When young George had his ears boxed by his French teacher with very good reason, he could not understand why the teacher should be dismissed from the school, and he told his father so. His father said he was too young to understand. The biographer comments in his usual dense and platitudinous manner: "Thus it is that a childhood life is filled full of imponderables. There are many things which a child does not understand, and I am not sure that the attitude of our fathers, of refusing to discuss certain matters with their young, was not fully as wholesome as the frank and detailed explanations which are retailed to the child of the present." Thus he manages to ignore the point of the episode—that the family pride and injustice of the father were allowed to override the better instincts of the child, who thus received one of his most impressive lessons in social conduct and the Apley code.

The style of the Berkeley Club biographer is uniformly trite and stilted, and a trifle flowery, suited to the literary pretensions of a Harvard graduate. But what he tries to say is often a little beyond his scope, so that he falls into many ineptitudes of expression. He uses "rationalization" where he means "reason" or "rationale." He speaks of society molding an individual "in conformation to its principles" where he means "conformity." He speaks of a brilliant and successful career which was "clouded by an unbalanced preoccupation over social injustices." He runs from flowery figurative into platitudinous literal: "These two had played together in childhood and had trod the same paths of youth with a similarity of upbringing which could not but make them congenial." He speaks of an "explanation—tedious though it may be, and one already consciously felt, if not consciously analyzed, by all who read these pages." Such writing is an ironic commentary on the Boston "pride in intellectual attainments."

Altogether, it is an ingenious and amusing device by which the apologist for the Apleys is made their prime betrayer. The trouble is that the method is pursued in such minute and fussy ways that it often misses fire. I doubt whether the casual reader is aware how badly this literary clubman writes, or whether, observing this, he realizes that the ineptitudes are his and not the author's. It may seem strange for me to complain of subtleties in Marquand after I have spent so much time defending them in Hemingway and Caldwell. But there is, I feel, a difference. In Hemingway and Caldwell, the subtlety is sharper. It cuts deeper. It is more of the essence of their art. It reflects the greater intensity of their imaginative conception. If the work of Marquand fails to keep its hold on readers in the future, it will probably be for this reason, that it is a product grown more on the surface of the mind than that of the other men considered.

XIII. JAMES T. FARRELL

Tragedy of the Poolroom Loafer

"Those who offer us the Puritan type of life offer us a
religion not true, the claims of intellect and knowledge not satisfied, the claim of beauty not satisfied,
the claim of manners not satisfied. In its strong sense
for conduct that life touches truth; but its other imperfections hinder it from employing even this sense
aright."

—ARNOLD

XIII. JAMES T. FARRELL

Tragedy of the Poolroom Loafer

There is, in *Studs Lonigan,* a minor character named Danny O'Neill, who is supposed to be modeled on the author as a child. This young student is shown to us on one occasion planning to be a writer. "Some day," he promised himself, "he would drive this neighborhood and all its memories out of his consciousness with a book." That is, I imagine, the best clue to the psychological motivation of James T. Farrell in the composition not merely of *Studs Lonigan* but of most of what he has written.

Farrell was, one gathers, the child of an Irish-American family inhabiting a quarter on the South Side in Chicago which has since been absorbed by the black belt. It was his lot to grow up in the dreary streets of that depressing neighborhood—not slums, as he insists [1]—to play rough games with the boys of that district, to join them in their fights and savage pranks, to listen to their crude jokes and dirty talk at the poolroom on the corner. It was his lot to witness the gradual degradation of many of his companions under the life of fighting, boozing, sexual promiscuity in youth; and then in maturity the life of narrow piety, family quarrels, financial worry and ill health. The chief models of success for a boy in this community were the cunning and windy lawyer and the backslapping ward politician. The sole training of the boy's mind was that furnished by the

[1] See Farrell's illuminating account of the origin and conception of *Studs Lonigan* in "A Novelist Begins," in the *Atlantic Monthly* for September 1938.

saintly or sour-tempered nuns of the parochial school. The most wholesome of activities in which he engaged were the games of baseball and football, in which he was proficient. By some miracle of chance and temper, Farrell conceived the idea of attending the University of Chicago, an institution feared and hated by his associates for its supposed atheism. He there came under the influence of a famous teacher of composition. It is clear that he read with avidity the books which would admit him to the world of ideas, the world of history and poetry and science and social theory, and that largely through them he was able to make his escape from the purgatory of his environment.

In his volume of tales entitled *Guillotine Party* (1935), Farrell has a story which is presumably somewhat autobiographical, and which gives a pathetic picture of the university student returning at night to the home of his aunt and uncle, his old father, and his cousins. He has come back for an evening of study, to an environment of prejudice, piety, wrangling and dissipation. The one thing they all hate is any knowledge that can be had in books, any idea which might tend to explode their passionate and unreasoned prejudices. They understand his wanting to make his way in the world by the road of education; but they cannot forgive him for taking the way of enlightenment. After supper, while his cousin Tommy is off to his poolroom friends to get drunk and his uncle and aunt have gone to a movie, Joe the student settles down to review his Political Science notes. He has great difficulty concentrating his mind on work.

He lacked confidence in himself. And he felt that he knew why. His home, his background. It was only after having started at the university that he had become aware of the poverty of his home life, his background, his people, a poverty not only of mind, but of spirit, even a poverty of the senses, so that they could scarcely even look at many things and enjoy them. And he, too, had been afflicted with poverty. He wanted to live more, he wanted to know more, he wanted to see and enjoy more life, and this limitation of his background was like a hook pulling the confidence out of him.

Poor Joe! he is in a difficult predicament, between his people whom he loves and his terrible need to free himself from the toils of ignorance, ugliness and hypocrisy before it is too late, before his life is permanently dwarfed and crippled and his chance for something better is past. He has vainly tried to enlighten his people, to break down some of their prejudices. But he cannot hate his own people.

How could he hate his own father, sitting at the dining-room table, his hands palsied, thin and sunken-cheeked, that ghastly dried up look on his face? How could he hate his own past, even though it was part of a world that would kill anything that was honest within himself?

But a sharp break with the past was what Farrell must have had to make before he could ever have started on a course of humane living and artistic production. And his literary performance is determined by his pity and loathing for all that was mean, ugly, and spiritually poverty-stricken in the *mores* and culture to which he was born. All his work is a representation, patient, sober, feeling, tireless, pitiless, of a way of living and a state of mind which he abhors, and from which he has taken flight as one flees from the City of Destruction. Farrell is, I believe, some kind of a Marxian materialist—one who holds that states of mind, ideologies, are in the last analysis the product of economic and industrial conditions. But he is no doctrinaire theorist, no party bigot. He obviously knows that states of mind, whatever their material origin, have the power of reproducing themselves, perpetuating themselves, and of influencing in turn the material conditions and behavior of those subject to them. The main theme of all this writing is a state of mind widely diffused in the world he knows best—a social state of mind highly unfavorable to the production of full and happy lives, to beauty of thought and sentiment, or any of those spiritual values that characterize human civilization at its best. It is much the same condition as that to which Matthew Arnold devoted so much attention, which he found to be prevalent throughout the middle and lower classes in Victorian England, and which he characterized as a want of "culture" or of "sweetness and light." Only, in Farrell it seems something more positive and even more noxious. It is like some poisonous gas that blights and discolors all living things which it touches. It was from this state of mind that Farrell was determined to free himself. In the course of doing so he made a social study of great interest to all who concern themselves with maladies of the spirit which affect whole cultural groups. Social and psychological. For essentially *Studs Lonigan* is a psychological study of a normal American boy infected by a disease of his environment. —

Studs Lonigan is a dramatic creation as significant in his way as the Soames Forsyte of Galsworthy's famous saga. And if I can trust my own impressions, he is an even stronger, more consistent and more movingly human creation than Soames Forsyte. The first of the series was entitled *Young Lonigan: A Boyhood in Chicago Streets* (1932). Young William Lonigan is here shown to be a boy as full of natural promise as the average adolescent youth. He has a strong healthy body, a love of games and sunlight and swimming. He is of an emulous nature. He wishes to be a man and to be treated as such. He wishes passionately to be admired. With the girls he is shy; but he has the capacity for idealized passion. He is full of energy waiting to be employed. He is mentally no fool. Under favorable conditions he might have found a good life, a life of pleasure in his work, of love of woman and family, even a life enriched by the normal working of mind and imagination.

Alas! this promising youth is shown from the start exposed to all the wrong influences. There is nothing anywhere in his environment to direct his energies in lines favorable to a good life. His mother's sole idea is to make him a priest; but he has no call that way. His father is a building contractor who has worked hard for a competence; but there is never any suggestion that satisfaction may be taken in a man's work. The big men of the community are small-time political hangers-on, most unattractive characters, who have nothing to recommend them but their meager success. The parish school has done nothing to rouse the mental faculties of the boy or to suggest that satisfaction may be had in the workings of the mind. Toward all the arts of beauty there is a general attitude of scorn and derision; the music-hall song, the obscene story and the sensational moving picture are the sole respected forms of artistic creation. The imaginative life of the women is mainly confined to the supernatural offerings of the Church. That of the men is served by the frantic dreams of alcoholism and the sexual indulgence which the Church forbids and which can only be had in shame and filth. The youth have this advantage over their elders that they can divert themselves with physical games and sports; they have not yet fallen into the slatternly pot-bellied lassitude of settled middle-age. But they are haunted already by that unconscious disease of boredom which hangs over them all and drives them to alternations of brutal pleasure and nostalgic melancholy. It should be added that a puritan conscience nags and bullies them all. The elders are deeply concerned to bring up their children as decent men and women. Unfortunately they have no idea how to make goodness attractive; and their efforts are wasted in scolding admonitions which only serve to fan the spirit of revolt.

Like most healthy natures, these people are dominated by a need to think well of themselves and a craving to make others respect them. But they have the most limited notion of how their aims are to be served. Their first impulse is that of the gangster, to make themselves strong by force and violence.

And when that fails—when they feel themselves weak—their instinct is to compensate with boasting and making light of all those unlike themselves. They are inherently sentimental and good-natured; they like to think of themselves as hearts of gold. But they are mainly dominated in their conduct by the ideal of the tough guy. The gentle and generous feelings of the Irish peasant have been transformed by some American witchcraft into the brutal cynicism of the gangster.

This is the poison that rots and corrodes all the good impulses of young Studs Lonigan. He has the impulse to make himself a person of distinction. But no form of activity is presented to his imagination in such a light as to make it take hold upon him. "He thought of himself on a scaffold, wearing a painter's overalls, chewing tobacco, and talking man-talk with other painters; and of pay days and the independence they would bring him." He would like to be heroic, and the movies have taught him to dream of the heroism of an Al Capone. The code of the poolroom loafer has forbidden him to think of school as offering anything worthy of his manhood. Ideas, if the school had offered ideas, were taboo in the South Side code. He plays hookey as the more honorable line of conduct. This is the worst of all his misfortunes. His manly ideal condemns him to idleness; and idleness is the mother of boredom and vice. There is in Studs a love of beauty and an almost mystical sense of himself as a part of the beauty of nature. "There was something about the things he watched that seemed to enter Studs as sun entered a field of grass; and as he watched, he felt that the things he saw were part of himself, and he felt as good as if he were warm sunlight." He has a bent toward peace and purity of mind; but boredom and the cynical code drive him to brutal and violent indulgence. He admires his strong, well knit body. He wants to grow up to be strong and tough and the "real ticket." He is somewhat under the average height, and in order to establish his prestige is obliged to make himself an expert pugilist and a game fighter. From the age of fifteen he swaggers through life like a gangland bully. Daytime is one continuous contest among the older boys as to who can get away with the worst pranks and practical jokes; the gang is the terror of janitors, storekeepers, property owners and small boys, and the admiration of the police. There is nothing to do at home; and night after night sees Studs on the poolroom corner winning his place in that society by the brutality of his talk. It generally ends with his getting drunk on bootleg gin and sneaking in after midnight.

For an adolescent boy, the greatest problem next to that of work is the problem of his sexual adjustment. Studs is naturally pure-minded, and in addition he has a religious fear of sin and hell-fire. He has a craving to be understood and a desire for nobility. His imagination has been caught by a certain Lucy Scanlan, who stands for breeding, decency and womanly charm. There is one blissful day when he strolls with Lucy in the park. They pass over to the wooded island and climb into a tree. They sit there for hours swinging their legs and singing. It is a glimpse of perfect happiness to Studs. When he left her at her door in the summer evening, while the spray from the sprinkler on her lawn tapped his cheeks, "the boy, Studs, saw and felt something beautiful and vague, something like a prayer sprung into flesh."

But this, again, is contrary to the code. Such a sentiment cannot live in the atmosphere of the poolroom, where every woman is a "broad" or a "jane" and must be regarded solely as a means of sensual gratification. Besides, this youth is furiously shy and awkward in the presence of decent girls. He is deeply sensitive to ridicule; and in his world it is the custom to chalk up on the fences the names of amorous boys. The children kid him; his parents warn him he's too young for love. The poolroom pours its filth into his mind. Everything conspires to make him lose the game of love. Throughout his life he can never forget the dream of happiness and beauty

associated with the word Lucy. But all his dealings with
women are cheap and vile till the time when he is a man
broken in health and glad to take up with second best. And
by that time old man death has caught up with him. And he
has never found that "something more" of which he had always dreamed and "didn't even know what it was."

I will not give the items of this painful history. I would
not even advise one to read it, unless one is prepared to take
that high ground in which the painful facts of human experience are transformed into tragic art and become the means
of esthetic satisfaction. William James divided people into
two classes, whom he called the tough-minded and the tender-
minded. If you happen to belong to the class of the tender-
minded, it will not pay you to read *Studs Lonigan*. Everyone
has the right to choose his own reading, consulting the needs
of his own spirit, and to do it without apology or rationalizing. For myself, I belong professionally to the class of the
tough-minded, as a critical student of literature. It is our business and our pleasure to review the accomplishments of the
human spirit in this line. We regard literature as, among
other things, a record of human experience. There is nothing
in human experience, we hold, that is too painful to be recorded in literature provided it is done with art—with what
Matthew Arnold calls "high seriousness."

I don't know whether Arnold would have judged that
Studs Lonigan is done with high seriousness. We have to
make our own judgment. It so happens that, in our day and
in the United States, the most serious literary artists are
much inclined to that tendency in literature which goes by
the name of naturalism. Farrell is consciously of that school.
And he is of that school partly, I suppose, because his personal need is to tell the unvarnished truth about the world
from which he made his difficult escape. He had to get it out
of his system. This is, psychologically considered, one of the
chief functions of literary art. It is a therapeutic and health-

giving function. It is one of man's chief instruments for getting the best of ugliness and evil. In *Studs Lonigan,* Farrell achieved his great triumph over hooliganism by thus objectifying it.

But this is not the whole story. Farrell considers that naturalism is the major trend of our literature today; he describes it, in his *Note on Literary Criticism,* as the school which "chooses understanding rather than myth, truth rather than comfort." And he regards it as more than the personal therapeutic referred to above. He has a very serious view of the educational function of literature today.

It makes the reader more intensely conscious of the problems of life, of the predicaments of people, the possibilities and the limitations of living, the diversities in human experience. It makes value judgments on conditions, actions, thoughts, situations, environments, hopes, despairs, ideals, dreams, fantasies. . . . It points [the readers'] emotions, their impulses, their wishes, and their thoughts toward or away from certain goals. It creates . . . the consciousness of an epoch, and is thus one of the instruments that work toward the molding and remolding of the human consciousness.

Thus it is clear that Farrell regards naturalistic fiction as properly more than a mere recording of truth. It is a criticism of life, making value judgments on actions and attitudes, setting ideal objectives for thought and feeling, and molding the spirit of men in more desirable patterns.

With such a humanistic program, and with his personal experience, he could not regard this thing which I have called hooliganism with anything but deadly seriousness. It was not possible to treat it in the romantic or sentimental vein, for that would falsify its essential nature. It was not possible with this theme to be entertaining in the ordinary story manner, or witty. The characters of this story were not conceived as people of fine feelings and noble aims at odds with a cruel and cynical world, triumphing over it in the end. They are rather people of the average neutral sort who take on the prevailing color of their environment, and who, being subjected to a social state of mind ugly and vile, are inevitably reduced themselves to the same uniform color of vileness and ugliness. Their instincts and intentions are normal enough, and with a different set of stimuli they might have developed into something fair and rich. But there is nothing in their environment to suggest ways of gratifying their instincts, or realizing their intentions, which might lead to fair and rich living.

The process of their degradation is a long and gradual one. It cannot be adequately presented in anything short of an extended narrative. In order to do justice to this process it was necessary for the author to set down scene after scene of talk and action gross, dreary, brutal, repelling, in an ascending scale of ugliness. The reader is caught in the pitiful web of this narrative; the people are so real and their plight so arresting that he cannot escape. He cries out over and over again at the cruelty of the thing; but he is held by its fatal fascination. When he is done, his first reaction is to repudiate it as one repudiates what is foul and wicked. But he cannot quite do that. It is too real, too serious, and too human. As time passes and he looks back on the thing from a certain distance, the ugliness gives place to a sense of pathos. His dominant feeling, so far as the characters are concerned, is that of pity. Poor bewildered humans who, by the circumstances of their lives, were condemned to live in hell! And so far as the literary work itself is concerned, he has the feeling of having looked upon some structure great and monumental in its proportions, something solidly based in earth and occupying space with an obstinate persistence like Dante's Hell or the Canterbury Tales or the novels of Zola.

There can be little doubt that Farrell's purpose was well served on the strictly esthetic side. On the moral side, and having in mind his own statement of the function of literature, there are two objections that might be raised. It is possible to hold that his record is more detailed and prolonged than is necessary to make his point. And as for "pointing emotions, etc., toward or away from certain goals," it might be urged that in this book he is too exclusively engaged in pointing away from undesirable goals, and does too little pointing toward desirable ones.

But I am not inclined to urge either of these objections.[1] It is always questionable business trying to check the flow of imaginative creation. Too much is the fault of great artists. And while pointing toward ideal goals is certainly one of the noblest functions of literature, it cannot be required of everyone nor in every context. To require it of Farrell in *Studs Lonigan* might well mean the spoiling of something that is good in its own way in order to make it good in another.

[1] Some further discussion of these points will be found in the following chapter and in the second chapter on Steinbeck.

XIV. JAMES T. FARRELL

The Plight of the Children

"The hungry sheep look up, and are not fed."

XIV. JAMES T. FARRELL

The Plight of the Children

The three books of the *Studs Lonigan* series amount to less than half of Farrell's output so far in the novel. Before the completion of the trilogy, he had already published *Gas-House McGinty* (1933), and since its completion he has brought out the first three volumes of a series of four—*A World I Never Made* (1936), *No Star Is Lost* (1939), and *Father and Son* (1940). These books deal with much the same class of people as *Studs Lonigan,* but in somewhat different aspects and more comprehensively, so that we have a greatly enlarged view of the social conditions of which Studs was a product. In *Studs Lonigan* it is the life of the young man on the streets that is featured; in *Gas-House McGinty* it is the working life of the adult; in the beginning novels of the new tetralogy it is, more broadly, family life. Many of the same basic motives of action are present in all the novels; but in *Studs Lonigan* they are shown leading a young man into gross and dreary dissipation; in *Gas-House McGinty* we see how they are affected by conditions of employment and display themselves under those conditions; in the later series we see them working in the larger theater of family life, with the effect on parents at home and on their families of growing children.

Gas-House McGinty has for its special subject the men who drive the express wagons and the men who take the calls and route the wagons for the "Continental Express Co." in Chicago. Most of the action takes place in the office, where the men fill in the time between taking calls wisecracking and playing practical jokes. The central character is Ambrose J. McGinty, who is boss in the call office until he is transferred and put on the street as the result of a shindy in the office. The narrative is almost entirely made up of what the men say to one another, together with some sprinkling of their thoughts, their daydreams, and their dreams at night. But out of this unplotted pandemonium we gather a very adequate notion of the ways of life, and above all of the dominant preoccupations, ideals and motives in this little industrial microcosm.

These men are of course concerned with keeping their jobs, supporting their families, and bringing up their children. And they are also bent on finding entertainment and relaxation in their leisure time. But all this would seem to be secondary to the more essential compulsion to maintain their self-esteem, to keep up, each one, a sense of his personal importance or build up defenses against the realization that he is a "mutt." The work is hard and leads nowhere; employment is precarious, subject to the whim of a boss or to the accident of ill-health or crippling injury. They work not in their own vineyards but are constantly subject to command and abuse from patrons and superiors. They live meanly, and enjoy only the social prestige which attaches to having fairly steady jobs. In spite of this they are men, and they have the ineradicable need to demonstrate to themselves and to all the world their force and worth as men. No Epictetus has taught them how dignity is won through stoicism. Of Christianity they comprehend little but hell-fire. They must find means less elusive than those of religion and philosophy for salving a self-esteem which is hourly bruised and lacerated and trampled in the dust.

For some of them—and notably for Ambrose McGinty (Mac)—the chief of such means is the satisfaction he takes in his work, his personal efficiency, and the importance he derives from his connection with the Continental—great and powerful organization indispensable to the carrying on of the world's work. Mac has in the business a position of responsibility and command. He can be proud of the order which he puts into things; he has even worked out the percentage of reduction in overhead which he has brought about.

But he has his troubles too. His wife is a despotic, suspicious woman, a mountain of flesh, and he has not the satisfaction of being master in his own house. He has no children to make him proud of his manhood. And for some reason which he cannot comprehend, he is the object of constant razzing on the part of the other men, who regard him, in spite of his efficiency, as a "fat slob." It is impossible for the reader to make out whether or not to like Mac, he is such an assorted bundle of natural impulses, the mean and generous all mixed up together. Which means, I suppose, that he is all too human, or, as the French say, *l'homme moyen sensuel.*

He certainly has his provocations. His friends humiliate him by getting a "fairy" to make up to him and then joking him in the office on his Oscar Wildean propensities. When in a fit of showy generosity he gives his last dime to a beggar, expecting his friends to pay his street car fare, they decline to acknowledge his acquaintance until he is on the point of being put off by the conductor. When he brings pillows to the office to lighten his suffering from the piles, they hide the pillows and provoke the hullabaloo that results in his being demoted. And, dirtiest trick of all, they telephone his wife that back pay has been distributed, so that she thinks he is keeping his pay envelope from her. This results in a period of sourness and alienation under which he suffers acutely. He tries to be friendly to his little stepdaughter Josephine, of whom he is very fond; but Mame breaks this up with her sarcasm. He is denied the restorative consolations of sexual intercourse. His self-esteem is flattened out completely. He has urgent need of psychological compensa-

tions, and the mechanism works automatically. He falls
asleep and dreams.

The account of his dream, which fills one of the longest
chapters, is a perfect primer in the ways of the unconscious—
at least in the more direct and obvious ways. The dream
takes its start from his bodily condition, and the "manifest
content" is much of it derived from the experiences of the
day. But the dreaming mind ranges widely among images
and symbols that free him from the restrictions of commonplace reality and morality. Long passages of anxiety, shame,
fear, and baffled seeking resolve themselves in a burst of
triumph and liberation. The dream begins with naked
girls inviting him to join them. But shame and confusion
come upon him when a girl he is chasing turns out
to be Josephine, his little stepdaughter. He finds himself
in hell, but even Satan cannot abide him and he is thrown
out and told to go dig his own hole in the bottom of the
sea. All through there is much made of this theme, derived
from Mac's dream-identification with the hero of the popular
song. McGinty jumps from towers, defies lions, and lands in
a dreary Nowhere. Then begins his process of recovery. He is
soothed by a sweet girl-voice (the voice of Josephine) bidding him arise and fight. The man in him asserts himself.
"McGinty arose, brandishing a sword with monkey-glands
tied to the handle, faced the blankly forward-marching
Legions of Death, and declaimed: McGinty never, never
dies!" There are many relapses into fear and humiliation;
there is long searching for a woman whom he cannot identify
or visualize. But at length the notes of victory prevail. Mc-
Ginty is crowned King of all Ireland, and St. Patrick himself
says a nuptial mass and inaugurates "the marital ceremonies
of McGinty, first King of all Ireland, to My Irish Molly-O,
Rosie O'Grady, My Wild Irish Rose, Peggy O'Neill, the
Colleen of the River Shannon, Ellen May Mahoney the girl
of his youthful dreams, Little Annie Rooney, and Sweet Sue,

the fairy from the Jew's cigar store, who stood with sprouting wings and an orange tie about his long hair." But McGinty has not reached the zenith in his dream-flight until he has slain God and freed himself from the last constraint and mastership under which mortal man must labor.

Thus by the fantasy of dreams McGinty has raised himself above the humiliations to which he has been subject and set his manhood above all question. A similar process is shown in the daydreaming of Danny O'Neill, the office boy, who is supposed to be more or less modeled after the author; in the boastful lies of Dusty Anderson, who pretends that he keeps his driver's job merely for exercise and to relieve his mind, that his main earnings are from his tony gambling house, or that he has turned down lucrative offers from big league baseball teams; and in the vicarious adventures indulged in by men at the moving pictures. In all of this, as well as in McGinty's dreams, we are often reminded of the fantasies of Leopold Bloom and other characters in Joyce's *Ulysses*.

In many cases the men support their sense of manhood in more socially constructive ways. They are concerned for the coming child; they take satisfaction in the thought of educating their little girls, sending a sick boy to a farm out West to restore his health, or putting their mother in steam heat. The most touching case is Jim O'Neill, Danny's father, a poor teamster with a large family, who has served the company for many years, and now has an office job, with some prospect of a raise if he can stand the gaff. But he has much to suffer from the insolence of his bosses, and he has had a stroke and is in fear that his health will not hold out. As he looks at himself in the washroom mirror his heart rises up in desperate prayers. "If God would only give him ten more years. God, please! God, please give the kids a chance." He was nothing but a workman; but he had been honest. He had done his share of drinking, but a man had a right to some diversion, and he had provided for his wife and kids with his hands and his back. He prays God to make his kids tough and give them guts. "God, they'll be workingmen, and they'll have to fight like workingmen. Give them fight, God, and two big fists."

More prominent, at least as a subject of conversation, are the pleasures of the bed, which are rightly understood by Farrell as having far more than a sensual character—as constituting, quite as much, a means of gratifying the vanity and restoring a man's sense of his own dignity and importance. Indeed, I cannot think of an author who has shown a better understanding of the psychological importance—we might almost say the spiritual importance—of the sexual act. These teamsters and route inspectors are often embarrassingly frank on this theme, and sometimes foul enough; but there is occasionally a simple eloquence in reference to the subject on the part of married men that should not be mistaken for obscenity. And the author is clearly aware of the unique value of this common experience for relieving nervous tensions and delivering poor devils from the indignities of life and from the burden of themselves.

With unmarried men the whole business has a more unsavory cast, because of its casual, promiscuous and huggermugger nature, the social irresponsibility, and the mainly commercial and mechanical character of the transaction. There is nothing very appetizing about the atmosphere of the Elite Hotel where the expressmen assuage their carnal hungers. But it is clear how large a part is played in the whole affair by the ideal or psychical element in these men's make-up—the need they have to satisfy the demands of the "persona" or ideal image a man has of himself, including the view of himself as a virile being. Even the diseases incident to purchased love are invested with some of the glamour attaching to the whole subject. The risk of disease adds to the adventurous nature of the enterprise; a man shows himself more manly by recklessness in the face of danger, and "you ain't a man till you get a dose."

But an even more constant and unattractive way for men to raise themselves is by lowering others. It is not that these men are by nature unfriendly or disinclined to do a good turn to one who needs it. But they are constantly eaten up with a gnawing sense of their being nobodies. There is so little chance to establish their worth by skill and knowledge; of doing so by goodness of heart or urbanity of manner the idea has not occurred to them. Where someone rises above the common level the impulse of the rest is to bring him down with ridicule. The language of these men is racy and vivid within a narrow range; but the use of any words from beyond that range, however exact or expressive, is universally frowned upon as affectation and show-off. These men would profit materially by a little education, but they make no end of fun of those among them who take pains to acquire it. This is no conspiracy, but the automatic working of an instinct to depreciate whatever you do not have. These men have a natural gift for conversation, but it takes the form of wisecracking and scurrility. You salve your own wounds by getting under the skin of another; and when he retaliates, it is a question of who can be most insulting. Your wife and in-laws are subject to abuse, and nothing is too intimate to be dragged in the mud.

If you have authority, however humble, you use it to humiliate those beneath you. You bawl them out on the slightest occasion. You make them toe the line. The blackest mark against McGinty was his procuring the discharge of Jimmy Horan, who was a good workman and had nothing against him except that he was sick of his job and had expressed the usual grudge against the boss. The report of this came to McGinty at a time when he was peculiarly down in the mouth. There is no indication that he understood the reasons for his action. His superior had told him that the call department needed jacking up. His vanity demanded a victim, and he persuaded himself that the firing of Horan was necessary for the good of the service. When the other men protested that Horan was a good workman, it was too late to reverse his decision without losing face. He had to go through with his injustice in order not to fall into lower depths of self-depreciation. McGinty was not a bad sort as human nature goes, but the strongest urge of his nature was to establish his own superiority.

The same mechanism is shown at work in his meeting with Jim O'Neill. Jim is a sad and dreary figure since he has had his stroke and goes limping about. And Mac is really sorry for him. But his dominant sentiment is self-congratulation over his own good health. "Mac strode away, feeling sorry for Jim. Jim was through. Well, it hadn't gotten him yet, he thought with a pride that he immediately regretted. It was lousy for a healthy man to feel proud when he sees a sick friend. But he couldn't help feeling that it hadn't gotten McGinty yet."

Self-maximation is the word applied by some psychologists to the motive here at work. It is the clue to nearly every aspect of human nature displayed in this novel. It is a motive that may work for good or ill; and here, through lack of enlightenment, it comes out almost altogether in cheap and ugly ways. These lives are like pictures painted in a mean tradition through want of knowledge or through bad instruction. The fine energies of the ego are turned into foul channels. It is a pitiful want of economy of spiritual forces from which there was so much to be hoped. Instead of fair and goodly lives we are left to mourn "the expense of spirit in a waste of shame." [1]

*   *   *

[1] A special instance of this sort of motivation is given by Farrell in *Tommy Gallagher's Crusade* (1939), a brand of self-motivation which is capable of having disastrous effects in the political life of a nation. Tommy Gallagher is

A broadly similar motivation is much in evidence in the later novels, *A World I Never Made, No Star Is Lost,* and *Father and Son.* Only, here the scene is transferred from the office to the home, and we have the more tragic spectacle of young children subjected to the same blighting and deforming influences. The central character here is Danny O'Neill as a young boy. The series is not completed. We know that in the end this boy was destined to break the evil spell and make his way out of the foul labyrinth, though it is not yet clear by just what turn of fortune he was granted light and strength to perform this feat.

The scenes are laid in two households, those of the O'Flahertys and the O'Neills. Mrs. O'Flaherty is Danny's grandmother, who is kept in steam heat and electricity by her son Al, a traveling salesman in shoes. She lives with her daughter Margaret, a cashier in a hotel. Lizz O'Neill is Danny's mother. She is supported by his father Jim, the teamster, whose acquaintance we have made in *Gas-House McGinty.* In the period covered by the first two books, he has not had his stroke; he is strong and hard-working. But he has too many children, and they must live in squalid quarters, with-

---

not content with the ordinary steady jobs held by his father and brothers. He is the kind who thinks the boss is against him, that he has always been a football to be kicked around. His brothers consider him lazy; for instead of working, he prefers to stand about all day trying to sell a few copies of Father Moylan's *Christian Justice* (anti-Semitic). He thinks himself that he is making sacrifices for the noble cause of Americanism. His craving for excitement leads him to join with other hoodlums in attacking Jews and breaking up "radical" meetings . . . where the risks are not too great; and by such activities, too, he drugs the consciousness of his own cowardice. Like so many of Farrell's characters, Tommy Gallagher is long on fantasy, making up in his imagination for what he wants in fact. Scorned by his family and baffled in his craving for a girl, "He lay awake, pitying himself, telling himself that he was brave, vowing over and over again that his day was coming, and assuring himself that when it did come, it would be a day of bitter vengeance. Look at Hitler in Germany! Hitler had known days like this, too!" Farrell, in this slight work, makes no pretense of describing political phenomena. But he does make an illuminating psychological study of one of the types that have played a major part in the Nazi movement.

out even gas or water-closet, and in neighborhoods infested with negroes and other undesirables.

The O'Flahertys have come to the rescue, taking Danny and later his little sister Margaret to live with them. The old woman is "shanty Irish"—completely illiterate, vain, boastful, foul-mouthed, violent, superstitious, stingy, and as hard as nails. But she is fond of her children and grand-children. She claims Danny for her son, does her best to spoil him, and centers on him her hopes for the future honor of the family. She is proud of her son Al and grateful to him for making her comfortable. She is ashamed of the poverty of Lizz and Jim, and on public occasions dissociates herself from them as persons beneath her notice. She never admits being Irish, since in the old country only landlords and the English had social caste. And yet in her cups she often speaks of the time when she was "a wisp of a girl running the bush in the old country, barefooted and with her backside show-ing through her dress." Jim O'Neill is deeply resentful of her vulgar toploftiness and of having his son brought up to scorn his father; and this is the occasion of many quarrels between him and Lizz. At bottom they are tenderly devoted to each other and to their children; but poverty puts a heavy strain upon them. It has turned Lizz into a slattern and brought out in her the gutter strain she had from her mother.

The other O'Flahertys are all in reaction against this gutter strain. Ned has married someone who passes for a lady. Al has remained a bachelor, his heart set on lifting the family out of the bog of vulgar indigence. He reads the letters of Lord Chesterfield; he shuns the drinking and obscene storytelling of his comrades of the road, their boasting and fighting; he strives to improve the speech of his relatives, and recommends to his drummer friends "the touch delicate and the retort adroit." He takes seriously his obligations to Danny O'Neill, teaches him to walk properly, plays baseball with him, disciplines him considerably. In the family circle he strives for harmony, good feeling, urbane manners, and "constructive" ideals. He dreams of a happy fireside, with the "Rosary" sung by self-respecting wives or "Kathleen Mavourneen" played on the victrola while children sport about the Christmas tree. It is only the dread of vice in the home that rouses his temper and leads him to violence and brutality. Altogether, Al O'Flaherty is one of the great creations of modern fiction—a slightly ridiculous old bachelor, priggish and limited, but a man of genuine character and goodwill, struggling valiantly with circumstances that make of him a profoundly pathetic figure.

His sister Margaret is a tragic figure. She is by endowment the richest and finest of all the family. She is warmly affectionate and generous by nature, an Irish heart of gold, full of romantic sentiment. She should have been a devoted wife and the life-giving mother of a family of children. Her fine nature has been warped by unhappy experiences—dreary meanness and quarrelsomeness in the home, cruel beatings as a child, the cynical construction placed by Irish puritanism on her association with boys. Her romantic nature has found satisfaction not in marriage and home but in a secret liaison with a married man—a Protestant lumber tycoon—who after a few years of furtive meetings ceases to answer her letters and leaves her to blank misery and despair. She tries to console herself with other men and with gin; she falls into terrible fits of drunkenness culminating in attempts at suicide and fearful visions of snakes and devils. There are dreadful scenes where her mother calls her a whore, puts upon her the curse of a parent, or exorcises the devils with prayer and holy water. And the worst of it all is the presence of terrified young children, who must stay up all night to keep their aunt from turning on the gas, or sit by helpless while aunt and grandmother engage in foul exchanges of insult and recrimination.

The real subject of the whole study is the plight of children reading in such a book their first lessons in the art of living. One hardly knows which of the children are the more unfortunate—Danny and little Margaret, who pay for cleanly surroundings and steam heat with subjection to spectacles like these, or the children who remain in the slums with their mother, or the one who passes back and forth between the two infernos and picks up on the way the criminal inspirations of the street. This one is Bill, Danny's older brother (an incipient Studs Lonigan), who comes to play with Danny and teach him the facts of life as observed in his home.

As for the younger children, we see them in their sordid home playing the games of children, sedulously copying their parents in every detail of speech and behavior, especially in the scolding exercise of authority and in the use of foul and abusive language. As babies they are adorable little animals; their parents sincerely love them and fiercely defend them against all comers. But it is alarming to see how fast they take on the less attractive features of adulthood; and one looks forward dolefully to a new generation repeating the errors and imbecilities of the last.

It is the moral blight that is most distressing to contemplate. But more immediate is the physical peril. They live in filth and ignorance, with no defense against disease but prayers and holy water. *No Star Is Lost* concludes with a series of scenes in which the baby of the family is struck down with diphtheria and dies before a doctor or priest can be had, and all the other children are bundled off in the police wagon to a hospital for contagious diseases. Meantime, at the O'Flahertys', little Margaret has been taken down with the same malady. But the O'Flahertys have better standing with the doctor, and he comes promptly to their call. What is most bitter for Jim O'Neill is the thought that his poverty is so great he cannot even command a doctor for his dying child. No doubt, with a little more enterprise or imagination, he could have had free medical care; but enterprise and imagination do not thrive in the midst of so much ignorance.

Perhaps I have laid too much stress on the unfavorable influences brought to bear on these children. After all, their father and mother were honest, religious, well-intentioned people; the father wrought manfully to support his family; and they and all the other relatives duly preached the gospel of industry, sobriety and Christian goodness. In *Father and Son,* Farrell shows the O'Neills in a period of greater prosperity, with Jim now in the supervision end of the express business and Bill, too, settled down and bringing home his pay envelop from the express company. It is not quite clear what turn of heart has brought Bill to a sense of responsibility. But there is every prospect of his marrying and setting out on a way of life that is an exact duplication of his father's.

Danny is destined to emerge upon another cultural level, but the process of his emancipation is distressingly protracted. The psychologist would doubtless find in this record plentiful indications of how the character of Danny O'Neill was beaten into shape and given its bent by his childhood experience. And the discerning psychologist could even make clear how the most apparently unfavorable influences were working, by some logic of reaction, to free him from the dark web which circumstance was weaving about him. We see him playing the games and thinking the long, long thoughts of youth. Every defeat begets daydreams of success and triumph. His older brother leads him into various mischief, which fails to take strong hold upon him. He labors with the problems of theology and suffers from a sense of guilt and the consciousness of making bad confessions. He engages in bloody fights with bullies, and he does not always tell the truth. He witnesses scenes of hatefulness and violence.

It is perhaps a congenital defect which proves in the end his great advantage. From early years he has had to wear glasses and be nicknamed Four Eyes. He suffers from the imputation of being tied to his grandmother's apron strings, and then from the social stigma of having a drunkard for an aunt and a beer-guzzling grandmother.

The most poignant scenes in *No Star Is Lost* are those of his birthday party. Danny has managed to secure the attendance of several of the most attractive girls from school, and the refreshments are of the best. His great dread is that Aunt Peg will get drunk and cause a scandal; but she is persuaded to stay in her room and babble tearfully of her innocence as a child. Danny hopes by this party to make himself popular with the kids and get pretty Virginia Doyle for his girl. But the kids resent his choosing the prettiest girl for his partner, and the girls do not take to the game of postoffice. The net result is that the girls avoid him and the boys kid him more than ever. He is greatly relieved when the family moves to a new neighborhood. He hopes that Aunt Margaret will give up drinking and he may make a fresh start in his social life. One of the first acquaintances he makes in the new street is young Studs Lonigan. Ominous portent! But Danny O'Neill has not the making of a tough guy. His very deficiencies will drive him into the larger life of the mind, the liberator.

But that is a long process, which will take more than the four years at St. Stanislaus high school, recorded in *Father and Son*. This is one of the most frank and convincing studies of adolescence ever made in fiction. It is a most uncomfortable affair for all concerned. Young O'Neill is determined to make himself respected by the boys and admired by the girls, and this he achieves in some degree by dint of thoughtful application to the arts of pugilism, baseball, football and basketball. But he never succeeds in getting himself accepted by the other boys as quite one of them, in spite of being an athletic star, dressing like a dude, and spending all his money on fraternity dances. As a ladies' man he is a flop, and the harder he tries the less he enjoys himself. He cannot seem to strike the right tone with boys or girls, and is censured by his fraternity brothers for wisecracking and want of dignity. Everybody insists on treating him as a goof, and he is more and more impressed with his ineptness and his difference from other boys. For a time, under the suggestions of Sister Magdalen, he thinks he has a call to the priesthood; perhaps his awkwardness with the girls is an indication that way. But he is glad enough to have the support of father and uncles in giving up that idea. In the final year at high school he does a good deal of heavy drinking, but that satisfies nothing but his social vanity. Altogether it is a painful and obstinate case of growing pains— a disease common enough at Danny's age, but likely to be most severe and protracted under conditions that do nothing to feed the mind or employ the faculties of the growing organism, and hardest of all perhaps on the boy whose faculties are the greatest, since he is likely to suffer most from an obscure sense of frustration, boredom and bewilderment, and beat his wings most wildly against the invisible bars.

Dramatically, the most interesting and moving theme in the last book is Danny's relation to his father—Jim crippled, dying and anxious over the fate of his family, Danny all absorbed in the crude desires and ambitions of adolescence. It is the familiar tale of a father angered and dismayed at the sight of a son precariously entrenched on the top of "Tom Fool's Hill" (to use the term most often on my own father's lips) and a son too much preoccupied by his own urgencies to appreciate his father's merits or understand his point of view. There are many beautiful and poignant touches in the account of Jim's decline. As for the blind egotism and crudity of the boy, they were a measure of his inexperience and the desperation of his spirit, starved and bewildered in a world that had so little to offer for its satisfaction. In his conscientious portrayal of Danny's relation to his father, Farrell has done bitter penance for us all.

On his father's death, Danny came down to earth. He went to work dutifully for the support of the family and gave up his dreams of life as a college man. Work in the wagon call department was anything but congenial, and leaden skies closed down upon him.

But there is a lightening on the horizon in one direction. Danny has sometimes thought that he might be a writer. He has read much in a battered volume of poetry cherished by his father, and in the little blue books of his Uncle Al. The men at the express office make fun of him for reading Shakespeare between calls. But the reader knows better. The reader knows that the written word is the key for which he is seeking, the key to all the doors of the mind and imagination, freeing him from the prison house of Ambrose McGinty and admitting him to the open world of Plato and Dewey, of Housman and Tolstoy. The reader knows that what Danny is seeking is just the magic word that makes the difference between a Studs Lonigan and a Robert Burns.

Farrell's writing is perhaps the plainest, soberest, most straightforward of any living novelist. There is nothing commonplace about it, for there is none of the prosing self-consciousness of an author displaying his skill or his wisdom. The acts and thoughts of the characters are stated in the simplest terms, and the rest is their very speech, with the edge and tang of what is said in deadly earnest. It is, in Wordsworth's phrase, a "selection from the real language of men." Selection because the author eliminates everything trivial and superfluous, leaving only what will illuminate the primary concerns of his people. Real language of men; for it has an unmistakable ring of authenticity. There is no attempt to point up the dialect, exaggerate the slanginess, or give phonetic representation to the local accent. Nor, on the other hand, is there any prudish toning down of the grossness of language. There is nothing facetious, nothing smartly satirical in the author's tone. These are linguistic documents, as they are social documents, of high seriousness and value, but not slavishly photographic. Farrell is obviously more concerned with the spirit than the letter of truth.

The fictional method is purest naturalism, unrelieved by the traditional interest of plot and drama, mystery and suspense, unalloyed with "idealism," with theory, moralizing, sentimentality, or humorous comment. The pathos is the pathos of human suffering; the tragedy is the tragedy of act and fact. The naturalism is not that of elaborate documentation; there is no suggestion of the notebook and the subject worked up for literary use. Nor is there any suggestion of data collected and forced into the frame of theory. The documentation is really prodigious, but it did not require the author's going beyond the limits of experience and memory. Scene crowds on scene with suffocating profusion, till the reader cries out for mercy. But no scene has the air of being made up; none is forced, not many can be spared. They spring like geysers from the seething burdened depths of the author's being. They are not the cold and labeled cases of the sociologist. Each one is presented in the concrete terms of story; the appeal is first to the imagination, and only in retrospect to the mind and conscience.

In so far as anything is lacking it is some principle of relief. And this is felt most in the third volume of the Danny O'Neill series. Too many of the episodes are on the same level of interest. This is the price paid for fullness and sobriety in the recording. One is conscious of something like monotony of effect. When the series is completed this may seem a frivolous objection. The level stretches of *Father and Son* may fit in perfectly in the planned perspective of the whole. Let it be stated then not as criticism but as simple matter of fact that one grows a little tired of the delays and repetitions of Danny O'Neill. One is impatient to see him get his toes and fingers in the clefts and make a start at scaling the cliff that towers above him.

The best single test for a writer of fiction is the creation of characters that live in the imagination. Farrell has brought to life an unusual number of such living characters. Studs Lonigan, Ambrose McGinty, Jim O'Neill, Al O'Flaherty, Aunt Margaret, and grandmother O'Flaherty are among the memorable people in English fiction. I have not been able to do justice to any of them, and above all to Mary O'Flaherty.

There is one scene that must not be passed without mention—that in which the old woman visits the grave of her dead husband. It will remind us that Farrell is not unprovided with that type of imagination which we associate with poetry and with the most famous of the Irish dramatists. The old woman sits on a bench in a well-tended plot, nibbling her sandwiches, and looks toward the weed-grown sandy lot where her husband and daughter Louise are buried. She thinks of the hard days they led together in the past and of the evil life of her daughter Margaret, of the grievous sorrow which her Tom has been spared by death. Her indignation is roused at the thought of how her daughter has neglected the father's grave. And as she sits there in the gentle breeze from the lake, with the sounds of the city distant and dreamlike, the limits between real and imaginary fade away. She sees her husband rise from the grave in his habit as he was; and she finds herself talking with him, complaining of her daughter, recalling their days together as children in the old country—their first communion—and exchanging views at last on his character and hers, and the obligations laid upon her as the spiritual head of the house. He asks her if she "do be missing" him. "Indeed, I do," she answers. "You were a good man, but I had to make you toe the mark." "You're a good woman yourself, Mary, but, ah, you're a hard woman, you are," he seemed to say. And to this she agrees, taking it as a compliment. "Hard I am, and hard I'll be till they'll be carrying me sorry old bones out here to be laid at rest beside you, Tom," she said. And almost the last thing he has to say to her is to bid her make the children all toe the mark— "Be hard on them, Mary," he seemed to say.

It is a ticklish undertaking for anyone to record the visions of an old woman communing with the spirits of the departed, and doubly ticklish in the context of hard facts provided by Farrell. But this whole scene is managed with a simple naturalness (born of a grudging tenderness) which is a signal triumph of literary tact. To any reader who thinks that in Farrell he has to do with a commonplace or insensitive spirit, I heartily recommend this eighth chapter of *No Star Is Lost*.

Farrell's type of naturalism is not of a kind to appeal to the common run of readers. It has little to offer those who go to fiction for light entertainment, the glamour of the stage, or the gratification of their bent for wishful thinking. There is no reason why the squeamish or tender-minded should put themselves through the ordeal of trying to like his work. But there will always be a sufficient number of those whom life and thought have ripened and disciplined, who have a taste for truth however unvarnished provided it be honestly viewed, deeply pondered, and imaginatively rendered. For many such it may well turn out that James T. Farrell is the most significant of American novelists writing in 1940.

XV. JOHN STEINBECK

Journeyman Artist

"The best form is that which makes the most of its
subject—there is no other definition of the meaning
of form in fiction. The well-made book is the book
in which the subject and the form coincide and are
indistinguishable—the book in which the matter is all
used up in the form, in which the form expresses all
the matter."

—Percy Lubbock

XV. JOHN STEINBECK

Journeyman Artist

The last of the novelists I shall discuss is the one who has
recently been the most widely read—a man whose great
reputation has sprung up during the last five years and has
been crowned with the international fame of *The Grapes
of Wrath*. That is certainly a very fine book; but its tremendous vogue is founded partly on what we call an accident—the fact that it concerns itself with one of the major
economic problems of our day, the problem of seasonal labor
in California, and with the largest scale agricultural catastrophe of American history, the catastrophe of the dustbowl.
It is, we might say, an accident that so great a talent as John
Steinbeck's should have come upon so great and so topical
a theme. But that so great a talent should have come to
flower in our time is not in the same sense an accident. It is,
let us say, the bounty of nature; and it is, moreover, what
we have all been looking for, the fruit of long cultivation—
the ripening of American literary culture in our day.

And the first thing we should take note of in Steinbeck is
the sheer literary genius with which he is endowed. The
dustbowl might never have thrown its dreary blight over the
vast empire of the cattle lands; the state of California might
never have been faced with this terrible labor problem. But
the connoisseurs in the written word would have known—
and they did know—that an American writer had appeared
with a sure and subtle sense for literary effect, a storyteller
worthy to be compared with Chekhov or Anatole France for

his skill in shaping up the stuff of human lives in forms that delight the mind and imagination. This is a rare event in our day or any day. It is like what we mean when we speak of a born musician—having reference to a composer—a finder of melodies, a natural shaper of harmonies—a Schubert or a Brahms. And *The Grapes of Wrath* was simply to demonstrate, what was already apparent to the discerning, that this was an unusually versatile talent, capable of being turned to themes of various sorts, and suiting itself to the theme like hand and glove.

Let me illustrate what I mean by his versatility. I have spoken of Chekhov. In our day the most distinguished writers have a disposition to feature characters like those in *The Grapes of Wrath,* who live on the barest subsistence level, and whose besetting concern is therefore with the primary needs of the animal organism. Or if the people are not so depressed economically, the disposition is still to represent them largely in terms of sensations and urges but one remove from the animal level, with small regard for the refinements of thought and sentiment which, we pride ourselves, are the distinguishing mark of our more civilized manner of life. They seem not to have "souls," or spiritual personalities, in the sense that we feel ourselves and our friends to have them. Now, the characters of this Russian storyteller, whatever their economic status, seem invariably to have "souls." There is a depth, a feeling quality, a diversification to their personal experience which makes them seem important—important individually for what they are in themselves over and above what they are as members of the tribe of men, as hungering and sex-ridden gregarious animals with the gift of speech. Chekhov is not a sentimental writer. He is objective and realistic enough and sets down what he has observed without any shrinking. But his people are so interesting for their individual quality, their inner world is so rich and diversified, his report on human nature so fresh, direct and authentic, that one always comes away from one of his stories moved and diverted and with a heightened sense of the interest of living. These people are suffused with the feeling which we attach to the living experience, as if bathed in the atmosphere of sensibility and aspiration which makes up our sense of life.

Well, there are many of Steinbeck's short stories that remind one of the Russian writer. There is the opening story of the volume entitled *The Long Valley* (1938). It is called "Chrysanthemums." It gives us the picture of a wholesome and attractive woman of thirty-five, wife of a rancher in that enchanting Salinas Valley where Steinbeck lived as a boy. This woman has what are called planter's hands, so that whatever she touches grows and flourishes. She is shown on a soft winter morning working in her garden, cutting down the old year's chrysanthemum stalks, while her husband stands by the tractor shed talking with two men in business suits. Nothing is said about the relationship of this married pair, but everything shows that it is one of confidence and mutual respect. He refers with simple pleasure to the size of her chrysanthemums. She applauds his success in selling his three-year-old steers at nearly his own price. And she welcomes his suggestion that, since it is Saturday afternoon, they go into town for dinner and then to a picture show. But she wouldn't care to go to the fights. The feminine note is sounded in the unaffected shrinking of the refined woman from the brutality of a sport which men enjoy. "Oh, no," she said breathlessly, "I wouldn't like fights." And he hastens to assure her he was just fooling; they'll go to a movie. It is not the author who tells us that he is making a sacrifice, and that he is glad to do so, for he likes his wife better thus than if she wanted to go to the fights. The beauty of this kind of storytelling is that the author does not waste words and insult his reader with that sort of explanation. He gets his effects with an elegant economy of words, and leaves some scope for the reader's imagination.

And now is introduced a third character, picturesque and individual, and a new balance of forces in human relations. The new character is an itinerant tinker who comes driving up in his queer covered wagon from the country road that runs along the bank of the river. He is a big stubble-bearded man, in a greasy black suit, graying but not old-looking, with dark eyes "full of the brooding that gets in the eyes of teamsters and of sailors." He is a shrewd, dynamic personality. And there ensues between him and Eliza Allen a combat of wits in which she shows herself a person of right feeling, one who doesn't let her charitable instincts run away with her, but who has at the same time a soft side where you can get round her. That is her love of flowers, and the pride she takes in her way with chrysanthemums. The author says nothing of this tug-of-war, nor of the shrewdness of the tinker, nor of the quality in Eliza Allen that makes her a victim. All these things he *shows* us in the brief dialogue—again with a richness of reference which makes us feel the whole quality of these two by no means commonplace lives. Among other things he makes us feel how, beneath her brisk and contented exterior, this woman harbors an unsatisfied longing for some way of life less settled than that of the rancher's wife, something typified by the shabby tinker camping nightly in his wagon underneath the stars.

Eliza Allen has nothing that needs mending, but the tinker does not want to leave without something to feed his hungry frame. He has the inspiration to take an interest in her chrysanthemums; he begs her for some of the shoots to take to a lady down the road who has asked him to bring her some. The upshot of it is that she finds some old pans for him to mend and he goes away with fifty cents in his pocket and a pot of chrysanthemum shoots. She watches him go down the road by the river, and is filled, as the author manages to make us know, with a kind of troubled joy at the thought of him on his vagabond trail.

And now she turns to the bustle of washing up and dressing for the trip to town. I wish I knew how the author manages here to convey the sense he does of the energy and well-being of this rancher's wife moved by thoughts unnamed and perhaps not brought above the level of consciousness. Her husband observes how "strong" she seems, but has no notion of the special occasion for it.

But Eliza Allen has a grief in store, and we have still the pleasure of seeing how mad and hurt she can be when she realizes that she has been outwitted by the man who means so much to her in the obscure places of her imagination. As she drives along to town with her husband she discovers a dark spot on the pavement where the tinker had thrown her chrysanthemums the moment he was out of sight of the ranch. The pot he kept. The thing remains a secret with her. She says nothing of it to her husband. We know it only by the tone she takes in asking him again about the fights. She asks him if the fighters do not hurt each other very much. "I've read how they break noses, and blood runs down their chests. I've read how the fighting gloves get heavy and soggy with blood." He is surprised and rather shocked that she should ever have thought of things like that; but he is willing to take her to the fights if she really wants it. "She relaxed limply in the seat. 'Oh, no. No. I don't want to go. I'm sure I don't.' Her face was turned away from him. 'It will be enough if we can have wine. It will be plenty.' She turned up her coat collar so that he could not see that she was crying weakly—like an old woman."

This is no tragic grief. But it does assure us that Eliza Allen is very much of a woman, and of the same flesh and blood with ourselves—that she shares with us our sensitive pride, our reluctance to let someone get the best of us, and more than that, our secret romantic longing for something more than "human nature's daily food." She is one of the most delicious characters ever transferred from life to the pages of a book. There is no doubt that she has a "soul." And she is much less simple than she seems.

The most famous story in *The Long Valley* is "The Red Pony." This is dedicated to a boy's passion for animal pets, and is quite in a class with Mrs. Rawlings' *Yearling*. It represents a more privileged level of human living than that, and aspects of nature more benign and lovely. It has its own splendor and pathos. I mention it here as another case of human types and relationships as fine and subtle as any in Chekhov. There is the opening enchantment of a boy's world in touch with the primitive joys of wild life. And there is the boy's shyness and secretiveness—the sternness of responsibilities laid on him as a member of a serious farming community—the ticklish balance of his relation to a stern but just and loving father—and the suffering inflicted on him by the indifferent cruelties of nature. The finest thing of all is the relation between the boy Jody and Billy the hired man, whose pride of skill as well as his affection for the boy is involved in his effort to save the lives, first of the red pony, and then of the mare who is chosen to be the mother of Jody's colt.

There is in Steinbeck much of the romantic poet and of the mystic, at least the love of themes embodying mystical attitudes. I will say little of his first experiment in psychological romance—*Cup of Gold* (1929)—which has for its subject the life of the buccaneer, Sir Henry Morgan. It opens with a glimpse of his hero as a boy at home in a Welsh manor house, and starts his adventures with an interview on a mountaintop with the sage magician Merlin. Altogether it is a very interesting performance and is another illustration of Steinbeck's versatility. But he did not know quite what he was after. There are echoes of many different manners, including, I think, that of the author of *Jurgen*. But he had not quite found himself in any of the several distinct genres in which he later became a master.

Very much more successful, and altogether delightful as imaginative evocation, is *To a God Unkown* (1933). This is the story of a man devoted to the land, who left his New England farm to establish himself as a pioneer in the fertile secluded valley of Nuestra Señora, not far from the sea in California. He was followed there by his brothers and their families, and they made altogether a highly prosperous and idyllic colony of ranchers while the good years lasted. But the main interest of the story lies in the mystical feeling of Joseph Wayne in regard to the land and his relation to it. He was the one of the brothers to receive the patriarchal blessing of their father. He has a nature poetic and aloof, regarding himself as a sort of priest, whose paramount concern is to promote the fertility of the earth and of the men and cattle who live upon its surface. He has great sympathy with the pagan superstitions and rituals which survive among the Indians and the Mexican half-breeds; and has notions and practices of his own which are sinful and blasphemous in the eyes of his Christian brother, while to the other brother they come to seem the infliction of madness. He believes that the spirit of his dead father has followed him West and is lodged in the great live-oak tree that shades the farmyard. He is possessed by the pagan theory of sacrifice, and in the end he makes a sacrifice of himself to bring back the rain upon a country made barren with drought. His favorite resort in times of joy and sorrow is a great moss-covered rock, which stands in a temple-like grove of pines, and beneath which in a mysterious cave is the source of a spring regarded by the Indians as sacred. It was there that his wife met her death by accident, herself a sacrifice to the unknown god of the earth.

Steinbeck's subject here is one suggested in part by his deep feeling for the land, especially in its virgin phase, and for the life of the early settlers in this lovely wilderness, partly by the more intellectual interest in primitive psychology and religion. It is a theme of utmost delicacy, hard to carry through in the right key, without sentimentality or self-consciousness in the handling of the fantastic and uncanny. Steinbeck has brought to his task a most unusual literary tact and a sympathetic imagination capable of fusing the diverse elements into a consistent and plausible whole. He has brought a style remarkable for its expressiveness without loudness or eccentricity, and a sense for rhythm and for right English idiom most unusual among contemporary writers; a manner of expression in which a strong reflective bent is felt beneath the surface of simple sentences shaped by the sensuous imagination and the proprieties of narrative. The style is strictly of today, but without the slightest suggestion of what is bizarre in the Hemingway manner, the Faulkner manner or the Wolfe manner. With a theme broadly suggestive of Arthur Machen, there is no hint of that romantic effusiveness, à la De Quincey, which repels the fastidious reader in *The Hill of Dreams*. Steinbeck's style in this book is the nearest to what we mean by "classical" of almost anything in contemporary fiction, but without dryness or coldness.

To a God Unknown belongs to the world of dreams rather than that of urgent realities. It has not the strength of Steinbeck's later work. It has not the emotional power of Hudson's *Green Mansions,* to name perhaps the greatest of novels of fantasy. But it has much of the charm of Hudson, and an intriguing quality of its own in the treatment of a local American subject. There is not the remotest suggestion of the proletarian themes which came to the fore in Steinbeck's later work. It is another reminder of his extraordinary versatility.

But it is time we were coming to what will be our special subject, which is Steinbeck's dealing with children of the earth. By this I mean human beings more lowly than prosperous ranchers—I mean those helpless children of earth who can never raise themselves more than a few feet from its surface, and for whom the question of the next meal remains a major obsession.

But here again I must distinguish types and dwell more on the versatility of this author, who has a d. manner for each class of subject matter which he trea fore the publication of *The Grapes of Wrath* (1939) S beck had already produced two books which were wi read and hailed by critics as masterpieces. The first of th was *Tortilla Flat* (1935) and the second was *Of Mice and Me* (1937).

Tortilla Flat is, I believe, the favorite with academic readers, and this for the obvious reason that it is most unmistakably among his books a literary feat. It is a very skillful blend of several varieties of comic writing; it recalls *Don Quixote* and *Gil Blas* and Anatole France and Charles Lamb. And in addition it recalls the simple heroic manner of Malory's *Morte d'Arthur* and the sweet simplicity of the *Little Flowers of Saint Francis*. So that any lover of these classic masterpieces is bound to have his palate titillated by its grave and playful cadences. Steinbeck was for several years, off and on, a student at Stanford University, where he followed only such courses as pleased his fancy and quite neglected to take a degree. And it is clear that he used his time to as great advantage as the average faithful student who comes away with a B.S. in Education or a B.A. in Sociology.

Steinbeck's subject in *Tortilla Flat* is the paisano of Monterey. The paisano is, as he tells us, "a mixture of Spanish, Indian, Mexican, and assorted Caucasian bloods. His ancestors have lived in California for a hundred or two years. He speaks English with a paisano accent and Spanish with a paisano accent. When questioned concerning his race, he indignantly claims pure Spanish blood and rolls up his sleeve to show that the soft inside of his arm is nearly white." The paisano lives in a special district in Monterey where town and pine forest intermingle. He has little property and is little subject to the civic and financial worries of other citizens. Steinbeck's particular subject is one Danny and his friends Pilon and Pablo and Portagee Jo, Jesus Maria Corcoran, and a certain ragamuffin called the Pirate. For the most part these men have no occupation, but work occasionally on ranches or cutting squibs in a canning factory. Most of them were enlisted in the war with Germany. On his return from the army, Danny, who had preferred as a boy to sleep in the woods, finds that his grandfather, a man of exceptional wealth in this community, has died and left him two small unpainted houses in Tortilla Flat. So for the first time in his life he is a man with a roof over his head and burdened with the cares of property. Unable to support this condition alone, he invites his friends to join him. They rent his second house, but never pay him any rent except an occasional purloined chicken or gallon jug of red wine. When the Virgin Mary gently admonishes them for their careless life by burning down their rented house, they move in with Danny, who welcomes them to his small room on condition that no one occupy his bed but himself. When the Pirate is added to the group with his five mangy dogs, a special corner is assigned to the dogs, and they all live happily together.

They lead an eventful life. These are true stories, Steinbeck assures us, though sometimes elaborated by the people of Tortilla Flat in oral narration. "It is well," he says, "that this cycle be put down on paper so that in future time scholars, hearing the legends, may not say as they say of Arthur and of Roland and of Robin Hood—'There was no Danny nor any group of Danny's friends, nor any house. Danny is a nature god and his friends primitive symbols of the wind, the sky, the sun.' This history is designed now and ever to keep the sneers from the lips of sour scholars."

The first reviewers of the book perceived that these people

were curious or quaint, dispossessed or underdoggish. Steinbeck's feelings were hurt, so he tells us. He had never thought that they were anything of the sort. They were friends of his, people whom he liked, and if he had thought they were quaint he would never have written of them. This disclaimer it is impossible to take at its face value. He liked these people and they were his friends. Well and good. That we can heartily believe. It is clear throughout his writing that Steinbeck is fond of the underdog; and that for good and sufficient reasons. Because he *is* the under dog, and because of his many virtues. And then, because in him the primary human impulses are less overlaid with disguise, and stand out in stark simplicity. But this last, observe, is an artistic reason, a literary reason. The likings of an artist are always open to suspicion; and we have to distinguish between his liking for people themselves and his liking for his *subject*. The paisanos are doubtless likable in themselves; but they are still more likable as subject for the literary artist. And they are all the more likable, it may be, for traits of which the artist could not well approve. Danny and his friends were frank and courtly in manner, fond of wine and women, full of charity, piety and good nature, ingenious and enterprising in odd ways of securing food and drink; and these may well be regarded as virtues as well as subjects for artistic representation. But they were also shiftless and lazy; they were inveterate if petty thieves; they were ignorant and superstitious; they were something very like drunkards; and these are hardly traits which their author could regard as moral virtues.

He likes them, he says, because they are people who merge successfully with their habitat. Well, that may be argued. On his showing they do make shift to live with satisfaction according to their notions; perhaps they have adapted themselves instinctively to the conditions imposed on them by race and the social set-up. But I doubt whether any jury of sociologists would rate them high as members of the body politic, or would give a clean bill of health to the social set-up which calls for this sort of adjustment.

The fact is, of course, that Steinbeck is not thinking primarily in sociological terms. The blending of these people with their background is an artistic circumstance, like that of Millet's peasants in the Angelus and the Man with the Hoe. We'll not call it quaint if that hurts his feelings, but he can hardly estop us from calling it picturesque. And the proof that he himself regards these people as at least curious is that he has written an essentially comic history of them. If he doesn't know that this is funny, then he doesn't know what he has done; and that is quite obviously contrary to fact.

It is certainly funny when Danny, in pursuit of amorous designs on Sweets Ramirez, presents her with a vacuum cleaner though it is well known that there is no electrical power in Tortilla Flat to run it. It is funnier still that she should daily pass this vacuum cleaner over the floor "on the theory that of course it would clean better with electricity, but one could not have everything"; that her stock should rise so much in her community because of the possession of a machine that would not work; so that she grew puffed up with pride and dragged her sweeping-machine into the conversation on every occasion. It was funniest of all when, Danny growing tired of this lady, his loving friends took back the vacuum cleaner by stealth and sold it to Torelli the bootlegger for two gallons of wine, and when on their departure Torelli looked into the machine and found it had no motor—it had never had a motor.

The story of the Pirate is funny too in a way—this ragamuffin who lives in a chicken house with his five dogs, and every day in a secret place buries the quarter of a dollar he earns from the sale of firewood. Danny's friends conclude by some process of paisano logic that he must have a buried treasure; and with a view to making it theirs, they treat him with a friendliness that he has never known. They bring him to their house and install him there with his five mangy dogs. They use on him every wile they know to worm out of him his secret. What is their surprise when he finally brings to them his treasure of two hundred dollars and puts it under their special protection! He has dedicated this treasure to the Virgin, promising her a gold candlestick for the favor she had done him in saving the life of a sick dog. These scalawags have their honor and piety, and much as they crave this money for their own uses, they guard it sacredly for the Virgin Mary.

On the day when the candlestick was dedicated, the dogs were admonished not to enter the church. They did break into the church in their enthusiasm and interrupted the sermon on Saint Francis of Assisi and his love for dumb beasts. But Father Ramon was indulgent. He could not help laughing. "Take the dogs outside," he said, "let them wait until we are through." The Pirate took them out and gave them a good scolding. "He left them stricken with grief and repentance and went back into the church. The people, still laughing, turned and looked at him, until he sank into his seat and tried to efface himself. 'Do not be ashamed,' Father Ramon said. 'It is no sin to be loved by your dogs, and no sin to love them. See how Saint Francis loved the beasts.' Then he told more stories of that good saint."

This anecdote ends with the Pirate's taking the dogs out into the woods, ranging them as an audience, and telling them the story of Saint Francis. And then a miracle occurred.

The dogs sat patiently, their eyes on the Pirate's lips. He told everything the priest had told, all the stories, all the observations. Hardly a word was out of its place.

When he was done, he regarded the dogs solemnly. "Saint Francis did all that," he said.

The trees hushed their whispering. The forest was silent and enchanted.

Suddenly there was a tiny sound behind the Pirate. All the dogs looked up. The Pirate was afraid to turn his head. A long moment passed.

And then the moment was over. The dogs lowered their eyes. The tree-tops stirred to life again and the sunlight patterns moved bewilderingly.

The Pirate was so happy that his heart pained him. "Did you see him?" he cried. "Was it San Francisco? Oh! What good dogs you must be to see a vision."

The dogs leaped up at his tone. Their mouths opened and their tails threshed joyfully.

There is much more than humor here, and the book shows throughout a genuine love for the charm and virtue of these childlike paisanos. I will not quarrel with Mr. Steinbeck over terms to characterize his people. Let them not be quaint or dispossessed. The point I wish to make is that his artistic sensibility has led him to choose for his subject here a manner of living and feeling which is not much in evidence in contemporary America, which reminds us more of rural Mexico today or of Italy of the Middle Ages. He has invested his tale with the tender pathos of distance that attaches to Saint Francis and Robin Hood and Shakespeare's Forest of Arden. And this he has colored with the quaint humor—oh, excuse me—the delicious humor of Don Quixote, Sancho Panza and Dulcinea Del Toboso. I refuse to quarrel with Mr. Steinbeck. I am trying to praise him. I am trying to say that the author of *The Grapes of Wrath* and *Of Mice and Men* is one who can bring to his representation of American life today the subtle skills of the great tradition in European writing.

Steinbeck's next major literary venture was in a very different vein, as far as possible from the gentle comedy of *Tortilla Flat*. *Of Mice and Men* is a tragic story of friendship among migratory laborers. And it is told with the directness and severe economy of a tale of Maupassant. The economy is that of drama as well as short story. We are told that Steinbeck's aim was to see how near he could come in narrative to the form of a stage play. And the story was no sooner written than it was turned into a successful drama.

It is the tale of two men whose custom it is to move from ranch to ranch, spending their little stake in town as soon as they have made it and passing on to another place where work may be had. But as with the Okies in *The Grapes of Wrath,* the secret dream of these two men is to save up enough money to buy a little farm and live in peaceful and settled independence. One of them is the mentally defective Lennie, a huge man of colossal strength, but simple as a child and helplessly dependent on the care of his friend George. George had taken him after the death of Lennie's aunt. Lennie is a millstone round his neck, standing between him and everything he would like to do. But George is deeply attached to his backward friend, knowing that without him he would lapse himself into the dreary state of a friendless wanderer. The huge Lennie has a child's passion for small animals, which he loves to hold in his hands and stroke; but the strength of his hands is so great that the frail creatures are likely to be broken and killed without his meaning any harm. He wishes earnestly to keep from doing anything bad, so as not to incur the wrath of George, but with the best of intentions he is forever getting them into trouble. And when it is a woman and not a puppy who becomes the victim of his ill-directed force, there is nothing left for his friend but to put an end to Lennie. That is the only way to save him from lynching.

One who has not read the book can hardly be made to appreciate the tone of humanity and beauty with which Steinbeck invests this tragic episode. The almost paternal affection of George for his blundering witless pal, and the sore grief he suffers over the necessity of putting him away —all this you are made to feel without the use of sentimental phrase or direct statement. Back of this lies the life of the bunkhouse—the essential decency and pathos of these rough homeless men whom circumstance has condemned to a life of physical and moral squalor. There is no touching on the industrial and social problems involved, as in *The Grapes of Wrath*, though the tale may have its bearing on the treatment of certain types of mental defectives. In this as in the earlier books, Steinbeck was content with the imaginative, the basically human, factors in the drama.

I think I have said enough to indicate that, by the time Steinbeck came to *The Grapes of Wrath*, he had served his artistic apprenticeship. If in this greatest of his fictions he has shown himself a social propagandist of unusual power, it is not because he lacked the literary skills required for pure imaginative writing, or the disposition to regard the art of fiction as primarily a matter of esthetics. It remains to see whether he left his artistry behind when he dealt directly with a sociological theme.

XVI. JOHN STEINBECK

Art and Propaganda

"And because all men are members of one great whole, and the sympathy which is in human nature will not allow one member to be indifferent to the rest or to have a perfect welfare independent of the rest, the expansion of our humanity, to suit the idea of perfection which culture forms, must be a *general* expansion. Perfection, as culture conceives it, is not possible while the individual remains isolated."

—Arnold

XVI. JOHN STEINBECK

Art and Propaganda

The Grapes of Wrath is perhaps the finest example we have so far produced in the United States of the proletarian novel. This is a somewhat loose term to designate the type of novel that deals primarily with the life of the working classes or with any social or industrial problem from the point of view of labor. There is likely to be a considerable element of propaganda in any novel with such a theme and such a point of view. And it often happens that the spirit of propaganda does not carry with it the philosophical breadth, the imaginative power, or the mere skill in narrative which are so important for the production of a work of art. Upton Sinclair is an example of a man of earnest feeling and admirable gifts for propaganda who has not the mental reach of a great artist, nor the artist's power of telling a plausible story and creating a world of vivid and convincing people. One sometimes has the feeling with Sinclair that he starts with a theory and then labors to create characters who will prove it; that his interest in the people is secondary. And that is a bad start with a writer of fiction.

With Steinbeck, it is the other way round. He has been interested in people from the beginning, from long before he had any theory to account for their ways. What is more, he is positively fond of people, more obviously drawn to them than any other of our group of writers. More especially he has shown himself fond of men who work for bread in the open air, on a background of fields and mountains. They have always appealed to him as individuals, and for something in them that speaks to his esthetic sense. He sees them large and simple, with a luster round them like the figures in Rockwell Kent's engravings. He likes them strong and lusty, ready to fight and ready to make love. He likes to see the women nursing their babies. He likes to see people enjoying their food, however coarse, and sharing it with others, what there is of it. And when they are in distress. . . .

When people are in distress, you want to help them. If the distress is so widespread that anyone's help is a mere drop in the bucket, you begin to reflect on the causes. You develop theories. The people in distress themselves begin to ponder causes, the rights and wrongs of the case, and they develop theories. Their theories may not be scientific, but they have the merit of growing out of a real experience. The best of social philosophies, so far as fiction is concerned, is that which comes spontaneously to the lips of people trying to figure out a way through life's labyrinth. The best sort of story from the point of view of sociology is one that by the very nature of its incidents sets you pondering the most fundamental human problems.

Steinbeck has always had a liking for brave men, men who could fight when occasion served, who could take their punishment, and who would risk their lives without repining in the cause of justice and human solidarity. He likes men who have the courage, the cunning and the singleness of mind that make them leaders. That is what attracts him to labor organizers. Already in 1936 he published *In Dubious Battle,* which is one of the best of novels dealing with industrial disputes. It is the story of a strike in the apple orchards of California—of communist organizers who move in on a district where the wage has been cut below a living standard and lead the men in a desperate fight for higher pay.

It is not a communist tract; it was not favorably received by the party, I believe, in spite of the highly sympathetic way in which he treats the party leaders. The ideology is somehow wrong. Too much space is given to the doctor who comes to see to the sanitary arrangements of the labor camp. This doctor is too much of a philosopher, and too much of a sociologist—regarding himself and his communist friends too coolly as products of forces which have been at work through all history, creatures of mob sentiment, and seeing this particular fight as but an incident in a never-ending struggle and perpetual balance of powers. The communist organizers are a little too frank in acknowledging that their object is not so much to win this fight as to develop class consciousness in the workers and make recruits for the revolution. They are men of normal feeling, and they grieve over those who are killed or mutilated. But they eagerly seize on blood and death and use them to fan the fires of wrath and violence. Such is the technique of the class struggle; and while the author does not pass judgment on it, he shows it up perhaps too clearly for the purpose of propaganda.

It is not a good communist tract, but as between labor and commercial profit the author's sympathies are on the side of labor. The law, the guns, and the dirty tricks are all with the big producers. You are made to feel the absolute necessity as well as the rightness of organization among the workers. The alternative is starvation for themselves and their children. As for the organizers, what is never in doubt in this book is their good faith, their courage, and their self-devotion. All these are brought to their peak in Jim, the new recruit, who in the course of these few days of the strike develops fine qualities of leadership, and whose death at the end gives him the status of a martyr. His comrade does not fail to exploit his death in the speech he makes over his dead body. The book ends with the opening words of this harangue: "This guy didn't want nothing for himself. . . ."

The strength of proletarian fiction is in that note, of comrades who want nothing for themselves alone—who sink their personal interest in that of the whole tribe of underdogs.

Thus Steinbeck had already broken ground in the earlier novel for the subject matter he was to handle so magisterially in *The Grapes of Wrath*. But *In Dubious Battle* is a hole-in-the-corner thing in comparison with the later work. In the intervening years the subject had been growing in his mind and imagination. He had written up for a San Francisco newspaper his observations on seasonal labor and life in the bunk-houses. He had visited the Oklahoma dustbowl which sent so many homeless families to California, and had made the trek West along with them. He had seen the uprooting of men in its epic proportions. He had reflected on the broad social problems underlying the special predicament of the California orchards. And so, taking his departure naturally from what he had seen in his native valley, from the men and women of his own acquaintance in Monterey County, he had let his thought widen out and deepen down until he was ready to make of his story the vehicle of comprehensive and significant attitudes on the major topics of social philosophy. He had things to say of large scope on the home, the family, the community of those who live in one place, on mother-hood and fatherhood, as well as on such political and economic topics as the function of police, property in land, the nature of capitalistic enterprise, the balance of power between labor and management, and the strike as a weapon of the class struggle.

The story of *The Grapes of Wrath* is simple and uncompli-cated. A family of tenant farmers in Oklahoma, the Joads. The great dust storms ruin their crops, and then they are forced to give up their land. It is to be worked on a large scale by the bankers' syndicate. The huge tractors plow up the land for miles on end and topple over the poor shacks of the farmers as they shave their foundations. There is only one thing to do. They will go to California, where the handbills promise employment for thousands in the orchards. The Joads get themselves a rickety second-hand Hudson six and turn it into a sort of covered wagon. They slaughter pigs for food on the journey and load their truck with such of their possessions as are indispensable for the long overland trek. And then they pile in—grampa and grandma, ma and pa, six children, a son-in-law, Uncle John, and the preacher Casy.

They are self-respecting people of old American stock, who have never had more than enough to fill their bellies. Their ways and speech are crude; but there is in them a sound root of wisdom and generosity, of courage and persistence. The eldest son Tom has just been paroled from the penitentiary. He is a good sort, a reliable member of the tribe; but he had killed a man who stuck a knife in him in a drunken brawl. It is dangerous for him to leave the state, breaking parole, but he cannot abandon the family by staying behind. He will try to keep his temper down henceforth so as not to get back in the clutches of the law. Casy is the thinker of the group. He has been a preacher of the Holiness persuasion, a great exhorter, and much of a sinner where the women are concerned. He has lost his faith in religion, but is earnestly seeking to find the way of truth and right in human affairs. The strongest character of all is Ma. She is a tower of strength in all that concerns the family welfare and the great mission of keeping them together and intact. She is dreaming of the little farm and the little white house among the orange trees where they will live together in peace when they have once found a place to work and save. But it is her misfortune to see them fall away one by one under the terrible stress of their misfortunes.

The journey is a long one, since they do not dare to push their old jallopy more than a certain speed. It is a desperate race against time; they are determined to get to the promised land before their money and supplies give out. Every night they camp beside the road in some place where there is water. They give help to other desperate pilgrims and receive help in turn. The hardships of the trip are great, and both

Grampa and Grandma die on the way. In the promised land they find they are unwelcome and despised. They are called by the insulting name of Okies and regarded as scarcely human. They are pushed around by the police. They get employment gathering peaches; but they cannot make enough to meet the prices charged for food at the company store; and when the wage is cut in two, they move on to the cotton fields. Both Casy and Tom get involved in strikes; Casy is killed by the strikebreakers, and Tom becomes a fugitive and leaves the family so as not to bring trouble on them. He disappears into the anonymous band of those who give their lives to the cause of organized labor. Misfortunes pour down upon them. Rosasharn's husband deserts, and her baby is born dead in a box-car camp during the autumn floods. The last scene shows father and mother and the three remaining children taking refuge in a barn. Here they come on a boy and his father, the father dying of starvation; and Rosasharn nurses him back to life with the milk that nature intended for her child.

This final episode is symbolic in its way of what is, I should say, the leading theme of the book. It is a type of the life-instinct, the vital persistence of the common people who are represented by the Joads. Their sufferings and humiliations are overwhelming; but these people are never entirely overwhelmed. They have something in them that is more than stoical endurance. It is the will to live, and the faith in life. The one who gives voice to this is Ma. When they are driven out of their Hooverville and Tom is with difficulty restrained from violent words and acts against the deputies, it is Ma who explains to him what we might call the philosophy of the proletariat.

"Easy," she said. "You got to have patience. Why, Tom—us people will go on livin' when all them people is gone. Why, Tom, we're the people that live. They ain't gonna wipe us out. Why, we're the people—we go on."

"We take a beatin' all the time."

"I know," Ma chuckled. "Maybe that makes us tough. Rich fellas come up an' they die, an' their kids ain't no good, an' they die out. But, Tom, we keep a comin'. Don' you fret none, Tom. A different time's comin'."

"How do you know?"

"I don' know how."

That is, you will recognize, the philosophy of Sandburg in *The People, Yes*—the mystical faith of the poet in the persistence and the final triumph of the plain people. Sandburg knows no better than Ma how he knows. He feels it in his bones. And that feeling is, I suppose, with Ma the very mark of the will to live.

Rosasharn's gesture in the barn is not the only symbol of this will to live. Very early in the book the author devotes a whole chapter—a short one—to the picture of a turtle crossing the highway. It is an act of heroic obstinacy and persistence against heavy odds. This is a gem of minute description, of natural history close-up, such as would delight the reader of Thoreau or John Burroughs. There are things like this in Thomas Hardy's Wessex novels. And as in Hardy, so here—it is not a mere piece of gratuitous realism. It may be enjoyed as such. But it inevitably carries the mind by suggestion to the kindred heroisms of men and women. It sets the note for the story that is to follow.

This chapter is an instance of a technical device by which the author gives his narrative a wider reference and representative character. The story of the Joads is faithfully told as a series of particular incidents in their stirring adventure. We hang with concern and suspense over each turn of their fortunes. But the author is not content with that. He wishes to give us a sense of the hordes of mortals who are involved with the Joads in the epic events of the migration; and along with the material events he wishes us to see the social forces at play and the sure and steady weaving of new social patterns for a people and a nation. And so, to every chapter dealing with the Joads, he adds a shorter, more general, but often not less powerful chapter on the general situation.

There is, to begin with, an account of the dust storm over the gray lands and the red lands of Oklahoma—a formidable example of exact and poetic description matched by few things in fiction. Like Hardy with Egdon Heath, Steinbeck begins with physical nature and comes by slow degrees to humanity. The chapter ends with an account of the reactions of the men, women and children in the face of this catastrophe. The conception is large and noble. Humanity has been stripped of all that is adventitious and accidental, leaving the naked will and thought of man. Under the stress of desperate calamity the children watch their elders to see if they will break. The women watch the men to see if this time they will fail. It is a question of going soft or going hard; and when the men go hard the others know that all is not lost. The corn is lost, but something more important remains. And we are left with the picture of the men on whom they all depend. It is man reduced to the simplest terms —man pitted against the brute forces of nature—man with the enduring will that gives him power to use his brains for the conquering of nature. Man's thinking is an extension of his powers of action—he thinks with his hands. And so we read: "The men sat in the doorways of their houses; their hands were busy with sticks and little rocks. The men sat still—thinking—figuring." It is a kind of parable, summing up the theme of the book in its widest, most general form.

Most of these intercalary chapters have more particular themes. There is the theme of buying cheap and selling dear —the wonderful chapter of the second-hand automobile dealers. There is the theme of social forms coming into being as occasion requires. In the roadside camps the separate families are quickly assembled into one community; and community spontaneously develops its own laws out of its own obvious needs. There is the theme of large-scale production for economy and profit—the land syndicates in California who ruin the small owners. There is the theme of spring in California —its beauty, the scent of fruit, with the cherries and prunes and pears and grapes rotting on the ground to keep up the price. There are hungry men come for miles to take the superfluous oranges; but men with hoses squirt kerosene on the fruit. "A million people hungry, needing the fruit—and kerosene sprayed over the golden mountains." And there is the theme of the blindness of property in its anonymous forms.

And the companies, the banks worked at their own doom and they did not know it. The fields were fruitful, and starving men moved on the roads. The granaries were full and the children of the poor grew up rachitic, and the pustules of pellagra swelled on their sides. The great companies did not know that the line between hunger and anger is a thin line. And money that might have gone to wages went for gas, for guns, for agents and spies, for blacklists, for drilling. On the highways the people moved like ants and searched for work, for food. And the anger began to ferment.

There is the theme of a common interest as opposed to a private and exclusive. "Not my land, but ours." "All work together for our own thing—all farm our own lan'." And finally we have the theme of man who has lost his soul and finds it again in devotion to the common cause.

Some of these themes are expressed in the spontaneous utterance of the Okies; some of them in the more abstract and theoretical language of the author. In general we may say that he is most effective when he puts his views in the mouths of the characters. For this is fiction; and fiction has small tolerance for the abstractions of an author. Still, there are cases where the theme is too broad and too complicated to find adequate expression in the words of a single man on a particular occasion. This is a great challenge to the ingenuity of a writer, and Steinbeck has found a number of ingen-

ious and effective means of dramatizing the thought of a
whole group of people faced with a difficult problem in economics. There is one remarkable chapter in which he shows
us the debate between the tenant farmers and the agents of
the banking syndicates come to put them off the land. It is
a debate which recurs over and over again with each unfortunate family; and Steinbeck has presented it in a form that
is at the same time generalized and yet not too abstract and
theoretical. We are shown the farmers squatting on their
heels while the owner men sit in their cars and explain the
peculiar nature of the institution which they represent. It is
a kind of impersonal monster that does not live on side-meat
like men, but on profits. It has to have profits all the time,
and ever more profits or it will die. And now that the land is
poor, the banks cannot afford to leave it in the hands of men
who cannot even pay their taxes.

And at last the owner men came to the point. The tenant
system won't work any more. One man on a tractor can take the
place of twelve or fourteen families. Pay him a wage and take all
the crop. We have to do it. We don't like to do it. But the monster's sick. Something's happened to the monster.

But you'll kill the land with cotton.

We know. We've got to take cotton quick before the land dies.
Then we'll sell the land. Lots of families in the East would like
to own a piece of land.

The tenant men looked up alarmed. But what'll happen to us?
How'll we eat?

You'll have to get off the land. The plow'll go through the
dooryard.

And now the squatting men stood up angrily. Grampa took up
the land, and he had to kill the Indians and drive them away.
And Pa was born here, and he killed weeds and snakes. Then a
bad year came and he had to borrow a little money. An' we was
born here. There in the door—our children born here. An' Pa had
to borrow money. The bank owned the land then, but we stayed
and we got a little bit of what we raised.

We know that—all that. It's not us, it's the bank. A bank isn't like a man. Or an owner with fifty thousand acres, he isn't like a man either. That's the monster.

Sure, cried the tenant men, but it's our land. We measured it and broke it up. We were born on it, and we got killed on it, died on it. Even if it's no good, it's still ours. That's what makes it ours—being born on it, working it, dying on it. That makes ownership, not a paper with numbers on it.

We're sorry. It's not us. It's the monster. The bank isn't like a man.

Yes, but the bank is only made of men.

No, you're wrong there—quite wrong there. The bank is something else than men. It happens that every man in a bank hates what the bank does, and yet the bank does it. The bank is something more than men, I tell you. It's the monster. Men made it, but they can't control it.

Thus, in a kind of parable, with allegorical figures, and with Biblical simplifications, our author has managed to give in summary, in essence, what must have gone on a million times all over the world, when the two groups were confronted—two groups that represent two opposed and natural interests, and both of them caught in an intricate web of forces so great and so automatic in their working that they are helpless to combat them or even to understand them. This is not an individual scene of drama; but many of the remarks must have been made a thousand times in individual cases. It is not an economic treatise; but the substance of many such a treatise is presented in simplified form suited to the apprehensions of the men who speak. There is enough local color to make it appropriate to this story of the Okies; and sufficient differentiation of the manner of the two groups to give it a properly fictional cast. The apologetic tone of the one party, their patience and firmness; the bewilderment and indignation of the other party; the reasonableness on both sides—are admirably rendered. In each case the speaker is like a chorus in ancient tragedy, embodying the collective sentiments of a large group. Anyone who has tried to write will

understand the number of difficulties which have been overcome in the application of this literary device. Anyone, at
least, who has tried to write fiction, and who has tried in
fiction to present a general view of things without cutting
loose from the concrete and particular. This is but one of
many instances in *The Grapes of Wrath* of Steinbeck's resourcefulness in meeting his main problem—to reconcile the
interests of theory with those of imaginative art—to render
the abstractions of thought in the concrete terms of fiction.

It would take long to list the technical variations and com-
binations which Steinbeck brings to the solution of this problem. Often he is more direct and less dramatic than in the
passage quoted above. He will give a generalized account of
some development among the migrants, as where, with the
eye of a sociologist, he describes the spontaneous evolution of
social codes and governmental agencies among these people
in the camps and on the roads.

And as the worlds moved westward, rules became laws, although no one told the families. It is unlawful to foul near the
camp; it is unlawful in any way to foul the drinking water; it is
unlawful to eat good rich food near one who is hungry, unless he
is asked to share. . . . There grew up government in the worlds,
with leaders, elders. A man who was wise found that his wisdom
was needed in every camp; a man who was a fool could not
change his folly with his world. . . . Thus they changed their social
life—changed as in the whole universe only man can change.
They were not farm men any more, but migrant men. And the
thought, the planning, the long staring silence that had gone out
to the fields, went now to the roads, to the distance, to the West.

He tells in general terms, in a passage earlier cited, how the
companies and banks worked at their own doom without
knowing it, while the anger of the hungry began to ferment.
Here he is the social philosopher, commenting on a phase of
economic psychology.

Such passages are just frequent enough to offend some

readers having cut-and-dried notions of fictional technique, who make it a principle that no philosophy may show its head in fiction, and whose nose for propaganda is so keen that they are distressed at any hint of an idea. As a matter of fact, these general and theorizing passages are fairly rare and generally very short. They are interspersed with concrete instances and vivid images. And the style is so pithy and picturesque that it gives the whole an effect as different as possible from that of prosing science.

More often what we have is not generalized narrative but a *composite* of many short incidents and dialogues, racy and individual, but building up a general picture of some phase of the migrant life: people discovering common acquaintances back in the home county, small boys exchanging audacities, a man strumming his guitar while the people sing the old songs in the evening. Such is the bulk of the seventeenth chapter, from which I have quoted sociological observations, and of the twelfth, with its diversified picture of life on Highway 66. The most famous instance is Chapter Seven, with its dizzy riot of sales talk, frightened farmers, old tires, wheezy motors, glinting headlights, bargains, profits and overreaching. It is developed thematically like a tone poem by Roy Harris, and renders as nothing else could the sense of frenzied movement, confusion and anxiety which accompanies so much of our daily living, and particularly that of men caught like straws in the whirlwind of loss and misfortune.

The narrative method in these chapters is thus an extremely flexible medium, in which many different modes of statement are composed in a consistent whole diversified in coloring as a Persian carpet. What really needs stressing is the virtuosity of the performance, a virtuosity fully as great as—say—Thornton Wilder's, though it is likely to be passed over because of the homeliness of the subject matter, because Steinbeck is supposed to be simply rendering the plain reactions of plain people. And so he is, and much concerned not

to introduce any foreign element of preciousness or affectation. But he is rendering them, the reactions of plain people,
with tenderness, insight, and artistic detachment, and with
the power of modulating freely round the dominant key. He
is like an actor capable of doing things with his voice, vary-
ing his tone with the changing rôle and emotion. He has
more than usual of the storyteller's ventriloquism.

He is one who feels strongly on the subject of man's essential dignity of spirit and his unexhausted possibilities for
modification and improvement. It is natural that at times he
should slip into a prophetic tone not unlike that of our mid-
western poet.

For man, unlike any other thing organic or inorganic in the
universe, grows beyond his work, walks up the stairs of his concepts, emerges ahead of his accomplishments. . . . Having stepped
forward, he may slip back, but only half a step, never the full step
back. This you may say and know it and know it. . . . And this
you can know—fear the time when Manself will not suffer and
die for a concept, for this one quality is the foundation of Manself, and this one quality is man, distinctive in the universe.

Here let me lay my cards on the table. About such a passage
as this I have a divided feeling, as I do about some of the
quietly eloquent sayings of Tom to his mother when he leaves
her to take up the cause of labor. These statements of Tom
about his mission, these statements of Steinbeck about Manself, do not seem to me among the best things in the book,
considered as literary art; and yet I do not see how we could
dispense with them. I would not wish them away. For they
are important clues to the author's feeling—to his hope and
faith in humanity. But they do not seem to me altogether successful as imaginative shapings of the stuff of life in keeping
with the most rigorous demands of fictional art.

The passage about Manself and dying for a concept is considerably longer than what I have quoted. It is in substance

highly creditable to the author's feeling about man's nature and destiny. But there is something a trifle stiff about it, a trifle abstract, "talky," and magniloquent. It is as if at this point Steinbeck's art, generally so flexible and sure, had weakened—as if he was hurried or tired, and had for the moment allowed mere words to take the place of images or the dramatic evocations which are his most effective medium. In the case of Tom's remarks to his mother when he is setting out on his career as a labor organizer (Chapter Twenty-eight), they are cast, like all the dialogue, in the familiar language of the Okie, the untutored man of the people. Perhaps for that very reason, however, there is something just a bit questionable in the high seriousness, the wistful Christlikeness, of the sentiments he expresses. One does not so much question his harboring these sentiments, along with others less exalted in tone; what one questions is whether he could have brought himself to utter just these sentiments in just this tone. One asks whether the author has not a little too obviously manipulated his material here in order to point the moral of his tale.

And this reminds me of a statement of Farrell's about Steinbeck which is worth considering, and which involves a crucial problem in criticism. In an article dealing with the 1930's in American literature, Farrell comments on the work of younger writers who have come from the bottom or near the bottom of American society and have duly exploited the order of life with which they are acquainted. "Some of it is serious," he says, "in the sense that Matthew Arnold would have used that word in relation to literature. But this tendency has also created a new type of popular fiction, the hard-boiled novel. This type of novel relies on expressive language; it lacks any underlying structure, but does fit a Hollywood patter of action; it is swift; it has all the mannerism, and none of the substance of genuine realistic writing. . . . These books stand in a sort of intermediate position between genuinely serious works of realistic writing, and merely fictional entertainment." As examples of this sort of writing he cites Jerome Weidman, James Cain, and Steinbeck in *Of Mice and Men*.

This is an extremely interesting utterance, whatever we may think of it; and it would be too simple to suppose that Farrell is jealous of Steinbeck's skill and popularity and unwilling to give him credit for what he has done. There is, I believe, a serious opposition of temper underlying this criticism, and a serious divergence in literary theory.

Steinbeck does not ignore the function of literature as entertainment, or at least its function of refreshing man's spirit. He writes in one place of this attribute of some literature, and the book he names as an example of this refreshment is none other than the immortal story of *Alice in Wonderland*. Farrell can afford to like Alice's adventures because they are so frankly adventures in Wonderland. What he does not like is making a sugar-candy wonderland of real life, as Stark Young does in *So Red the Rose*—that is the example that Farrell gives.

What he has in mind in Steinbeck's tale is, I suppose, a certain theatricality in his treatment of his theme. You remember that *Of Mice and Men* was cut to the model of a play. The situation is greatly simplified, and so are the people. They are pointed up and colored so as to emphasize the characteristic—their decency where they are decent, their meanness where they are mean. The superhuman strength of the moron, his absolute devotion to his friend, the circumstances that lead to his death, make of him a character as picturesque and stagey as Hugo's hunchback of Notre Dame. Everything about the story is arranged so as to give it an effectiveness seldom found in actual life.

I don't know what Farrell thinks of *The Grapes of Wrath;* but I fancy that he would feel much the same way about that book. He would naturally be sympathetic to the sort of propaganda which it represents. But he would probably complain that it is more propaganda than literature. He would complain that both Casy and Tom are idealized for the sake of the social doctrine Steinbeck wishes to convey. Perhaps he would say the same of Ma, and of the final scene in which Rosasharn gives her breast to the starving man. He would say that, while much of the book is a faithful transcription of such reality as Steinbeck has observed, much of it is an invention for carrying the attitudes which he wishes to convey. And I have confessed that for myself some of the more idealistic passages do not ring quite true—that there is a slight suspicion here and there of a sentimental forcing of the note. But this is for me a question merely of an occasional slip in phrasing, and not of a radical fault in the conception of the book.

If I have rightly interpreted Farrell's position, I would say, in general, that I respect his view, and I believe that what he has in mind is a real danger to serious writing. But I doubt whether Steinbeck is a good example of the vice in question. Perhaps Farrell has too narrow and exclusive a notion of what makes good literature. Naturalism is one great school of fiction, and I have not the slightest disposition to question this way of writing when it is done well. But naturalism does not cover the whole ground, and taken by itself it does not fully satisfy the needs of the human imagination and the human spirit.

The life of the imagination has two poles—that of the real and that of the ideal. One of our strongest and most normal passions is the passion for the truth. Our intellectual nature and our moral nature alike drive us to the finding and the publishing of the truth. But there is another pole to the imagination which is just as valid and important as the realistic pole. Whatever the cold facts of life as they are, they derive all their meaning for us from our idea of what can be made of them. We believe that men have the faculty of fixing goals and striving for their attainment. We believe that such striving is itself a fact of life—the most important of all, since it is the means by which the will of man is given effect in the world of reality. We believe that certain goals are more worth while than others, since they represent our most persistent notions of human well-being. Such goals we call *ideals*. They have their origin in our moral sense, our vision of better and worse; and it is by reference to them that we organize our most serious activities.

Now, the ideal may be most faintly and imperfectly represented in the daily course of human life. But it is certainly present. And without some indication of its presence, we hardly know how to orient ourselves, how to read directions. One reason why Steinbeck is more widely read than Farrell at the present moment is that, while the element of reality is very largely present in his books, there is also a sufficient indication of ideal directions toward which the human compass points. The moral appeal is not merely negative, through revulsion from the ugly. It is also in some measure positive. We respond to the good qualities and impulses in Casy and Tom and Ma and in many of the minor characters. And we do not feel so lost and helpless in this world of positive directions as many readers feel in the world of Studs Lonigan.

A similar difference may be stated in esthetic terms. We are more aware in Steinbeck of the principle of selection for effect. This is a prime esthetic merit in all the arts, making for definition and appeal. Farrell piles up details in the same key without diversification of effect, with the result that a certain monotony is felt. This has long been noted as a characteristic weakness of naturalistic fiction, as in the novels of Zola and Dreiser.

On the whole we must say that Steinbeck is a more versatile and skillful craftsman, a more natural craftsman, than Farrell. This is not saying that he will turn out to be the greater writer of the two in the judgment of critical posterity. There are other things that may come in to determine a dif-

ferent verdict. Farrell is more obviously dealing with things
which he knows down to the ground from personal experience. There is an unmistakable sincerity and a passion of
earnestness in him which may tell in the long run. His monotony is one phase of his earnestness and substance. His record
of social fact may prove to be the more profound and reliable.
I will not undertake to say which of these two men is more
likely to take his place in the hall of the immortals. The
chances are good for both of them. And certainly they both
have much to say to us of this generation.

If I were asked to say just exactly what are the economic
theories of John Steinbeck, and how he proposes to apply
them in terms of political action, I should have to answer:
I do not know. The book offers no specific answer to these
questions. It reminds us of what we all do know: that our
system of production and finance involves innumerable instances of cruel hardship and injustice; that it needs constant
adjustment and control by the conscience and authority of
the sovereign people. This author is concerned with what has
been called the forgotten man; it is clear that he holds the
community responsible for the man without work, home, or
food. He seems to intimate that what cannot be cured by individual effort must needs be met by collective measures. It
is highly important that our people should be made aware
of the social problems which remain to be solved within the
system which is so good to so many of us. And there is no
more effective way of bringing this about than to have actual
instances presented vividly to our imaginations by means of
fiction. For this reason I regard *The Grapes of Wrath* as a
social document of great educational value.

Considering it simply as literary art, I would say that it
gains greatly by dealing with social problems so urgent that
they cannot be ignored. It gains thereby in emotional power.
But it is a notable work of fiction by virtue of the fact that

all social problems are so effectively dramatized in individual situations and characters—racy, colorful, pitiful, farcical, disorderly, well meaning, shrewd, brave, ignorant, loyal, anxious, obstinate, insuppressible, cockeyed . . . mortals. I have never lived among these Okies nor heard them talk. But I would swear that this is their language, these their thoughts, and these the very hardships and dangers which they encountered. They represent a level, material and social, on which the reader has never existed even for a day. They have lived for generations completely deprived of luxuries and refinements which in the life he has known are taken for granted as primary conditions of civilization.

And yet they are not savages. They are self-respecting men and women with a traditional set of standards and proprieties and rules of conduct which they never think of violating. Beset with innumerable difficulties, cut off from their familiar moorings, they are confronted with situations of great delicacy, with nice problems in ethics and family policy to be resolved. Decisions are taken after informal discussion in the family council organized on ancient tribal lines. Grampa was a rather flighty and childish old fellow. He was still the titular head of the tribe, but his position was honorary and a matter of custom. He had the right of first comment; but actual decision was made by the strong and wise, by Pa and Tom, and above all by Ma. Pa was the representative of practical prudence; Ma the voice of right feeling and generous impulse and the traditional code of decent conduct. It was she who decided that they should take Casy with them although they were already overcrowded. And she delivered the decision of the court in language pithy and judicial. Pa wanted to know, "Kin we, Ma?"

Ma cleared her throat. "It ain't kin we? It's will we?" she said firmly. "As far as 'kin', we can't do nothin', not go to California or nothin'; but as far as 'will', why, we'll do what we will. An' as far as 'will'—it's a long time our folks been here and east before,

an' I never heerd tell of no Joads or no Hazletts, neither, ever re-
fusin' food an' shelter or a lift on the road to anybody who asked.
They's been mean Joads, but never that mean."

And so the Joads and the Okies take their place with Don
Quixote, with Dr. Faustus, with Galsworthy's Forsytes and
Lewis' Babbitt, in the world's gallery of symbolic characters,
the representative tapestry of the creative imagination. Will
the colors hold? That is a large question, which only time
can answer. It depends on whether the dyes are synthetic ani-
line or the true vegetable product. And who at the present
moment can make sure of that?

I will put the question in another way. Is the subject too
special for this book to have continuing artistic appeal? Are
the issues fundamental enough in human nature to give it
what is called universality? Perhaps the best theme is a combination of a particular and local subject with one more general and lasting. The particular subject here is the Oklahoma
farmer and an oversupply of labor in the California orchards.
The general subject is hunger; the general subject is man
pitted against the forces of nature. There is much to remind
one of *Robinson Crusoe*. Steinbeck will certainly do well if
he can last as long and be as widely read as Daniel Defoe.

XVII. TAKEN ALL TOGETHER

"And ye shall know the truth, and the truth shall make you free."

The more one considers this group of writers, the more
impressive they become, whether individually or collectively.
With all their diversity, they have in common essential features that make them genuinely typical of their period. Not
everything in our life and nature is well represented in them,
but they do stand, I believe, for attitudes prevailing among
intellectuals during the interval between two world wars.
They do not, for example, give any proper view of people
living in settled peace and contentment in homes secure
against financial disaster, moral ruin, and sentimental breach
of faith. By one consent they have taken for their subject that
unsettlement and instability which we must acknowledge to
be a characteristic feature of our life both material and moral.
They are all realists in the sense of making no concession to
the demand for fiction as a vehicle of wishful thinking. There
is not a single success story in the entire output of these eight
men, unless we include the purely romantic tales with which
Marquand made the pot boil before he turned to George
Apley and the Brills. Their idealism has largely taken the
negative form of irony, tragedy, comedy, satire and pathos, in
which the positive ideal is simply implied in the author's reaction against what he deprecates and abhors. And yet in the
long run they impress one as deeply and humanly concerned
that men should attain to the spiritual dignity of which they
are potentially capable, and that the social forms which em-
body and determine relations among men should better re-

flect the ideals of democratic justice to which in this country we all pay at least lip service.

Each one of them offers a vivid and colorful picture of human nature under some aspect. But it is as a group that they have the most impressive effect on the imagination—with the many diverse phases combined in one brilliant and variegated tapestry or mural eloquently expressive of our times. Each one of them is highly significant in his social comment, but it is the united commentary of them all, so various and yet consistent, that most impresses the mind; and each gains importance from the collective testimony of the group.

Dos Passos subjects the whole of human behavior to the corrosive action of his analysis, bidding us observe in rich and poor, in failure and success, among the crude and the refined, the withering effects of materialism in action. Hemingway bids us beware of words that weave illusions; he wishes to study the most primary situations where feelings are naked and genuine; and so confines his exhibit for the most part to types and situations below the threshold of bourgeois "culture." Faulkner shows us a decadent society haunted by the ghosts of slavery and caste, burning with the fevers of pride and lust and madness, but with strange shoots of idealism waving their rootless blooms among the Spanish moss of the cypress swamps. Caldwell presents another aspect of the same unhappy South—the soil exhausted, and the poverty-stricken share-croppers seeking in religion and sex and nigger-lynching fantastic ways of satisfying the hunger of flesh and spirit for which there is no normal satisfaction provided. Farrell gives still another view of the same spiritual hunger and perversion of instinct—a whole society of peasants transplanted from the rural simplicities of Ireland to the competitive jungles of cement and steel, unable to bring their native culture with them or to replace it with any adequate nourishment for mind, heart, or imagination, and so falling—for want of alternatives—into philistinism, ugliness of spirit, and the gross and lethal excitements of vulgar dissipation. Marquand shows us the dried pods of once juicy New England culture, rattling their withered and infertile seeds like peas in a clown's bladder.

It is Steinbeck who gives us the most encouraging view of human nature in his Okies, rude and crude in outward show, struggling desperately with natural catastrophe and economic exploitation, deprived of all artificial aids to the good life, and now made homeless, but carrying with them still the saving traditions of home and organized society and many a sound root of sweetness, strength and loyalty. The true dignity and contentment of spirit he finds with them in an effort for the well-being of the social body. In Wolfe, as in Dos Passos, it is the whole of American life that is surveyed, and more especially the bourgeois levels from newsboys and boarding-house keepers to wealthy merchants and financiers. His vein is more romantic than Dos Passos', for he takes a poet's view of the aspirations of the heart, even when they are expressed in the struggle for money and power; whatever the heart desires is invested by him with a mystic rainbow luster. But he knows the ugliness and cruelty that accompany the process of men's seeking, the tragedy and ruin that follow on the conflict of dreams and ideals. What he particularly idealizes—since it is his own, and is less tainted with commercialism than the Babbitt type—is the artistic temperament, and the pursuit of love, of knowledge, and of fame. But he came to realize that none of these will fully satisfy the spirit, which craves a larger fulfillment. In the end, he is at one with Steinbeck, with Farrell and Dos Passos and Hemingway, in demanding of the individual participation in the common hopes of social man.

I have had almost nothing to say of these men's philosophy in the more special sense of the word. I mean their conceptions of essential reality, from which their ethical and social evaluations might be derived as corollaries. Professor Josiah Royce used to contend that everyone has a philosophy, a metaphysic, whether he knows it or not; it is implied in everything he does or thinks. And in this sense these men must have philosophies. Some of them, it is well known, are readers of philosophy—Steinbeck, for example; and I should not be surprised in the case of any one of them to learn that he was an assiduous student of that "gay" science. But the characters they portray are seldom philosophers, and the authors have no occasion to set forth their own views in the course of these narratives. Steinbeck's Joseph in *To a God Unknown* is imbued with a sort of pagan mysticism and given to rituals and sacrifices which imply a power in nature that must be propitiated by men in order to secure the success of their undertakings. But there is no reason to think that Steinbeck shares this attitude toward the cosmos, however sympathetically he may present it in his character. Both Wolfe and Faulkner display a kind of romantic idealism in their treatment of certain characters. By this I mean that they seem to attribute value to certain sentiments and ideals in and for themselves, almost without reference to the social implications and the type of behavior which accompany them or follow from them. These men are concerned with the flower and not the fruit. I think we might state with some measure of confidence that neither of these Southern writers is a utilitarian, certainly not in the full sense of the term.

It seems obvious from his *Note on Literary Criticism* that Farrell is somewhat inclined toward Marxian materialism; and this type of philosophy seems to me clearly implied in the work of Dos Passos, and somewhat less clearly in that of Caldwell and Steinbeck, and possibly even in Hemingway. By Marxian materialism I mean the disposition to trace back states of mind and moral attitudes to the material conditions (in the last analysis, economic and industrial conditions) to which the person or the group has been subjected through training, environment and social status. The disposition is here to emphasize the material factors as determinants in the ideology of individuals, social groups, cultures and schools of thought, and to assume that, under specified economic conditions, in such and such an industrial set-up, such and such ideologies are typical. This does not necessarily imply a strict metaphysical materialism, in which physical matter is regarded as the primary substance of all existing things, and spirit or mind as reducible to, or adequately explained by, the activities of material atoms. Still less does it imply the type of ethical materialism which holds that consideration of the material well-being, either of groups or of individuals, should be the sole rule in the determination of conduct.

Metaphysical materialism is rather too abstruse to come into question in the writing of fiction. As for ethical materialism, the writer of fiction is by nature too much of a humanist to be satisfied with anything so unimaginative. He is too much concerned with how a man feels within himself to be content with any exclusive consideration of his material well-being. It is man's emotional satisfactions and distresses which are the writer's prime concern—his self-esteem, the pride he takes in his own fineness and decency, the quality of his relations with others, his loves and hates, his sense of obligation to others or his want of it, his sentimental despairs and exaltations. Above all, with the writers we have in mind, a paramount concern is the sense of brotherhood among men, of common obligations, common aspirations, and a common cause. In all of this it is not so much what is shared that is felt to be important as the sentiment of sharing; well-being is measured less in terms of the material factors than in terms of the moral or sentimental.

The materialism of these men is best interpreted as an effort to bring the moral world within the framework of the natural. Natural does not here mean material exclusively. The natural is that which is subject to uniform laws and sus-

ceptible of explanation and understanding. In this it is opposed to the supernatural order, which is taken to be above
explanation and understanding, at least by men, and not
readily amenable to natural laws. Contemporary fiction is
overwhelmingly naturalistic in its main implications. Good
and evil are not thought of as autonomous forces moving
mysteriously behind the scenes of life and making their appearance from time to time in the realm of human behavior.
They are value-terms applied to objects and events and to
persons according as they give us satisfaction or the contrary;
and they may be promoted or diminished by the highly complicated but intelligible action of natural laws working in the
physical and the mental world. And then in a special sense,
we apply the terms good and evil in the realm of social relations. It is between man and man that moral good exists; for
it is there that we find our obligations, our responsibility for
the good of others and the crowning satisfactions of the
shared experience.

There is a common tendency of the mystical-minded to
ignore the importance of material circumstances in promot-
ing and determining good conditions. They think it enough
to hope and pray that the transcendent good may gain the
victory and the transcendent evil be defeated in the great
combat that is going on forever behind the clouds. This is a
comfortable attitude for the wealthy and privileged. It is
pleasant for them to think that the social order which has
brought them so much satisfaction is ideally suited to bring
good to all society, and that those who do not profit from this
order are the victims of their own vice and incompetence.
They interpret good and evil in terms of their personal convenience, and build themselves an ideology which is a rationalization of the existing order. It is against the complacency of such a procedure that our story writers invoke the
Marxian analysis. When the social order proves inadequate to
secure the well-being of the common man, they call in ques-

tion the ideology that supports it. Even if it is only material
well-being that is involved, they question the morality of
those who are willing to perpetuate poverty and starvation.

But what most distresses the writers of fiction is not so
much material poverty as the poverty of spirit which is so
widely prevalent under even our favored institutions. It is
only Caldwell and Faulkner (in one or two books) who present conditions of physical indigence so extreme that they
result by themselves in spiritual degradation; though Farrell
and Steinbeck show people carrying on a losing battle with
starvation and desperately crippled by it. But in Farrell it is
not physical undernourishment from which the Lonigans
and McGintys and O'Flahertys are suffering; it is spiritual
undernourishment—it is want of a humane culture adequate
to satisfy the normal demands of men and women with energies to be employed and with minds and hearts and imaginations to be fed. The same thing is true in Don Passos of businessmen, stenographers, promoters, actors and mechanics; in
Wolfe, of boarding-house keepers, investors in real estate,
small town merchants and city muckers. This is what, in *Culture and Anarchy*, Matthew Arnold deplored as the malady
of philistinism, the want of sweetness and light. It is a spiritual malady, but Arnold himself ascribed it in the last analysis
to social causes—to social inequality, a system of caste which,
he said, "has the natural and necessary effect, under the present circumstances, of materializing our upper class, vulgariz-
ing our middle class, and brutalizing our lower class."

The people of Dos Passos and Wolfe, and even the people
of Farrell, were not absolutely cut off from the sources of culture. The fruits of the spirit were available in schools and
libraries, in museums and laboratories and churches and con-
cert halls, in field and wood, in the political institutions of
democracy, and in the very newspapers. But they had not the
spirit to stretch forth their hands and take what was offered.
Or taking it, it did not nourish them. There was something

wanting in the atmosphere essential to health, or something positively unfavorable to the proper functioning of the organism. Their spiritual vitality had been so drained by greed and anxiety, by fear and boredom, that they could not assimilate what they took in. Their blood was thinned by a spiritual anemia till they grew languid and unenterprising. Or in their fever they desperately snatched at vulgar excitements or spent their strength in foulness, acrimony and disorder. In Caldwell and Steinbeck the cry is: Without bread the spirit cannot live. In Farrell and Wolfe and Dos Passos, it is: Man shall not live by bread alone. That is certainly not materialism in the common understanding of the word, but just the contrary: it is an earnest protest against this noxious and vulgar philosophy.

I have spoken of Hemingway's "behaviorism," referring to his disposition to play up action more than feeling and thought. This is not behaviorism in the strict sense as the word is used in psychology. It is more of a literary device. But it does derive from somewhat the same attitude toward the subjective. In Hemingway, I have suggested, it goes back to his distrust of fine words, so often the cloak for rationalization and sentimental self-deception. He was in violent reaction, with the intellectuals of his time, against the false pretensions of an earlier generation; reluctant to admit the abstractions of philosophy or moral systems handed down by the fathers. But in spite of all his caution, his insistence on giving the items, his stress on the thing done, we know how everything is referred back to the test of feeling—"what makes you feel good after." And if feeling is the test, there can be no proper behaviorism, which is materialistic with a vengeance. We have seen what stress Hemingway lays on the romantic sentiment of love, and on the virtues of faithfulness to comrades and loyalty to cause. We must conclude that he, too, is fundamentally devoted to the cultivation of the spirit, though he hates to admit it.

So that the simplest way of characterizing the thought of these men as a whole is perhaps to say that they are literary realists, philosophical naturalists, who attribute value chiefly to the spiritual states of men, but who are jealous of systems that flatter and inflate the ego, and are resolutely determined to place men's spiritual states squarely in the framework of material conditions and social relationships.

Few of these men are storytellers in the traditional sense, like Scott or Dumas, Hardy or Dickens, Tarkington or Sabatini. Marquand can tell a romantic story with the best. And *Wickford Point* has its elements of suspense and intrigue. But in *The Late George Apley* he gives us a novel as like as possible to the biography of some worthy whose life pursues its placid course without event from the cradle to the grave. Caldwell can relate an episode with spirit and point, and some of his tragi-comedies, like *God's Little Acre* and *Trouble in July,* have, in their slender way, admirably managed plots. Faulkner is in the whole group the one inventor of complicated plots, replete with mystery and suspense, which he conducts with an excessive delight in teasing and mystifying the reader. But the best of his novels—*The Sound and the Fury* and *As I Lay Dying*—have little plot interest, and that little duly subordinated to the dissection of morbid psychology and the elaborate exhibition of the characters' stream of consciousness. Hemingway has been in the main a short story writer, a recorder of episodes, and one who depends not on ingenuity of plot and trick endings, but on subtlety of interpretation and graphic suggestion of the characteristic in situation.

In all of these, the emphasis is not so much on the story as on the psychology or the social significance of the theme. With the rest, psychology and social significance are still more dominant. In Wolfe, it is the cloudy psychology of the romantic soul, with the narrative following pretty close the eventful but uncomplicated order of his own career. In Dos Passos, all is biography, case histories, either in snatches and fragments, or in minute detailed sequences of minor incident, without complication of plot, suspense, resolution, and without concern for dramatic issues or elaborated scenes. The inclusion in one composition with these private histories of thematic prose poems, representative excerpts from the newspapers, and biographies of noted public figures is a perpetual reminder that they are offered as sociological exhibits illustrative of American culture and mentality in our times. In Farrell, the incidents are more poignant and sometimes more dramatic, but they are even more intimately and painstakingly biographical—an extended, day-by-day succession of close-ups from business and family life and the street life of hoodlums, which, but for the touch of art in the narrative method, concreteness of presentation, and the complete absence of specialized scientific vocabulary, might well pass for documents offered in support of some theory about child psychology, causes of crime, the effect of environment on the individual, or other sociological topic. And finally, in Steinbeck, instead of the complications of a contrived plot, we have simply the forward march of events in the chronicle of tribal migration, once again illustrative of various phenomena of interest to students of the family, of seasonal employment in agriculture, the responsibilities of the federal government for industrial conditions, and similar social themes.

It is quite remarkable, when one reviews these men's work, how large a part is taken by the social institution of the family. In place of the romantic hero, we have the group including father and mother and children, or brothers, sisters and cousins, sailing life's stormy ocean in one boat—Faulkner's Compsons and Bundrens, Wolfe's Gants and Webbers, Caldwell's Jeeters, Steinbeck's Joads, and Farrell's O'Neills and O'Flahertys. The emphasis has passed from the wooing season and even from the troubled season of matrimonial adjustment to the period of final involvement with obligations and liabilities no longer purely sentimental.

And the same social emphasis appears in the importance of industrial occupation. Next to his family connections, the most important thing about a man or a woman is that his income is derived from typesetting or interior decoration, from trading in real estate or driving an express wagon, or from hoeing corn and picking cotton. These men mark the culmination in American fiction of a long realistic movement, which has rapidly gained momentum in the present century, in which the influence of home and trade is emphasized not merely for sociological reasons, but in the interest of richness and plausibility of characterization.

It is this preoccupation with people which in interbellum fiction has taken the place of the traditional story interest. Recognition takes the place of curiosity in the reader's reactions; intrigue and adventure yield to the daily struggle for existence. The characters are built up in our imaginations not by heroic deeds and sentimental refinements but through the day-by-day encounter with a world of reality narrowly circumscribed and the pursuit of satisfactions such as are available under the conditions and conceivable to people with their range of experience. The American frontier was long since closed. The year 1929 clearly marked the end of indefinite economic expansion. It had its large effect on the national imagination. Romance has retired to the past— *Anthony Adverse, Gone with the Wind*—to the murder-mystery, and the moving picture. In our most serious fiction of the present moment the story interest has given way to what we might call the human interest as such.

For it must not be supposed for an instant, because of their sociological emphasis, that these men are dull and prosy. Dullness is a function of the commonplace, the conventional and the half-hearted. Prosiness is a function of the abstract and the general. There is no period group of American novelists who are less chargeable with commonplaceness, conventionality, or half-heartedness. There is no one of these writers who is not vivid and fresh in his conceptions, ingenious and individual in his execution. If they are open to any criticism at all in this connection, it is that they have outdistanced the ordinary reader: their subjects are too "strong" for him, their technique too modern and original for his appreciation. For the most part in their style they have renounced the traditional blandishments of rhetoric, even when eminently well equipped to wield them. They offer no commentary and no explanations. Their pride is in self-suppression. Their verbal power and subtlety are spent not on description, characterization, and interpretation, but on rendering the very tone and complexion of the characters' thought and feeling. The reader must interpret for himself and draw his own conclusions. He may at times be puzzled, but he never can be bored. It is life itself speaking, and life is not dull.

As for abstraction and generalization, begetters of prose, there is less of these in our interbellum writers than in any earlier fiction, English or American. The interest may be sociological, but the method is not that of science or philosophy. Concreteness is the mark of all these writers. The characters are not verbal figments but men and women in action. The dialogue is not invented to suit some exigency of plot and drama. It is taken directly off the lips of human beings. It is vigorous, natural, idiomatic, racy, infinitely varied in tone and phrasing, and for the most part absolutely convincing. And this does not mean that it is not selective and esthetically pleasing.

These men are without exception artists of unusual gift and distinction. The energy which they have saved from description and rhetorical display they have turned to the essential business of disposing their subject matter in the most effective ways. Their problem is, by arrangement and emphasis, to mark the "values" and point them up with precision and calculated effect. Because the values are so often sociological, it does not follow that they are any the less esthetic. The best guarantee of their being esthetic is their being human. The social seriousness of American fiction today is one of its two chief sources of strength. But it is everywhere supported, in our most powerful writers, by an artistic seriousness and maturity such as we have never known before.

APPENDIX

AMERICAN FICTION 1920–1940

List of novels and main collections of short stories.[1]

1920. Dos Passos, One Man's Initiation—1917.
1921. Dos Passos, Three Soldiers.
1922. Marquand, The Unspeakable Gentleman.
1923. Dos Passos, Streets of Night.
1925. Dos Passos, Manhattan Transfer.
      Marquand, The Black Cargo.
      Hemingway, In Our Time (stories).
1926. Hemingway, The Torrents of Spring (parody).
      Hemingway, The Sun Also Rises.
      Faulkner, Soldiers' Pay.
1927. Hemingway, Men without Women (stories).
      Faulkner, Mosquitoes.
1929. Hemingway, A Farewell to Arms.
      Faulkner, Sartoris.
      Faulkner, The Sound and the Fury.
      Wolfe, Look Homeward, Angel.
      Steinbeck, Cup of Gold.
1930. Dos Passos, The 42nd Parallel.
      Faulkner, As I Lay Dying.
      Caldwell, The Bastard.
      Caldwell, Poor Fool.

[1] In drawing up this list, I am greatly indebted to the bibliographies provided by Fred B. Millett in his admirable volume *Contemporary American Authors*, Harcourt, Brace and Co., 1940. I do not pretend to absolute completeness, and in particular have made no attempt to give a complete list of Marquand's numerous historical works and mystery stories.

1931. Faulkner, Idyll in the Desert (stories).
       Faulkner, These 13 (stories).
       Faulkner, Sanctuary.
       Caldwell, American Earth (stories).

1932. Dos Passos, 1919.
       Faulkner, Light in August.
       Faulkner, Miss Zilphia Gant.
       Caldwell, Tobacco Road.
       Caldwell, Mama's Little Girl, a Brief Story.
       Steinbeck, The Pastures of Heaven (stories).
       Farrell, Young Lonigan, a Boyhood in Chicago Streets.

1933. Hemingway, God Rest You Merry Gentlemen (stories).
       Hemingway, Winner Take Nothing (stories).
       Caldwell, Brief Stories . . . We Are The Living.
       Caldwell, A Message for Genevieve, a Brief Story.
       Steinbeck, To a God Unknown.
       Farrell, Gas-House McGinty.

1934. Marquand, Ming Yellow.
       Faulkner, Doctor Martino and Other Stories.
       Farrell, The Young Manhood of Studs Lonigan.
       Farrell, Calico Shoes and Other Stories.

1935. Faulkner, Pylon.
       Caldwell, Journeyman.
       Caldwell, Kneel to the Rising Sun and Other Stories.
       Steinbeck, Tortilla Flat.
       Wolfe, Of Time and the River.
       Wolfe, From Death to Morning (stories).
       Farrell, Judgment Day (Studs Lonigan III).
       Farrell, Guillotine Party and Other Stories.

1936. Dos Passos, The Big Money.
       Marquand, Thank You, Mr. Moto.
       Faulkner, Absalom, Absalom!
       Caldwell, The Sacrilege of Alan Kent (included in American Earth).
       Steinbeck, In Dubious Battle.
       Farrell, A World I Never Made.

1937. Marquand, The Late George Apley.
       Hemingway, To Have and Have Not.
       Steinbeck, Of Mice and Men.
       Steinbeck, The Red Pony (included in The Long Valley).

1937. Farrell, Can All This Grandeur Perish and Other Stories.
Farrell, Fellow Countrymen (collected stories).

1938. Hemingway, The Fifth Column and the First Forty-Nine
Stories.
Faulkner, The Unvanquished (stories).
Caldwell, Southways (stories).
Steinbeck, The Long Valley (stories).
Farrell, No Star Is Lost.

1939. Dos Passos, Adventures of a Young Man.
Marquand, Wickford Point.
Faulkner, The Wild Palms.
Wolfe, The Web and the Rock.
Steinbeck, The Grapes of Wrath.
Farrell, Tommy Gallagher's Crusade.

1940. Faulkner, The Hamlet.
Wolfe, You Can't Go Home Again.
Caldwell, Trouble in July.
Farrell, Father and Son.
Hemingway, For Whom the Bell Tolls.

INDEX